Lecture Notes in Business Information Processing 277

Series Editors

Wil M.P. van der Aalst
Eindhoven Technical University, Eindhoven, The Netherlands
John Mylopoulos
University of Trento, Trento, Italy
Michael Rosemann
Queensland University of Technology, Brisbane, QLD, Australia
Michael J. Shaw
University of Illinois, Urbana-Champaign, IL, USA
Clemens Szyperski
Microsoft Research, Redmond, WA, USA

More information about this series at http://www.springer.com/series/7911

Ewa Ziemba (Ed.)

Information Technology for Management

New Ideas and Real Solutions

14th Conference, AITM 2016
and 11th Conference, ISM 2016, held as Part of FedCSIS
Gdansk, Poland, September 11–14, 2016
Revised Selected Papers

 Springer

Editor
Ewa Ziemba
University of Economics in Katowice
Katowice
Poland

ISSN 1865-1348 ISSN 1865-1356 (electronic)
Lecture Notes in Business Information Processing
ISBN 978-3-319-53075-8 ISBN 978-3-319-53076-5 (eBook)
DOI 10.1007/978-3-319-53076-5

Library of Congress Control Number: 2016963601

Printed on acid-free paper

This Springer imprint is published by Springer Nature
The registered company is Springer International Publishing AG
The registered company address is: Gewerbestrasse 11, 6330 Cham, Switzerland

Preface

The first edition of this book appeared in 2016 under the title *Information Technology for Management* (LNBIP 243). Given the rapid developments in information technology and its applications for improving management, there was a clear need for an updated version.

The present book includes extended and revised versions of selected papers submitted to the 11th Conference on Information Systems Management (ISM 2016) and the 14th Conference on Advanced Information Technologies for Management (AITM 2016) held in Gdańsk, Poland, during September 13–16, 2016. These conferences were organized within Federated Conference on Computer Science and Information Systems (FedCSIS 2016).

FedCSIS provides a platform for bringing together researchers, practitioners, and academics to present and discuss ideas, challenges, and potential solutions on established or emerging topics related to research and practice in computer science and information systems. Since 2012, the proceedings of the FedCSIS conferences are indexed in the Thomson Reuters Web of Science. In addition, FedCSIS full and short papers are included in the IEEE Xplore Digital Library.

ISM is a forum for computer scientists, IT specialist, and business people to exchange ideas on management of information systems in organizations and the usage of information systems for enhancing the decision-making process and empowering managers. It concentrates on various issues of planning, organizing, resourcing, coordinating, controlling, and leading the management functions to ensure a smooth operation of information systems in organizations.

AITM is a forum for all in the field of business informatics to present and discuss the current issues of IT in business applications. It is mainly focused on business process management, enterprise information systems, business intelligence methods and tools, decision support systems and data mining, intelligence and mobile IT, cloud computing, SOA, agent-based systems, and business-oriented ontologies.

ISM 2016 and AITM 2016 received 51 papers from 13 countries in all continents. From these, after a review process, only 15 papers were accepted as full papers and ten as short papers. Twelve papers of the highest quality as ranked by the Program Committee were chosen and the authors were invited to extend their papers and submit them for consideration to the LNBIP publication. Our guiding criterion for including papers in the book was the excellence of publications indicated by the reviewers, the relevance of subject matter for the economy, and promising results. The selected papers reflect state-of-art research work that is often oriented toward real-world applications and highlight the benefits of information systems and technology for business and public administration, thus forming a bridge between theory and practice.

This book provides a comprehensive overview of current research in the field of information technology for management. Its first two parts focus on information technology and information systems for knowledge management and business transformation. The third part of this book presents research on implementation and evaluation of information systems.

Finally, the authors and I hope readers will find the content of this book useful and interesting for their own research activities. It is in this spirit and conviction we offer our monograph, which is the result of the intellectual effort of the authors, for the final judgment of the readers. We are open to discussion on the issues raised in this book, and we look forward to the polemical voices as to the content and form.

February 2017   Ewa Ziemba

Acknowledgments

I would like to take this opportunity to express my gratitude to all those who contributed to the ISM 2016 and AITM 2016 research events. First of all, the authors, whose quality work was the essence of the conference, and the members of the Program Committee, who helped us with their expertise and diligence in reviewing the papers. I am deeply grateful to the program chairs of ISM 2016 and AITM 2016, namely, Witold Chmielarz, Helena Dudycz, and Jerzy Korczak, for their extensive organizational involvement in the conferences and the evaluation of papers. I acknowledge the chairs of the FedCSIS 2016, i.e., Maria Ganzha, Leszek A. Maciaszek, and Marcin Paprzycki for putting a lot of effort into organizing the big and excellent research event. Their work and commitment were invaluable. I extend my heartfelt thanks to Ralf Gerstner and Alfred Hofmann from Springer without whom this book would not come into being.

Organization

AITM 2016

Event Chairs

Helena Dudycz	Wrocław University of Economics, Poland
Mirosław Dyczkowski	Wrocław University of Economics, Poland
Jerzy Korczak	Wrocław University of Economics, Poland

Program Committee

Witold Abramowicz	Poznan University of Economics, Poland
Frederik Ahlemann	University of Duisburg-Essen, Germany
Frederic Andres	National Institute of Informatics, Tokyo, Japan
Ghislain Atemezing	Mondeca, Paris, France
Zbigniew Banaszak	Warsaw University of Technology, Poland
Anna Bobkowska	Gdansk University of Technology, Poland
Kenneth Brown	Communigram SA, France
Jaonna Bruzda	Nicolaus Copernicus University, Poland
Witold Chmielarz	University of Warsaw, Poland
Agostino Cortesi	Università Ca' Foscari, Venice, Italy
Beata Czarnacka-Chrobot	Warsaw School of Economics, Poland
Suparna De	University of Surrey, Guildford, UK
Jean-François Dufourd	University of Strasbourg, France
Maja Fosner	Faculty of Logistics, University of Maribor, Slovenia
Bogdan Franczyk	University of Leipzig, Germany
Beata Gontar	University of Lodz, Poland
Zbigniew Gontar	University of Lodz, Poland
Tamás Hartványi	Széchenyi István University, Hungary
Arkadiusz Januszewski	UTP University of Science and Technology in Bydgoszcz, Poland
Rajkumar Kannan	Bishop Heber College (Autonomous), Tiruchirappalli, India
Grzegorz Kersten	Concordia University, Montreal, Poland
Jerzy Korczak	Wrocław University of Economics, Poland
Ryszard Kowalczyk	Swinburne University of Technology, Melbourne, Victoria, Australia
Karol Kozak	TUD, Germany
Anna Križanová	University of Zilina, Slovakia
Neringa Langviniene	Kaunas University of Technology, Lithuania
Christian Leyh	Technische Universität Dresden, Germany
Antoni Ligęza	AGH University of Science and Technology, Poland
Ming K. Lim	University of Derby, UK

André Ludwig	University of Leipzig, Germany
Damien Magoni	University of Bordeaux – LaBRI, France
Marek Matulewski	Poznań School of Logistics, Poland
Krzysztof Michalak	Wroclaw University of Economics, Poland
Roberto Montemanni	University of Applied Sciences of Southern Switzerland, Switzerland
Mieczysław Owoc	Wroclaw University of Economics, Poland
Anna Pamuła	University of Łódź, Poland
Małgorzata Pańkowska	University of Economics in Katowice, Poland
Irena Patasiene	Kaunas University of Technology, Lithuania
Ilona Pawełoszek	Częstochowa University of Technology, Poland
Arnaud Quirin	University of Vigo, Spain
Eva Rakovska	University of Economics in Bratislava, Slovakia
Stefano Ricci	Sapienza University of Rome, Italy
Artur Rot	Wroclaw University of Economics, Poland
Aleksej Ivanovich Shinkevich	Kazan National Research Technological University, Russia
Pawel Sitek	Kielce University of Technology, Poland
Grazia Speranza	University of Brescia, Italy
Stanislaw Stanek	General Tadeusz Kosciuszko Military Academy of Land Forces in Wroclaw, Poland
Jerzy Surma	Warsaw School of Economics, Poland and University of Massachusetts Lowell, USA
Stephanie Teufel	University of Fribourg, Switzerland
Edward Tsang	University of Essex, UK
Waldemar Wolski	University of Szczecin, Poland
Cecilia Zanni-Merk	Université de Strasbourg, France
Ewa Ziemba	University of Economics in Katowice, Poland

ISM 2016

Event Chairs

Bernard Arogyaswami	Le Moyne University, USA
Witold Chmielarz	University of Warsaw, Poland
Dimitris Karagiannis	University of Vienna, Austria
Jerzy Kisielnicki	University of Warsaw, Poland
Ewa Ziemba	University of Economics in Katowice, Poland

Program Committee

Emad Abu-Shanab	Yarmouk University, Jordan
Saleh Alghamdi	University of Sussex, UK
Andrzej Bialas	Institute of Innovative Technologies EMAG, Poland
Zane Bicevska	DIVI Grupa Ltd., Latvia
Tsungting Chung	Douliou Yunlin Uniwersytet, Taiwan
Beata Czarnacka-Chrobot	Warsaw School of Economics, Poland

Gary DeLorenzo	California University of Pennsylvania, USA
Ioan Constantin Dima	Valahia University of Targoviste, Romania
Yanqing Duan	University of Bedfordshire, UK
Helena Dudycz	Wrocław University of Economics, Poland
Ibrahim El Emary	King Abdulaziz University, Saudi Arabia
Susana de Juana Espinosa	University of Alicante, Spain
Nitza Geri	The Open University of Israel, Israel
Tanja Grublješič	University of Ljubljana, Slovenia
Leila Halawi	Embry-Riddle Aeronautical University, USA
Jarosław Jankowski	West Pomeranian University of Technology in Szczecin, Poland
Dorota Jelonek	Czestochowa University of Technology, Poland
Andrzej Kobyliński	Warsaw School of Economics, Poland
Krzysztof Michalik	University of Economics in Katowice, Poland
Roisin Mullins	University of Wales Trinity Saint David, UK
Marian Niedźwiedziński	University of Lodz, Poland
Mieczysław Owoc	Wroclaw University of Economics, Poland
Necmettin Ozkan	Turkiye Finans Participation Bank, Turkey
Zbigniew Pastuszak	Maria Curie-Sklodowska University, Poland
Jayanthi Ranjan	Institute of Management Technology in Ghaziabad, India
Kun Ren	Yale University, USA
Nina Rizun	Alfred Nobel University, Dnipropetrovs'k, Ukraine
Marcin Schroeder	Akita International University, Japan
Marcin Sikorski	Gdańsk University of Technology, Poland
Vered Silber-Varod	The Open University of Israel, Israel
Robert Skovira	Robert Morris University, USA
Andrzej Sobczak	Warsaw School of Economics, Poland
Jerzy Surma	Warsaw School of Economics, Poland
Urszula Świerczyńska-Kaczor	Jan Kochanowski University in Kielce, Poland
Symeon Symeonidis	Democritus University of Thrace, Greece
Edward Szczerbicki	University of Newcastle, Australia
Ali Tarhini	Brunel University London, UK
Bob Travica	University of Manitoba, Canada
Bartosz Wachnik	University of Technology in Warsaw, Poland
Jarosław Wątróbski	West Pomeranian University of Technology in Szczecin, Poland
Janusz Wielki	Opole University of Technology, Poland
Waldemar Wolski	University of Szczecin, Poland
Paweł Ziemba	The Jacob of Paradyż University of Applied Science, Poland

Contents

Information Technology and Systems for Knowledge Management

Towards Context-Aware Supervision for Logistics Asset Management:
Concept Design and System Implementation 3
  Fan Feng, Yusong Pang, and Gabriel Lodewijks

Paired Transactions and Their Models 20
  Frantisek Hunka and Jiri Matula

Extension of Intelligence of Decision Support Systems: Manager
Perspective. 35
  Jerzy Korczak, Helena Dudycz, Bartłomiej Nita, Piotr Oleksyk,
  and Adrian Kaźmierczak

Use of Information and Communication Technologies for Knowledge
Sharing by Polish and UK-Based Prosumers. 49
  Ewa Ziemba, Monika Eisenbardt, and Roisin Mullins

Information Technology and Systems for Business Transformation

Analysis of Predispositions of E-gamers and Its Relevance
in the Use of Computer Games Didactic Process. 77
  Witold Chmielarz and Oskar Szumski

Assessing the IT and Software Landscapes of Industry 4.0-Enterprises:
The Maturity Model SIMMI 4.0 103
  Christian Leyh, Thomas Schäffer, Katja Bley, and Sven Forstenhäusler

The Role of ICT Solutions in the Intelligent Enterprise Performance 120
  Monika Łobaziewicz

Evaluation of User Specific Privacy Policy Architecture for Collaborative
BPaaS on the Example of Logistics. 137
  Björn Schwarzbach, Michael Glöckner, Bogdan Franczyk,
  and André Ludwig

Implementation and Evaluation of Information Systems

Examining the Antecedents and Outcomes of ERP Implementation Success:
An Explanatory Study 157
  Prodromos Chatzoglou, Dimitrios Chatzoudes,
  and Georgia Apostolopoulou

Examining the Critical Success Factors for ERP Implementation:
An Explanatory Study Conducted in SMEs   179
    Prodromos Chatzoglou, Dimitrios Chatzoudes, Leonidas Fragidis,
    and Symeon Symeonidis

Patterns of Communication Management in Project Teams.   202
    Karolina Muszyńska

Using PEQUAL Methodology in Auction Platforms Evaluation Process.   222
    Jarosław Wątróbski, Paweł Ziemba, Jarosław Jankowski,
    and Waldemar Wolski

Author Index   243

Information Technology and Systems for Knowledge Management

Towards Context-Aware Supervision for Logistics Asset Management: Concept Design and System Implementation

Fan Feng[✉], Yusong Pang, and Gabriel Lodewijks

Transport Engineering and Logistics, Delft University of Technology,
Mekelweg 2, 2628 CD Delft, The Netherlands
{f.feng,y.pang,g.lodewijks}@tudelft.nl

Abstract. Innovations of information and communication technology (ICT) open plenty opportunities to promote internal operation efficiency and external service level in logistics. As current logistics developments tend to be more complex in operation and large in scale, recent practices start to pay more attentions on improving asset (e.g. equipment and infrastructure) management performance with new ICT development. One of the primary concern is to improve system robustness and reliability. It not only requires the supervision system be capable of diagnosing the condition of the system, but also proficient to find the intrinsic relationship between different conditions and resources thus lead to an integrated decision making process. Moreover, recent ICT innovations, such as WSN and IOT, could record and deliver system descriptors (physical measurements, virtual resources, operational configurations) in real time. Such large-stream and heterogeneous data requires an integrated framework to process and management. To address such challenges, in this paper, a novel concept of context-aware supervision is proposed. An intelligent system with integration of semantic web and agent technology is developed, which aims at providing condition-monitoring and maintenance decisions to relevant user. A generic ontology-agent based framework will be illustrated. The developed system will be applied for the supervision of a large-scale material handling system-belt conveying system as a proof-of-concept.

Keywords: Logistics asset management · Context-awareness · Ontology-agent integration · System supervision

1 Introduction

As the scale of transport and logistics system tremendously expanded, the attention of researchers and engineers have been shifted from improving operational efficiency towards enhancing system reliability. Takata [4] revealed this paradigm shift by demonstrating that the ultimate objective for a manufacturing is not only to produce products in an efficient way but also to provide the functions needed by society in a sustainable and reliable way. It is well known that operations of large logistics infrastructures are heavily rely on reliable and efficient equipment, such as container transportation, production assembling line and etc. And such equipment, like automated

© Springer International Publishing AG 2017
E. Ziemba (Ed.): AITM 2016/ISM 2016, LNBIP 277, pp. 3–19, 2017.
DOI: 10.1007/978-3-319-53076-5_1

assembling line machinery, AGV and belt conveying system, are normally have complex structures and massive capital investment. If a malfunction of single component or process has not been detected and corrected timely, it could lead to an expensive downtime and furthermore impose a great impact on the entire logistic activities. Consequently, a system with decision support becomes an essential element to provide relevant users a consistent understanding regards the system status and enabling an effective planning and execution of maintenance.

To implement an efficient supervision system, ICT is seen as a key enabler. Indeed, the ICT has been widely used for assisting information intensive tasks in logistics such as resource planning, order processing, crew scheduling and so on [1–3]. With respect to asset management, it demands an efficient supervision system to delivering right information (e.g. system condition, maintenance decisions) to right person (inspector, technical engineer) at right time to right place. Specifically, how to determine the 'rightness' with respect to fault condition identification, information integration, information presentation and information delivering becomes critical. Several challenges are summarized as follows:

- Heterogeneity: The heterogeneity is defined as system entities have different types of data model, properties, operation mechanisms and even different hardware and operating system [5]. As for TEL management especially for asset management and supervision, different data resources, operational information, past experiences and knowledges are characterized as heterogeneous resource, thus impose difficulties in integration.
- Interoperability: With respect to interoperability, three perspectives can be identified [6], (1) organizational level: generic approaches and shared understanding of concepts, process, beliefs and terms [7]. (2) system level: interconnection between independent systems. (3) data level: consider the data properties include data format, data availability, data representation and semantic meanings. With respect to asset supervision, the interoperability challenges are inevitably presented at all three levels.
- Integrated decision making: Logistics asset normally depicted as large-scale and complex equipment. If a malfunction of single component or process has not been detected and corrected timely, it could lead to an expensive downtime and furthermore impose a great impact on the entire logistic activities. Consequently, a system with decision support becomes an essential element to provide relevant users a consistent understanding regards the system status and enabling an effective planning and execution of maintenance, such functionality could be referred as integrated decision making.

To confront with above mentioned challenges, the concept of e-maintenance which utilizes ICT technology to implement a web-based monitor system is suggested [8]. Candell et al. [9] presented an e-maintenance framework that integrated maintenance and ICT perspectives to support maintenance task in aviation industry. Arnaiz et al. [10] applied e-maintenance in manufacturing and logistics operations by means of advanced ICT technologies. Though attractive, the e-maintenance system still has limitations [11]: (1) instead of introducing a layer of semantic, the use of e-maintenance system focused on expanding the descriptive scope of existing models which results in an inefficient support for format generalization and standardization and eventually too complex for users to process; (2) direct working on large stream of data could limit contributions to share knowledge and expertise. Followed by e-maintenance, a new paradigm has emerged named context-aware monitoring system [12]. It was firstly designed as a component of ubiquitous computing environment and recently been introduced to the system monitoring domain. Galar et al. [13] presented a hybrid context-awareness model to facilitate the asset life cycle management. Evchina et al. [14] proposed a context-aware middleware to assist the data-intensive monitoring tasks, and the framework is validated by means of case study in the domain of building automation. Pistofidis et al. [15] proposed a context-awareness system for asset management based on mobile and cloud technology. Inspired by the concept of context-aware monitoring, in this paper, the concept of context-aware supervision will be initiated.

The works presented in this paper is a continues work with respect to [36]. In [36], the concept of CASS is briefly introduced. In this paper, we elaborate the detailed implementation of the CASS. The purpose of CASS will be further motivated. The developed system will be applied to assist the practical maintenance tasks for a large-scale belt conveyor system. Moreover, the software packages used to system development will be specifically explained.

The remaining part of the paper is organized as follows: Sect. 2 will introduce the concept of context-aware supervision system (CASS) and the motivations behind it. Section 3 will provide key technological enablers that could support the implementation of a CASS system. Section 4 will first present the system design with an abstract structure perspective and the design of each functional block. Section 5 will present a case study of applying CASS for intelligent supervision of a large-scale belt conveying system. The conclusion and future works will be addressed in Sect. 6.

2   The Concept of Context-Aware Supervision

The definition of context is given by [16] as *any information that can be used to characterize the situation of an entity. An entity is a person, place or object that is considered relevant to the interaction between a user and an application, including the user and the application themselves.* And a system can be termed as context-aware if *it uses context to provide relevant information and/or services to the user, where relevancy depends on the user's task* [16]. A context-aware system (CAS) adapts and provides relevant information and the most appropriate service to users in an active and autonomous manner while requires little interactions [13]. Take advantage of such property, the CAS has been applied in various domains such as health care [17], pervasive computing [18], data intensive monitoring [14], enterprise application model [19] and so on. It is noted that the mentioned CAS are represented with a layered framework which is generally composed of sensor layer for data acquisition, data layer for storage, processing layer for context modelling and application layer for context delivery and representation. The ultimate goal is to deliver right information with right format to right user in right time.

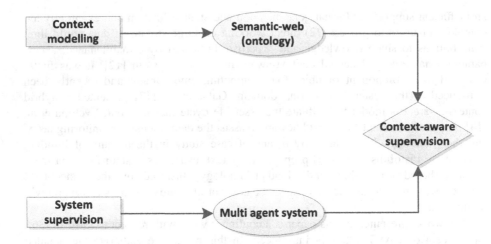

Fig. 1. General philosophy of a context-aware supervision framework

In this research, we focus on investigating the potential of applying CAS for asset supervision service. In essence, the supervision services include system monitoring, failure/abnormality diagnosis/prognosis and maintenance planning. Apart of being context-aware of delivering meaningful information to user, it also requires a transparent flow from data to supervision method. The objective of a supervision system is to deliver accurate and timely information regards system conditions and propose effective maintenance actions to ensure reliability and availability of the system. Its success relies on integrating different diagnosis/prognosis methods and such methods most often have certain scope of applicability and input context. As such, it put additional requirements on CAS to systematically integrate and manage system supervision processes. To integrate CAS for system supervision and fulfil additional requirements, a novel concept of *Context-aware supervision* is initiated as:

A context-aware supervision system (CASS) should include a series of functionalities include monitoring, supporting and advising in relation to system events. It not only focuses on diagnosing and prognosis failures, but also responsible for managing and organizing system knowledge, reasoning facts, integrating resources and analysing problems. As such, the failure context can be given in a more meaningful manner that delivers information include: the specification of fault condition, recorded data linked to it, maintenance or operating actions linked to it, users that responsible for it and method that been used to determine it.

The characters of *context-awareness* are presented at two levels in CASS: (1) the supervision method should be aware of the context information it operates upon; (2) the end user should comprehend the created supervision context. In literature, several works have been established which attempt to consolidate the concept of context-aware with asset management such as context-awareness predictive maintenance [20], context-aware E-maintenance [15] and context-aware condition monitoring [13]. Two limitations are drawn from previous works: (1) the scope of applicability of proposed concept is limited given the fact that it only concerns partial aspect of the supervision process, For instance, the work of [20] concerns predictive maintenance, it lacks details regards how context been modelled and processed, (2) most works stay on a conceptual level which lack of sufficient technical details on how to put the concept into practice.

A context-aware supervision system is used for information integration and supervision of large-scale asset service in TEL domain. The key ICT enablers are semantic web and autonomous agent and its philosophy is depicted in Fig. 1. Specifically, the ontology is used to model the semantic connections for heterogeneous data and various entities in supervision domain, thus enable information integration, data filtering and problem decomposition for specific supervision tasks. The use of agent system intends to provide intelligent diagnosis and decision making function-alities through agent intelligence and cooperation. Our work contribute to the literature by first introducing the concept of CASS, then we will discuss the technology been selected for putting such concept into action. Finally, a case study would demonstrate how the system works.

3 Key Methodologies for CASS Implementation

This section will discuss the key technological enablers for implementing a CASS, which include the method for context-modelling and system supervision.

3.1 Context-Modelling Methodology

Intuitively, large amount of context information is either acquired or derived from sensor devices. Normally, there exist gaps between raw data and the level of infor-mation which is useful to applications [21]. The context-modelling is used to bridge this gap by processing and transforming raw data before passed to context-aware services. Krummenacher et al. [22] have proposed several criteria for context model selection which include applicability, comparability, traceability, quality and so on. Meanwhile, Hoareau et al. [21] conducted an extensive review for existing modelling choices such as key value models, makeup scheme, logic based models, object oriented models, ontology and so on. According to their in-depth discussion, the use of ontology is proposed to be the most expressive models to fulfil our requirements [23]. A formal definition of ontology is given by [24] as *an explicit specification of a conceptual-ization* which was used to describe a specific domain knowledge where concepts and relationships are unambiguously defined and checked.

Recent works extensively applied ontology to facilitate the context modelling, its applicability covers domain include risk management of cold chain logistics [25], enterprise application [26], process supervision [27] and so on.

3.2 System Supervision

A system supervision process considers providing users with decision support before/during/after the occurrence of system failure or abnormal situations. A typical supervision process consists of data acquisition, condition diagnosing/prognosis and maintenance planning. In this paper, rather than considering specific method or algorithm, we focus on how to provide a generic and adaptive environment to incorporate and integrate different methodologies and mechanisms operate together with flexibility and scalability. Several requirements are given as below:

- Flexibility: Be aware of and accommodate to different system conditions and retrofits seamlessly.
- Cooperative: It should cooperate and coexist with different software system and third party interface. Be capable of accessing information and providing diagnosis result in meaningful form.
- Collaborative: Enable collaborative decision making process with different diagnosis/prognosis methods. Support seamlessly information exchange between different supervision modules to achieve cohesive judgment of overall system conditions.
- Extensibility: The system should be able to incorporate new supervision method or update existing one without significant change of the system architecture. New measurement, supervision intelligence and human expertise could be deployed seamlessly as needed.

Agent, as a tool in artificial intelligence domain, provides a way of dealing with complex engineering problem and establishing adaptive system for decision making and information management through agent intelligence and collaborations [28]. State-of-arts demonstrate that agent system have been largely applied to support system supervision functions, which include condition monitoring [29], risk management [30] e-maintenance [31] and so on. Given such facts, agent technology is chosen as the key enabler for supervision system design, reasons are given as: (1) agent could cooperate and deploy on top of existing software; (2) in a multi-agent-system, agents could collaborate with each other to communicate and exchange information; (3) agent system could be deployed in distributed environment where new agent could easily join the system or leave the system as needed.

3.3 Ontology-Agent Integration

Key technological enablers have been chosen in previous section. We select ontology as the context-modelling method and agent system as the environment to support system supervision integration. In order to implement CASS, a next step is to consider the integration issues. In literature, several works have been established that concerns the integration of ontology and agent system. Natarajan et al. [32] developed an ontology-agent framework for condition supervision of large chemical plant. Dibley et al. [33] presented a work of building monitoring system where three ontologies are developed to capture the major semantics of a building environment and agent system is deployed to facilitate the monitoring tasks. For most of existing works, attentions are paid on using ontology to assist agent communication and knowledge retrieving. To implement CASS, potentials include information analysis, problem decomposition, agent status control are needed. To achieve this, a novel ontology-agent integrated framework is proposed, it will be elaborated in next section.

4 System Framework

The key framework will be given in this section. We first present a comparison between a context-aware system and the proposed context-aware supervision system. It used to emphasis the purposes and objective of the concept. Then aspects such as context model design, agent system design and ontology-agent integration mechanism will be elaborated in different sections.

4.1 Comparison Between CAS and CASS

Figure 2 presents a comparison between a context-aware system and the proposed context-aware supervision system from an abstract structure perspective. A classical context-aware system follows five key processes [17]: (1) context information acquisition: gather information from virtual resources and physical sensors; (2) context-information persistent: data filtering and storing; (3) context-aggregation/reasoning: interpretation and transfer low-order data to high-level applicable information via aggregation and reasoning; (4) context information utilization/delivering: apply context information to implement application-specific service; (5) context representation.

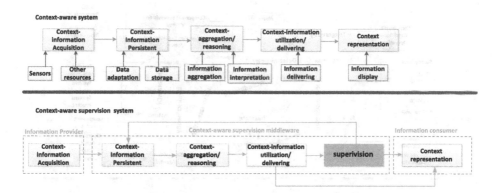

Fig. 2. System abstract architecture: a comparison between CAS and CASS

The abstract structure of a CASS can be found in Fig. 2 as well. All of the functional blocks from CAS are inherited and implemented in CASS. The major difference is distinguished from two aspects:

- The supervision block: The key objective of CASS is to assist system supervision with aspects include equipment monitoring, condition diagnosis and maintenance planning. Such tasks are unable to perform well by only using context-modelling (e.g. ontology reasoning). In most cases, it requires advanced platform/engine for decision making. As such, the supervision block is introduced.

The information flow: The information flow is also adjusted. In CAS, the information flow follows an open loop style where data is gathered from ground layer, processed through each functional block and becomes context-aware. For CASS, a partial closed-loop is formed. In essence, the aggregated and processed context information will be the input source for supervision module. The output of supervision module will be feedback for further processing. It will be first stored in data base and then processed by context model. By doing so, not only the measured data from ground layer would be context-aware but also the supervised result will be aggregated with other relevant information together to make result meaningful to end user. Moreover, it would be helpful to use the returned supervision information to infer new knowledge and propose further actions.

The major abstract module for a CASS is explained, the detailed system design will be given in the following sections.

4.2   Context Model Design

We design an ontology termed *ontoSupervision* to capture major concepts and relationships related to system supervision process. The schematic of *ontoSupervision* is given in Fig. 3 and the explanations of each taxonomy are given below:

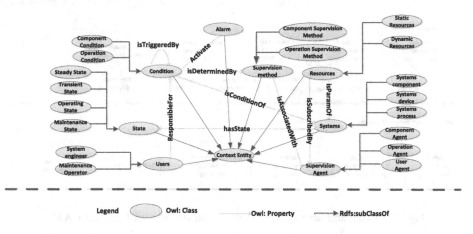

Fig. 3. Upper ontology taxonomy: definition of classes and object properties

System taxonomy is the core concept that presents a description of the system. It includes notions of system fundamental components and operations that needs to be supervised. In addition, the subclass *system devices* contains peripheral devices. Other taxonomies either direct or indirect connect with system through well-defined relationships.

Condition taxonomy incorporates the notion of condition in the system. Two subclasses are included, namely operation condition and component condition. The former one concerns the system abnormal condition during operations and the latter one addresses the physical condition of system at different levels (component, instrument and equipment).

Resources taxonomy represents all relevant information resources that need to be accessed by supervision method. It is composed of two subclasses, namely static resources and dynamic resources. The former one can be thought as the resource that does not change over time such as system specification, historical information and system configurations. The latter one represents the notion of resources that change in real time, such as data acquired from sensor devices and any updated supervision results.

Supervision agent & method represents all available agents been deployed in current system and its associated supervision method. In essence, it serves as a bridge that connects context model with agent system.

State taxonomy represents possible state of the system. In current model, four states are considered namely maintenance state, transient state and operation state and steady state.

Alarm taxonomy represents the notion of possible alarm level that been activated by supervised conditions in the system.

User represents the information consumers in the system. It specifies the responsibilities and point of interests of respective user.

Apart of taxonomy definitions, a complete ontology also includes the design of properties. The object property is used to specify the relationship between two individuals (instance of classes), where the data property is used to link individual to data values. For *ontoSupervision*, the object properties are depicted in Table 1.

Table 1. Object properties of *ontoSupervision*

Property	Domain	Range
isAssociatedWith	Supervision method	Supervision method
isParameterOf	Resources	System
isSubscirbedBy	Resources	Supervision agent
isDeterminedBy	Condition	Supervision method
Activates	Condition	Alarm
hasState	System	State
hasCondition	System	Condition
isTriggeredBy	Condition	Condition

4.3 Multi-agent System Design

Regardless of the models, scopes and design tools, all supervision methods require system measurements as input and transform system conditions (operation and component condition) to supervision result. The supervision result refers to the one that is understandable by respective users. Such common structure allows the supervision methods to be represented as supervision agent [27]. The multi agent system can be perceived as a wrapper which provides environment for different supervision intelligence to perform supervision tasks. It also enables integrated decision making by taking the advantages of agent communication and collaboration. In the proposed framework, three kinds of agent are employed:

- Supervision Agent: Two categories of agent groups are considered as supervision agent. The first one is termed healthiness agent (HA) which is responsible for fault diagnosis at different level of system granularity. Single HA could be used to assess the condition of piece of equipment while multi HAs could work together for evaluating the overall healthiness of the whole system by consolidating different conditions. Another one is termed operation agent (OA) which is used to capture the abnormality during system operation. Typically, it is used to identify the abnormal deviation from normal operations or improper configurations. The agent intelligence, scope of interest, input information and responsibility are determined by its associated methods.

- Information Mediator Agent: The information mediator is used to manage and control the agent execution and interactions. Its necessities are given as (1) It serves as an information portal for supervision agents.; (2) it keeps an active connection between agent system and ontology knowledge model.

- User Agent: It contains the information consumer of the system. Any on-going supervision conditions will be relayed to it via IMA. Sophisticated GUI will connect with it to provide end user a friendly interface.

The overall agent system framework is given in Fig. 4 which follows a *subscription* interaction protocol. The initiator (supervision agent and user agent) sends subscription request to the participator (information mediator agent) indicating its desired information. If the subscribe action success, a permanent communication channel is established between the initiator and participator. The advantage of adapting subscription protocol is given that only information needed would be delivered to target agent with efficiency and accuracy.

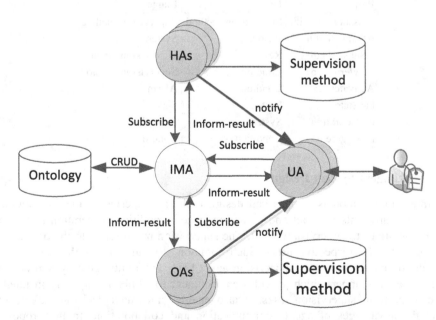

Fig. 4. Agent system framework: topology and communication protocol

4.4 Agent-Ontology Integration

The key of agent-ontology integration is achieved via the interaction between information mediator agent and ontology knowledge base. Such interactions aim at manipulating ontology to acquire information and knowledges where actions include create, read, update and delete entities in ontology. We identified three major processes:

- *Information acquisition*: In this case, ontology is treated as a hybrid database which is used to locate and retrieve information. A typical scenario can be that when a new sensor measurement is available in ontology, the IMA could retrieve it by executing well defined query template. An example of a query template is shown in Fig. 5.

```
SELECT ?par ?agent ?system ?method ?timeStamp
?state ?measurement
WHERE {
            ?par onto:isSubscribedBy ?agent.
            ?par onto:isParametersOf ?system.
            ?agent rdf:type onto:AgentName.
            ?method onto:isAssociatedWith ?agent.
            ?system onto:hasState ?state.
            ?par onto:hasTimeStamp ?timeStamp.
            ?par onto:isMeasuredBy ?measurement.}
```

Fig. 5. Example of information acquisition template

- *Knowledge acquisition*: It fully utilizes the reasoning capability of an ontology model. When certain information is available, the ontology could infer new knowledge by executing context-rules. For instance, if a belt idler temperature is over 70 degree, the ontology could use rules to determine that such context indicates a idler is in fault condition.

- *Knowledge reasoning and agent control*: As discussed previously, a partial closed loop is formed in the structure of CASS. The key motivation is given that any returned supervised information could be further processed by ontology. And the inferred knowledge could be useful in coordinating agent activities. For instance, a misalignment condition often occurs during the running of a belt conveyor and such condition could be induced by multiple reasons (improper power supply, overloading and so on) and such casualty relationships could be pre-defined in the ontology via proper object properties. By doing so, when a misalignment condition is supervised and returned, the ontology could running context rules to find the relevant condition relate with it. Consequently, the associated agent will be activated to allow a depth investigation of the root cause.

5   Case Study

The concept of CASS and its implementation framework has been proposed. Key technology enablers and their integration have been elaborated. To demonstrate how it works, a prove-of-concept is presented in this section. We applied CASS for a large scale material handling system- belt conveying system.

5.1   Background

Belt conveyor system (BCS) is widely accepted as a major equipment in continues material handling domain. Its usages are well developed in various logistics domains, such as container/dry bulk terminals, airport and mine industry. Normally, the BCS is deployed in an open and harsh environment, as such, major components could suffer severe damage as system ages. Consequently, a monitoring and supervision system with decision support is essential to help users (from operations, maintenance, reliability and other departments) gain a consistent understanding about the system status and enabling effective planning and execution of maintenance. Due to the limit space of the paper, we demonstrate a typical fault supervision process- belt tear condition supervision which is made up for 85% among all system component damages for a BCS [34].

5.2   Belt Tear Condition Supervision

This scenario demonstrates the CASS capability of the system. Specifically, when inspection of tear shape is available, the system should analyse the damage level and propagation pace of the damage by intelligent supervision method, and create decisions in the form of possible maintenance activities and/or warning/alarm message if needed. We identify three key processes of implementing the context-aware supervision service for belt tear condition:

- Context modelling: It concerns extending the upper ontology (ontoSupervision) with definition of new entities for application purpose. Such extension is termed domain-specific ontology and partial illustration for BCS supervision (*ontoBeltCon*) is depicted in Fig. 6. The semantic meaning is given as: a tear shape (TS) *isMeasuredBy* a human inspection tool(HIT), which *isParameterOf* belt (belt Sect. 01). To supervise the tear condition, a belt tear supervision agent (BTSA) is designed. The BTSA *hasAssociatedMethod* belt tear supervision method (BTSM1). For supervision purpose, TS and a belt tear condition log (BTCL) *isSubscribedBy* BTSA. Upon successful decision making, a belt tear condition (BTC) is supervised which *isDeterminedBy* BTSM1 and *activates* alarm (alarm level 1). Finally the BTC *isResponisbleFor* user (maintenance operator 01). Besides newly added entities and its individuals, the data properties for a belt tear shape and belt tear condition is also available in Fig. 6.
- Context supervision: After context information are collected and pre-processed by ontology, the agent intelligence should be invoked. For a belt tear condition

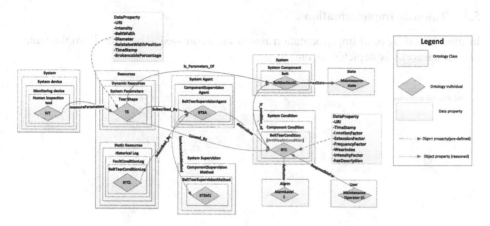

Fig. 6. *OntoBeltCon* configuration for belt tear condition supervision: include class, subclasses, data properties and object properties

supervision, a fuzzy logic based approach is applied [34]. Decisions are made based on the current tear shape measurement and history inspection log for the same shape. Two indicators (belt wear index and inspection frequency index) are provided to deliver a consistent understanding and interpretation of the supervision result and give straight forward suggestions for possible maintenance actions.

• Response actions: The supervised condition will be send back to ontology model for further processing before finally delivered to end users. In essence, it will use the supervision indicators to quantify the alarm level by running defined rules. For the given scenario, the rules can be given as Eqs. (1) and (2):

$$
\begin{aligned}
&BeltTearCondition(?condition), greaterThan(?level, 0), hasWearIndex(?condition\\
&, ?level), lessThanOrEqual(?level, 0.7) - > AntiHealthCondition(?condition)
\end{aligned}
$$
(1)

$$
\begin{aligned}
&BeltTearCondition(?condition), greaterThan(?level, 0), hasWearIndex(?condition\\
&, ?level), greaterThanOrEqual(?level, 0.7) - > FaultCondition(?condition)
\end{aligned}
$$
(2)

The semantic meaning is explained as: if a belt tear condition is confirmed and its wear index is go beyond 0.7, then a fault condition is inferred, while if the value is below 0.7 then an anti-health condition is given. Based on the triggered condition type, different alarm level is reasoned followed by rules given in Eq. (3):

$$
\begin{aligned}
&AntiHealthCondition(?condition) - > activates(?condition, AlarmLevel2)\\
&FaultCondition(?condition) - > activates(?condition, AlarmLevel3)
\end{aligned}
$$
(3)

5.3 Towards Implementation

In this section, several implementation issues are addressed. The overall implementation frameworks is depicted in Fig. 7.

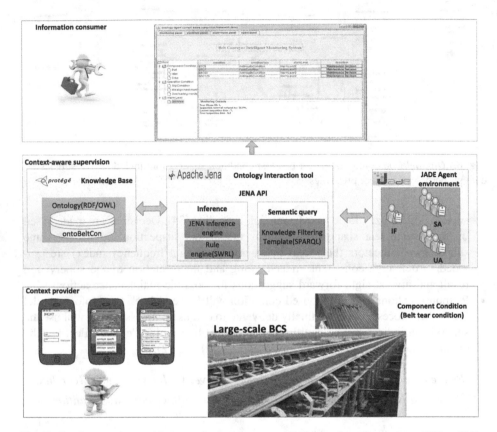

Fig. 7. Implementation architecture: ground layer: mobile inspection of tear shape [35]; middle layer: CASS; upper layer: GUI programmed uses Java-Swing

For the belt tear shape inspection, a mobile based tool is implemented [35]. It is used to assist human inspectors to register and record inspection data. The information will be pre-processed and send to CASS remotely for further processing.

The context model *ontoBeltCon* is created using open source tool Protege[1] and the ontology inference is realized via Pallet reasoner[2]. It has been saved as an owl file and persisted in remote server.

---

[1] Protégé, http://protege.stanford.edu/.

[2] Pallet, https://www.w3.org/2001/sw/wiki/Pellet.

For agent system implementation, a JAVA-based agent development environment (JADE)[3] tool is adapted. The JADE compliant with FIPA-standard[4] and provides an rich libraries and tools for controlling and managing agent behaviour. The supervision method is programmed in java and packaged in the agent behaviour. The inter-communication between agent is supported by the build-in ACL messages.

For agent-ontology integration, Apache-JENA[5] is used. It is a middle-ware that allow any Java-based program to interact with ontology. Through Jena, the JADE agent could interact with ontology and perform actions include create, update, read and delete (CRUD). And all the operations is done by implementing and executing SPARQL queries.

Finally, for demonstration purpose, a simple GUI is programmed by using Java swing to show how the system behaves.

6 Conclusion and Future Works

In this paper, a novel concept of context-aware supervision and its associated implementation techniques are proposed. The motivation behind the concept is to enable an efficient and transparent information flow for asset supervision tasks. We implement such system for supervision of a large-scale material handling system to demonstrate its major functionalities and potential usage in the domain of logistics. The designed system properly addresses the challenges mentioned in Sect. 1 as follows:

- Heterogeneity: A key concept of managing heterogeneity is to make such resources transparent. The use of ontology captures the capabilities and structure of such resource into a suitable representations and provide uniform storage platform that assist the work flows of heterogeneity environment.
- Interoperability: The data level interoperability is dealt with by means of ontology. The system level interoperability is addressed by establishing a uniform agent-ontology integration mechanism. The one in organization level is approached by means of context-aware service.
- Integrated decision making: The integrated decision making for asset supervision is achieved by designing and deploying a multi agent system that running and collaborating different intelligence together.

By integrating ontology with agent system, a novel ICT framework is created. The developed system together with the technological enablers are generic. As such we conclude that the system and concept is free to use in other similar domains. Future works include further extending the ontology model to incorporate more generic entities and concept in the system supervision domain. Moreover, to cope with more complex diagnosis/prognosis problem and enable more sophisticated decision making engine, the agent intelligence can be future investigated.

---

[3] JADE, https://jena.apache.org/.

[4] FIPA, http://www.fipa.org/.

[5] JENA, https://jena.apache.org/.

Acknowledgement. This research is supported by the China Scholarship Council under Grant 201307720072.

References

1. Neng Chiu, H.: The integrated logistics management system: a framework and case study. Int. J. Phys. Distrib. Logistics Manage. **25**(6), 4–22 (1995)
2. Gunasekaran, A., Ngai, E.W., Cheng, T.E.: Developing an e-logistics system: a case study. Int. J. Logistics **10**(4), 333–349 (2007)
3. De La Cruz, A.L., Veeke, H.P.M., Lodewijks, G.: Prognostics in the control of logistics systems. In: Proceedings of IEEE International Conference on Service Operations and Logistics, and Informatics, pp. 1–5 (2006)
4. Takata, S., Kirnura, F., Van Houten, F.J.A.M., Westkamper, E., Shpitalni, M., Ceglarek, D., Lee, J.: Maintenance: changing role in life cycle management. CIRP Ann. Manuf. Technol. **53**(2), 643–655 (2004)
5. Thomas, G., Thompson, G.R., Chung, C.W., Barkmeyer, E., Carter, F., Templeton, M., Fox, S., Hartman, B.: Heterogeneous distributed database systems for production use. ACM Comput. Surv. (CSUR) **22**(3), 237–266 (1990)
6. Winters, L.S., Gorman, M.M., Tolk, A.: Next generation data interoperability: it's all about the metadata. In: IEEE Fall Simulation Interoperability Workshop (2006)
7. Clark, T., Jones, R.: Organisational interoperability maturity model for C2. In: Proceedings of the 1999 Command and Control Research and Technology Symposium (1999)
8. Chioreanu, A., Brad, S., Porumb, C., Porumb, S.: E-maintenance ontology-based approach for heterogeneous distributed robotic production capabilities. Int. J. Comput. Integr. Manuf. **28**(2), 200–212 (2015)
9. Candell, O., Karim, R., Söderholm, P.: eMaintenance—Information logistics for maintenance support. Rob. Comput. Integr. Manuf. **25**(6), 937–944 (2009)
10. Arnaiz, A., Iung, B., Adgar, A., Naks, T., Tohver, A., Tommingas, T., Levrat, E.: Information and communication technologies within E-maintenance. In: E-maintenance, pp. 39–60. Springer, London (2010)
11. Pistofidis, P., Emmanouilidis, C., Papadopoulos, A., Botsaris, P.N.: Modeling the semantics of failure context as a means to offer context-adaptive maintenance support. In: Proceedings of Second European Conference of the Prognostics and Health Management Society, pp. 8–10. PHME (2014)
12. Hong, J.Y., Suh, E.H., Kim, S.J.: Context-aware systems: a literature review and classification. Expert Syst. Appl. **36**(4), 8509–8522 (2009)
13. Galar, D., Thaduri, A., Catelani, M., Ciani, L.: Context awareness for maintenance decision making: a diagnosis and prognosis approach. Measurement **67**, 137–150 (2015)
14. Evchina, Y., Puttonen, J., Dvoryanchikova, A., Lastra, J.L.M.: Context-aware knowledge-based middleware for selective information delivery in data-intensive monitoring systems. Eng. Appl. Artif. Intell. **43**, 111–126 (2015)
15. Pistofidis, P., Emmanouilidis, C.: Profiling context awareness in mobile and cloud based engineering asset management. In: Emmanouilidis, C., Taisch, M., Kiritsis, D. (eds.) APMS 2012. IAICT, vol. 398, pp. 17–24. Springer, Heidelberg (2013). doi:10.1007/978-3-642-40361-3_3
16. Dey, A.K.: Understanding and using context. Pers. Ubiquit. Comput. **5**(1), 4–7 (2001)
17. Forkan, A., Khalil, I., Tari, Z.: CoCaMAAL: A cloud-oriented context-aware middleware in ambient assisted living. Future Gener. Comput. Syst. **35**, 114–127 (2014)

18. Garrido, P.C., Ruiz, I.L., Gómez-Nieto, M.Á.: OBCAS: an agent-based system and ontology for mobile context aware interactions. J. Intell. Inform. Syst. **43**(1), 33–57 (2014)
19. El Kadiri, S., Grabot, B., Thoben, K.D., Hribernik, K., Emmanouilidis, C., von Cieminski, G., Kiritsis, D.: Current trends on ICT technologies for enterprise information systems. Comput. Ind. **79**, 14–33 (2016)
20. Kumar, U., Ahmadi, A., Verma, A.K., Varde, P.: Current Trends in Reliability, Availability, Maintainability and Safety: An industry Perspective. Springer, Switzerland (2015)
21. Hoareau, C., Satoh, I.: Modelling and processing information for context-aware computing: a survey. New Gener. Comput. **27**(3), 177–196 (2009)
22. Krummenacher, R., Strang, T.: Ontology-based context modelling. In: Proceedings (2007)
23. Schmohl, R., Baumgarten, U.: A generalized context-aware architecture in heterogeneous mobile computing environments. In: Proceedings of the Fourth International Conference on Wireless and Mobile Communications, ICWMC 2008, pp. 118–124 (2008)
24. Staab, S., Studer, R.: Handbook on Ontologies. Springer Science & Business Media (2013)
25. Kim, K., Kim, H., Kim, S.K., Jung, J.Y.: i-RM: An intelligent risk management framework for context-aware ubiquitous cold chain logistics. Expert Syst. Appl. **46**, 463–473 (2016)
26. Nadoveza, D., Kiritsis, D.: Ontology-based approach for context modelling in enterprise applications. Comput. Ind. **65**(9), 1218–1231 (2014)
27. Natarajan, S., Srinivasan, R.: Implementation of multi agents based system for process supervision in large-scale chemical plants. Comput. Chem. Eng. **60**, 182–196 (2014)
28. Feng, F., Pang, Y., Lodewijks, G.: Integrate multi-agent planning in hinterland transport: design, implementation and evaluation. Adv. Eng. Inform. **29**(4), 1055–1071 (2015)
29. Mahdavi, I., Shirazi, B., Ghorbani, N., Sahebjamnia, N.: IMAQCS: design and implementation of an intelligent multi-agent system for monitoring and controlling quality of cement production processes. Comput. Ind. **64**(3), 290–298 (2013)
30. Dawson, R.J., Peppe, R., Wang, M.: An agent-based model for risk-based flood incident management. Nat. Hazards **59**(1), 167–189 (2011)
31. Yu, R., Iung, B., Panetto, H.: A multi-agents based E-maintenance system with case-based reasoning decision support. Eng. Appl. Artif. Intell. **16**(4), 321–333 (2003)
32. Natarajan, S., Ghosh, K., Srinivasan, R.: An ontology for distributed process supervision of large-scale chemical plants. Comput. Chem. Eng. **46**, 124–140 (2012)
33. Dibley, M., Li, H., Rezgui, Y., Miles, J.: An ontology framework for intelligent sensor-based building monitoring. Autom. Constr. **28**, 1–14 (2012)
34. Lodewijks, G., Ottjes, J.A.: Application of fuzzy logic in belt conveyor monitoring and control. BeltCon **13**, 2–3 (2005)
35. Pang, Y., Lodewijks, G.: A remote intelligent belt conveyor inspection tool. In: Proceedings of 11th International Congress Bulk Materials Storage, Handling and Transportation. Newcastle, Australia (2013)
36. Feng, F., Pang, Y., Lodewijks, G.: An intelligent context-aware system for logistics asset supervision service. In: Proceedings of 2016 Federated Conference on Computer Science and Information Systems (FedCSIS), pp. 1147–1152. Gdansk, Poland (2016)

Paired Transactions and Their Models

Frantisek Hunka(✉) and Jiri Matula

University of Ostrava, Dvorakova 7, 701 03 Ostrava, Czech Republic
{frantisek.hunka,jiri.matula}@osu.cz

Abstract. Paired transactions or paired transfers have their origin in accountancy systems. Resource-Event-Agent (REA) ontology uses paired transactions as a basic building block for business process modelling. A business process (REA model) is composed of two kinds of paired transactions which stand for provide (give) and receive (take) transactions (transfers). The REA core pattern which comes from double-booking entry, constitutes the basic structure from which the REA model is further extended. The REA model was previously depicted by ER diagrams, and later by UML class diagrams. However, neither of these diagrams were designed to capture conceptual models which are more precise and comprehensible for domain experts, and easy to modify. ORM (Object Role Modeling) is a Fact-Based Modeling methodology that represents an approach to conceptual modelling that fulfils the requirements. The article presents fact-based models of paired transactions corresponding to the REA core pattern and REA exchange model. These models were created and verified by NORMA (Natural ORM Architect) and provide both semantic stability and semantic relevance, which is necessary for further incorporating the REA modeling approach into fact-based modeling methodologies of business processes.

Keywords: REA ontology · Paired transactions · Fact-based modelling · ORM method

1 Introduction

REA (Resource-Event-Agent) ontology can be classified as a domain-specific ontology that focuses on value-modelling of business processes. The term value-modelling, in this context, means that the REA modelling approach keeps track of primary and raw data about economic resource values. Economic resources can be exchanged for other economic resources within the scope of REA exchange processes or they can be consumed, used or produced within the scope of REA conversion processes. The three core REA concepts are *resource*, *event* and *agent*, from which the name of the modelling approach was derived. The aim of the REA modelling approach is to record any changes in property rights to resources, record resource usage, record resource consumption, or resource production, see [1, 6, 9].

The REA model records information based on the coherence between data of one or more economic events. The REA process is defined by related economic events and has at least two composite economic events: a *decrement event* that outflows, consumes or uses the outgoing resource(s), and an *increment event* that inflows or produces the

© Springer International Publishing AG 2017
E. Ziemba (Ed.): AITM 2016/ISM 2016, LNBIP 277, pp. 20–34, 2017.
DOI: 10.1007/978-3-319-53076-5_2

incoming resource(s). The REA process is called the *REA model* and represents the notion of a business process. The main benefit of the REA modelling approach is the possibility of keeping track of primary and raw data about economic resources, by [7]. All accounting artefacts such as debit, credit, journals, ledgers, receivables and account balances are derived from data describing exchange and conversion REA processes [6, 10]. For example, data describing a sale event is used in warehouse management, payroll, distribution, finance, and other application areas, without transformations or adjustments. This explains why the REA approach can offer a wider, more precise and more-up-to-date range of reports. The REA ontology also benefits from the presence of a semantic and application independent data model, an object-oriented perspective and abstraction from technical and implementation details [7, 9]. These features enable the possibility of calculating the value of the enterprise's resources on demand, as opposed to calculation at pre-determined intervals.

The quality of a database application depends essentially on its design, see [15]. To ensure correctness, clarity, adaptability and productivity, information systems should be specified at the conceptual level first, using concepts and language that both designers and customers can easily understand [8]. Object-Role-Modeling (ORM) is a fact-oriented approach for modelling information at a conceptual level. A fact is a particular arrangement of one or more objects. Depending on the number of objects that are involved in a fact, we speak of unary, binary, ternary, etc., facts. An example of unary fact is a *Vendor is a Person*. An example of a binary fact is that a *Customer receives a Pizza*. Unlike traditional approaches, ORM make no use of attributes such as base constructs, instead expressing all fact types as relationships [8]. This attributes-free-approach leads to greater semantic stability in conceptual models, and enables ORM fact structure to be directly verbalized and populated using natural language sentences.

ORM methodology provides a more precise way to capture and validate data concepts and business rules with domain experts. This methodology provides higher semantic stability and semantic relevance than ER and UML diagrams. Semantic stability is a measure of how well models or queries expressed in the language retain their original intent in the face of changes in the business domain, according to [8]. Semantic relevance requires that only conceptually relevant details need to be modelled, by [8]. ORM also focuses on structural changes in the application. By omitting the attribute concept, ORM allows communication in simple sentences. ORM diagrams simply capture the world in terms of objects (entities or values) that play roles (parts in relationships) which forms fact. ER notation, as well as UML notation, allow relationships to be modelled as attributes. ORM models that capture the world in terms of objects and roles have only one data structure – the relationship type. As a consequence, ORM diagrams take up more space than corresponding UML or ER diagrams. The aim of the paper is to apply the ORM modelling approach to REA core patterns and REA models to obtain easily comprehensible, verifiable, and easily implementable solutions.

This paper is an extended version of the shorter and less comprehensible contribution to the Federated Conference on Computer Science and Information Systems (FedCSIS), which was held in Gdansk in 2016. The extension covers the Fact-Based Model of the REA core pattern, a more precise description and explanation of the

Fact-Based Model of the REA model, and a verification of both models. Apart from these main features the whole text has been revised, corrected, and modified in order to increase comprehensibility and overall clarity.

The structure of the paper is as follows: An overview of business process modelling is provided in Sect. 2. Section 3 describes the REA modelling approach. A concise description of the possibilities of the ORM modelling method are mentioned in Sect. 4. The ORM model of the REA core pattern is described and illustrated in Sect. 5. Section 5 illustrates and depicts the ORM model of the REA model. Discussion of the results is featured in Sect. 6, and the conclusion is contained in Sect. 7.

2 Business Process Modeling

There are a number of methods that deal with business process modelling. Currently the most important methods are IDEF0; see [16], Business Process Modeling Notation, flowcharts, use cases, and data models. The approaches mentioned above model business processes using general-purpose concepts such as activities, data entities, etc., with or without poorly defined rules for formulating well-formed models of enterprise processes. These methods usually cannot offer an answer to questions such as how activities serve to increase the value of an enterprise's resources, and, consequently, these models cannot answer the question of why the enterprise performs its activities.

Research initiatives in the domain of accounting information systems have resulted in proposals of new data models in accounting, especially in models focusing on the modelling of the resource value. New modelling and system design techniques are required for information technologies that can support the enterprise in achieving and sustaining the necessary flexibility. However, traditional process models do not display resource control and value flows. This is the domain particular to value modelling ontologies. Currently, the most popular approaches within the area of enterprise ontologies are e3-value; see [17], and REA ontology for enterprise processes; see [1, 2].

The e3-value ontology stipulates that the actors exchange value objects by means of value activities. The value activity should yield a profit for the actor. Deeper insight into e3-value modelling (such as [17], shows that this method only covers the exchange and trade processes and omits production and conversion processes. The state-of-the-art e3-value model only focuses on the operational level (what has happened), but not on management policies (what could or should happen).

REA ontology links together business process modelling with underlying economic phenomena. It benefits from the presence of a semantic- and application-independent data model, an object-oriented perspective, and abstraction from technical and implementation details.

The REA model is the first semantic application-independent data model which utilizes an object-oriented perspective. The REA model originates from the domain of accounting; see [4] and matured to a conceptual framework and ontology for Enterprise Information Architectures; see [1, 3]. The REA model focuses on core economic phenomena and abstracts from technical and implementation details. The REA model provides concepts to store past and future data consistently.

On the other hand, REA ontology anomalies have their origin in the absence of a rigorous theoretical foundation. The REA model itself does not have given states from which a state machine can be derived. Instead, only the resource states are identified and frequently used as the states of the state machine. As a result, the REA model does not provide revoking operations such as cancellation and roll-back mechanisms. In addition, the REA model is predominantly designed to capture events that are concerned with resource values or resource features. Other events such as business events or information events are difficult to capture and process further. Consequently, REA has difficulty with so-called information or knowledge entities such as contract or schedule. It is possible to create them because creation indicates a value. But the real problem lies in determining the state for which the information entities are valid, see [10].

3   The REA Modeling Approach

The REA core pattern, which comes from double booking entry, underpins the fundamental part of REA ontology [4, 6]. It was McCarthy [4] who was first to recognize that an enterprise's economic activities follows the REA core pattern in which causally related *provide* (give) and *receive* (take) economic events are associated with resources and agents. The fundamental entities of the pattern are different events that are involved in various transactions which have something in common; there has always been a *decrement economic event* (one in which something is provided) and an *increment economic event* (one in which something is received). In addition to economic events, the economic agents that represent human beings partake in the exchange process. Resources are entities which are tracked because their property rights can be exchanged or they can be converted to create new resources. As mutually reciprocal events cannot happen at the same time, the claim entity is utilized for deferred revenue, prepaid expenses, accounts payable, and so on. The REA core pattern is illustrated as a Pizzeria shop in Fig. 1. Economic events in Exchange processes represent the permanent or temporary transfer of property rights to economic resources from one economic agent to another. The transfer of property rights represents the increment or decrement of the value of resources. That is why the term 'value' is utilized in the name of the *value-modelling* approach. The economic events in REA models usually encapsulate properties for *date*, *time* and *location* in space.

Economic events, and the duality relationship by which events are related, play a crucial role in this pattern. All other entities that participate in this pattern are related 'through' economic events. Both agents are related by increment and decrement events because they lose rights to given resources and gain rights to other resources. On the other hand, resources are related to corresponding economic events. The relationship between increment and decrement events is exchange duality. The purpose of exchange duality is to keep track of which resources were exchanged for which. In the REA value model of an exchange process, every increment economic event must be related by an exchange duality to a decrement economic event, and vice versa.

The REA model is an extension of the REA core pattern. The principal feature of the REA modelling approach is that it explicitly distinguishes between past and current events and events performed in the future for which it introduces the commitment

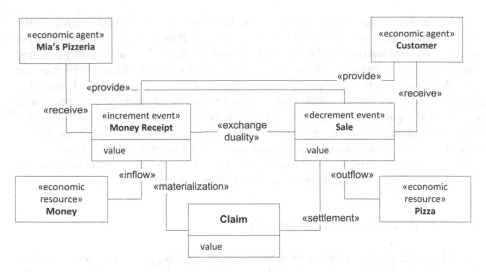

Fig. 1. The REA core pattern example

entity. This explicit distinction between these types of events has its origin in the progressive development of the REA Framework. Curiously, the utilization of a commitment entity is not obligatory but depends only on specific modelling circumstances. The REA core pattern is much easier and more straightforward to use for modelling than the REA model. When utilizing the REA core pattern, a database solution contains only real values of resources involved in transactions without planning events, which makes this approach incomplete.

The relationships of *committed provide* and *committed receive* mean that some agreement about the future exchange must be achieved between economic agents. The commitment entity addresses the issue of modelling promises of future economic events and the issue of reservation of resources. Commitment entities and their relationships with other entities are shown in Fig. 2. In this case, Fig. 2 is an extension of Fig. 1. To a considerable extent, the commitment entity copies the structure of the event entity, by which we mean the existence of an increment and decrement commitment and the exchange reciprocity relationship. The exchange reciprocity relationship between the increment and decrement commitments identifies which resources are promised to be exchanged for which other resources. The reciprocity relationship is one of many-to-many.

Each commitment is related to an economic resource by a reservation relationship which specifies which resources will be needed or expected by future economic events. The reservation relationship between the resource and commitment represents the obligation of economic agents to provide or receive rights to economic resources in exchange processes, and represents scheduled usage, consumption or production of economic resources in conversion processes.

The most important relationships of the REA model are the *exchange reciprocity* and *exchange duality* relationships, by [7, 11–13]. The exchange reciprocity relates a pair of increment and decrement commitment entities. The exchange reciprocity

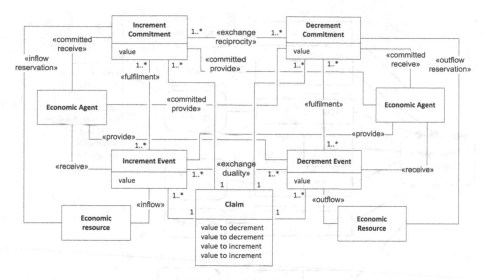

Fig. 2. REA model. Adapted from [7]

relationship identifies which resources are promised to be exchanged for which others. The exchange duality relationship, which relates corresponding increment and decrement economic events, keeps track of which resources were exchanged for which others.

4 ORM Conceptual Modeling Method

Object-Role Modeling (ORM) is a conceptual modelling method that ranks among fact-based modelling methodologies. ORM views the world as a set of objects that play roles (parts in relationships) according to [8]. For example, an individual may play the role of walking in the country (a unary relationship involving just the individual) or an individual may play a role reading this paper (a binary relationship between the individual and the paper). Thus a role in ORM corresponds to an association-end in UML, except that ORM also allows unary relationships. Object-Role Modeling is a conceptual modelling method that views the world as a set of objects that play roles (parts in relationships) according to [8].

The main structural difference between ORM and UML is that ORM excludes attributes as a base construct and treats them instead as a derived concept. The conceptual schema using ORM specifies the information structure of the application in the forms of: *fact types* that are of interest; *constraints* on these fact types; and *derivation rules* for deriving some other facts.

A fact is a proposition that is taken to be true by the relevant business community. A fact type is a kind of fact that may be represented in the database [5]. The constraints represent constraints or restrictions on populations of fact types. The derivation rules include rules that may be used to derive new facts from existing facts, see [8, 14].

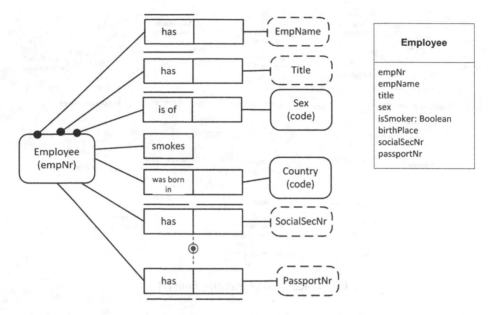

Fig. 3. ORM and UML model of Employee

The ORM model (left part of Fig. 3) indicates that employees are identified by their employee numbers. The top three roles (*EmpName, Title* and *Sex*) are mandatory roles. This is indicated by the black dots at the *Employee* box. The circled mandatory role dot depicts an *inclusive-or* constraint over the roles hosted by the Employee in the fact type. This indicates that an employee must have a social security number or a passport number or both. The uniqueness of constraints (cardinalities in UML) is indicated by vertical lines over roles. In Fig. 3 it means that *empNr, EmpName, Sex* and *Country* is unique for each employee. Two vertical lines over each roles (*SocialSecNr, PassportNr*) indicate that each employee number, social security number and passport number refers to a maximum of one employee. The dashed line over e.g. *PassportNr* indicates that this is a value not an object.

Graphically, object types are depicted as named boxes (solid for entity types, and dotted for value types). As in logic, a predicate is a proposition with object-holes in it. In ORM, a predicate is treated as an ordered set of one or more roles, each of which is depicted as a box, which may optionally be named. A fact type is formed by applying a predicate to the object types that play its roles. Fact type *roles* are depicted as *role boxes*, connected by a line segment to the object type that hosts the role.

In a similar way to UML class diagrams, ORM methodology also enables the use of sub-typing mechanism to classify object types. It enables specialization of some instances of an object type into more specific types. For example, people (persons) at a university may be roughly classified as staff and students.

5 ORM Model of the REA Core Pattern

The REA core pattern which was depicted in Sect. 2 comes from double-booking entry and deals with only current and past economic events. It is fully in compliance with the functional needs of double-booking entry. Figure 4 displays the ORM diagram of the REA core pattern. The left-hand side transactions represent *transfers of goods*, and the right-hand transactions stand for *transfers of money*. We consider the common example of a transfer, in which resources or services are exchanged for money.

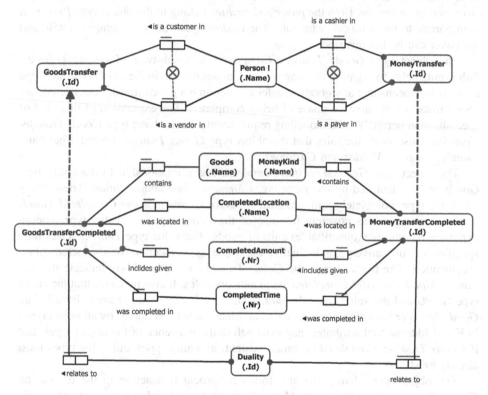

Fig. 4. ORM Model of the REA core pattern

Named boxes in the figure represent object types - more specifically entity types or value types. The object types *Duality, Goods Transfer, Money Transfer* and *Person* are primal types, and are not defined on the basis of other object types. Figure 4 indicates that the object type *Duality* has a relationship to the object types *Goods Transfers* and to the object type *Money Transfers*. The position of uniqueness constraint (vertical line over the roles) indicates that a *Duality* can be determined by one or more *Goods Transfer types*, as well as by one or more *Money Transfer types*. Goods may be delivered by several shipments and payments may be performed by several instalments, as in reality. The black dots at the *Duality* box indicate that the roles of *Duality* are mandatory roles. It means that the type *Goods Transfer* or *Money Transfer* may exist independently before the existence of the type *Duality*, and that the object type *Duality* must have s relationship to *Goods Transfer* and to *Money Transfer*.

The object type *Goods Transfer* has a relationship to the role of *vendor* and *customer*. Both roles belong to the object type *Person*. *Exclusive-or* relationship between two actor's roles means that these actor roles must be filled by different persons. The customer is an actor role that receives the goods in *Goods Transfer*. The *vendor* is an actor role that provides the goods for the transfer. Similarly, the corresponding object type *Money Transfer* is related to the payer and *cashier* actor's roles. Between both actor roles there is *exclusive-or* relationship with the same meaning as in the case of a *customer* and a *vendor*. Both the *payer* and *cashier* belong to the object type *Person*. It is important to use a proper actor role. The *customer* can be, for example, a wife and the payer can be her husband.

The object type *Goods Transfer Completed* is a sub-type of *Goods Transfer*. Sub-typing helps to organize the way we think about objects in the world. The sub-type relationship means that any goods transfer can become a goods transfer completed. So, goods transfer can enter the phase of being completed. The expression of this kind of specialization perfectly suits modelling requirements. Each object type *Goods Transfer Completed* also hosts the roles that the object type *Goods Transfer* hosted. These are, namely, the roles *Vendor* and *Customer*.

The object type *Goods Transfer Completed* has a relationship to the entity type *Goods* and is identified by the value types *Amount, Time* and *Location*. These entity and value types completely fulfil practical needs for *Goods Transfer Completed*. *Goods* in this case represents concrete instance of the entity type, the value type amount expresses measurable (quantifiable) units of goods. The value type *Time* indicates time specification of delivery, and, finally, the value type *location* is a concrete place specification. The black dots at the *Goods Transfer Completed* box indicate that the roles of *Goods Transfer Completed* are mandatory roles. It also indicates that the entity type *Goods* and the value types *Amount, Time,* and *Location* may have existed before *Goods Transfer Completed* became existent. Mandatory roles hosted by all object types in Fig. 4 indicate that attributes may exist before the existence of the object types. But if *Goods Transfer Completed* becomes existent, its entity types and value types must already exist.

The object type *Money Transfer* forms reciprocal transaction to the transaction *Goods Transfer*. The object type *Money Transfer Completed* is a sub-type of *Money Transfer*. Rationale for the object types and the roles hosted by the object types is very much the same as in the case of the object type *Goods Transfer Completed*.

REA model has also been modelled and verified by using NORMA (Natural ORM Architect). A human-readable definition of the model is automatically generated via verbalization browser integrated in NORMA. Such a method helps to discover inaccuracies in the model and allows to populate model with test data even before the actual implementation of the database application. This emphasizes the considerable expressivity of the ORM approach compared to ER diagram models. Here follows the example (Fig. 5).

The REA model being an extension of the REA core pattern, the ORM model of the REA model is also an extension of the ORM model from the previous section. The ORM model of the REA model is also composed of two kinds of transactions (left

Duality **is an entity type.**
Reference Scheme: Duality has Duality_Id.
Reference Mode: .Id.
Data Type: Numeric: Auto Counter.

Fact Types:
Duality has Duality_Id.
GoodsTransferCompleted relates to Duality.
Duality relates to CompletedMoneyTransfer.

Examples:

MoneyTransfer is paid by Person.
Each MoneyTransfer is paid by **exactly one** Person.
It is possible that some Person paid **more than one** MoneyTransfer.

Examples:
MoneyTransfer MTRN001 is paid by Person Joseph.

MoneyTransfer is accepted by Person.
Each MoneyTransfer is accepted by **exactly one** Person.
It is possible that some Person accepted **more than one** MoneyTransfer.

Examples:
MoneyTransfer MTRN001 is accepted by Person Phoenix.

CompletedMoneyTransfer includes MoneyKind.
Each CompletedMoneyTransfer includes **exactly one** MoneyKind.
It is possible that some MoneyKind is a part of **more than one** CompletedMoneyTransfer.

Examples:
CompletedMoneyTransfer CMTRN001 includes MoneyKind 'EUR'.

Person is a customer in GoodsTransfer.
For each GoodsTransfer **exactly one** Person is a customer in **that** GoodsTransfer.
It is possible that some Person is a customer in **more than one** GoodsTransfer.

Examples:
Person John is a customer in GoodsTransfer TRN001
GoodsTransferCompleted relates to Duality.
Each Duality is related to **exactly one** GoodsTransferCompleted.
It is possible that some GoodsTransferCompleted relates to **more than one** Duality.

Fig. 5. The example part of verbalized REA core pattern model in ORM

hand side, right hand side). Each kind of transaction is composed of three phases. The first initial phase and the final completed phase come from the ORM model of the REA core pattern.

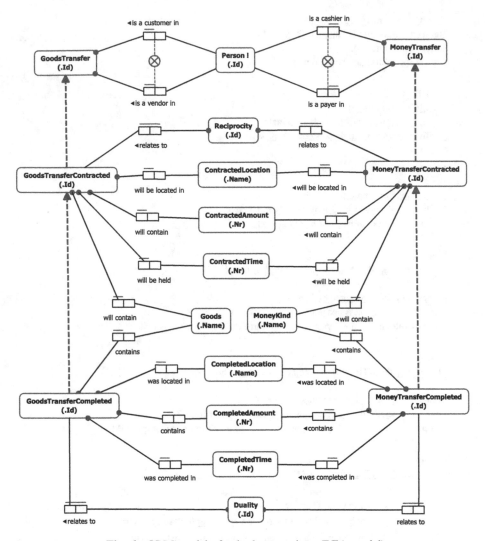

Fig. 6. ORM model of paired transactions (REA model)

The contracted phase is a new phase and is represented by the object types *Goods Transfer Contracted* and *Money Transfer Contracted*. This phase stands for future (planned) events (in REA notation – commitment). The ORM model of the REA model is shown in Fig. 6.

The ORM model of the REA model is extended by the object types *Goods Transfer Contracted* and *Money Transfer Contracted*. At first, we focus on a description of how these new object types change the overall structure of the model. The object type *Goods Transfer Contracted* is a direct sub-type of the type *Goods Transfer*. Next, the object type *Goods Transfer Completed* is a direct sub-type of the object type *Goods*

Transfer Contracted. It indicates that *Goods Transfer* first enter the phase of being contracted, and then enter the phase of being completed. In short, any *Goods Transfer* can become *Goods Transfer Contracted,* but only a contracted goods transfer can become a completed goods transfer.

The structure of the object type *Money Transfer* is similar to the *Goods Transfer* structure. The object type *Money Transfer* plays a fundamental role in this kind of transaction. The object type *Money Transfer Contracted* is a direct sub-type of *Money Transfer,* and the object type *Money Transfer Completed* is a direct sub-type of *Money Transfer Contracted.* By analogy with the previous paragraph, any *Money Transfer* can become *Money Transfer Contracted,* but only a contracted money transfer can become a completed money transfer.

The object types *Goods Transfer Contracted* and *Money Transfer Contracted* mutually express that the agreement specifying goods and their delivery, as well as the amount of money and conditions of payment, as reached. More specifically, the *customer* enters into an agreement about goods and their specification and the *vendor* promises to deliver the stated goods by certain time, in a certain location. The *payer* promises to pay according to the agreement, and the *cashier* promises to accept the money. Unless an agreement is reached, the exchange process will not continue. In order to express this condition explicitly, the object type *Reciprocity* that has a relationship to the object types *Goods Transfer Contracted* and to *Money Transfer Contracted* must be utilized. Its mandatory roles indicate that both *Goods Transfer Contracted* and *Money Transfer Contracted* have become existent.

Each object type *Goods Transfer Contracted* and *Money Transfer Contracted* has a relationship to contracted resource kinds (kind of goods and kind of money) and is identified by value types further specifying the entity type resource. The value types are *amount, time* and *location.* The structure of these entity and value types is the same as in the case of *Goods Transfer Completed* (*Money Transfer Completed*) but the meaning is different. These entities and value types represent planned values or kinds of resources. In reality, they may differ from the entity and value types stated at *Goods Transfer Completed* (*Money Transfer Completed*). On the other hand it is desirable to record both data concerning the contracted phase of the exchange process, as well as data concerning the completed phase of the exchange process.

The other transaction(s) of the paired transactions is represented by the object type *Money Transfer Contracted.* In this case, the payer has promised that he will pay for the goods and the cashier has promised that he will accept the amount of money (resource). At this point it is essential that the state of promise is achieved on both object types *Goods Transfer Contracted* and *Money Transfer Contracted* which is checked and validated by the object type *Reciprocity.*

6 Discussion of Findings

Designing an information system involves building a formal model of the application domain which requires a good understanding of the application domain and utilization of the proper methodology for modelling specifications in a clear and unambiguous way. ORM simplifies the design process by using natural language, and by examining the information in terms of simple and elementary facts. By expressing the model in terms of natural concepts, such as objects and roles, it provides a conceptual approach to modelling comprehensible also to domain experts.

The REA core pattern is directly based on double booking entry and captures modelling reality accurately. It is fairly comprehensible, but its drawback is its inability to model future events (commitments). However, this is brought about by the modelling paradigm (double-booking entry), which addresses only past and current economic activities. In addition, a temporally Claim entity is utilized to balance time differences between fulfilling transaction kinds.

The underlying object types of the ORM model of the REA core pattern are *Goods Transfer* and *Money Transfer*. These object types form the initial phase of the exchange process. *Goods Transfer Completed* is a derived sub-type from *Goods Transfer,* and *Money Transfer Completed* is a derived sub-type form *Money Transfer*. Derived sub-types create a completed phase of the exchange process. The sub-typing mechanism allows the introduction of state and state transitions. In reality, it means that first *Goods Transfer* becomes existent and then *Goods Transfer Completed* can occur. The same is also valid for *Money Transfer* and *Money Transfer Completed*. The crucial entity in the REA core pattern is the *Duality* entity that keeps different kinds of transactions together. In the ORM model of the REA core pattern, the object type *Duality* has a relationship to *Goods Transfer Completed* and to *Money Transfer Completed*. This is because this object type relates transactions in the completed phase. In other words, *Duality* indicates that both kinds of transactions have been successfully terminated. This approach enables the elimination of the entity type *Claim* from the ORM model.

Contrary to the REA core pattern, the REA model represents a solution which captures future events as an inseparable part. This is in compliance with reality, and not only with the requirements of double-booking entry. However, REA relationships between the commitment entity and event entity suffer from a number of deficiencies. Firstly, both entities are too separated from each other. They should create an integral unit, yet they do not. Secondly, they suffer from the absence of an REA transaction oriented state machine. The current REA state machine addresses the states of resource or resource type in question. Finally, these entities formally belong to different modelling levels; economic commitments belong in the policy level and economic events have their place at the operational level. A solution is rather difficult to implement.

The ORM model of the REA model represents the ultimate solution. The sub-typing mechanism is utilized to separate different phases of the exchange process. More specifically, it is used to discern the initial phase from the contracted phase and from the completed phase. Phase's design is intuitive and comprehensible. The contracted phase is a new phase which is added into the phases of the ORM model of the REA core pattern. It is important phase because this phase signifies the obligation to fulfil future economic events. The value types and entity types which identify both contracted transfers represent planned (promised) value types and entity types. Entity types represent a resource specification and value types represent an amount, time and location specification. Both in reality and in modelling, it is important to precisely determine whether the different kinds of transactions were contracted. For this reason, the object type *Reciprocity,* which has a relationship to both kinds of transactions, was introduced.

The object types *Goods Transfer* and *Money Transfer* form the beginning of the paired transactions process, which means that they identify partaking actor roles which will be involved in the process. They must be created first. After this, the object types *Good Transfer Contracted* and *Money Transfer Contracted* can be created. Mutual creation of these object types is checked and verified by the object type Reciprocity. Similarly, existence of *Goods Transfer Completed* and *Money Transfer Completed* is dependent on the existence of contracted transfers. Mutual existence of these object types is checked and verified by the object type *Duality*.

The ORM model which is exhibited in Fig. 6 is composed of 24 fact types. Mandatory roles, uniqueness constraints, and the sub-typing mechanism make the model comprehensible and complete.

7 Conclusion

The article presents fact-based models of paired transactions corresponding to the REA core pattern and REA exchange model utilizing the ORM conceptual modeling method. Presented models were created and verified by NORMA (Natural ORM Architect). They provide both semantic stability and semantic relevance, which is necessary for further incorporating the REA modeling approach into fact-based modeling methodologies of business processes.

The benefits of applying this method on paired transactions is mainly in distinction of the initial phase, the contracted phase, and the completed phase of the paired transactions ORM model and in support of unified transaction processing. The individual phases can be seen as the states of the REA exchange process.

The REA modeling approach is to some extent inherently confined to the changes in the value of economic resources. This aspect negatively affects creation of the complex REA concepts such as contract or schedule. On the other hand, mapping elementary facts delivered by a generic modeling methodology to the complex REA concepts could be an effective solution to the problem. This is the aim of further research.

Acknowledgements. The paper was supported by the grant provided by the Ministry of Education, Youth and Sport Czech Republic, reference no. SGS15/PRF2016.

References

1. Geerts, G.L., McCarthy, W.E.: The ontological foundation of REA enterprise information systems. In: Paper Presented at the Annual Meeting of the American Accounting Association, Philadelphia (2000)
2. Geerts, G.L., McCarthy, W.E.: Policy-level specifications in REA enterprise information systems. J. Inf. Syst. **20**(2), 37–63 (2006)
3. Geerts, G.L., McCarthy, W.E.: Using object-oriented templates from the REA accounting model to engineer business process and tasks. In: Paper Presented at European Accounting Congress, Gratz, Austria (1997)

4. McCarthy, W.E.: The REA accounting model: a generalized framework for accounting systems in a shared data environment. Acc. Rev. **57**, 554–578 (1982)
5. Dietz, J.L.G.: The Essence of Organization, 2nd edn. Sapio Enterprise Engineering (2015). http://www.sapio.nl
6. Dunn, C.L., Cherrington, O.J., Hollander, A.S.: Enterprise Information Systems: A Pattern Based Approach. McGraw-Hill/Irwin, New York (2004)
7. Hruby, P.: Model-Driven Design Using Business Patterns. Springer, Heidelberg (2006)
8. Halpin, T.: Object-role modeling fundamentals. A practical guide to data modeling with ORM. Technics Publications, New Jersey (2015)
9. Dudycz, H., Korczak, J.: Conceptual design of financial ontology. In: Ganzha, M., Maciaszek, L., Paprzycki, M. (eds.) Proceedings of the Federated Conference on Computer Science and Information Systems, FedCSIS 2015, pp. 1505–1511. Polskie Towarzystwo Informatyczne, IEEE Computer Society Press, Warsaw, Los Alamitos (2015)
10. Hunka, F., Zacek, J.: Detailed analysis of REA ontology. In: Aveiro, D., Tribolet, J., Gouveia, D. (eds.) EEWC 2014. LNBIP, vol. 174, pp. 61–75. Springer, Heidelberg (2014). doi:10.1007/978-3-319-06505-2_5
11. Hunka, F., Zacek, J.: A new view of REA state machine. Appl. Ontology **10**(1), 25–39 (2015)
12. Klimek, R., Szwed, P.: Verification of archiMate process specification based on deductive temporal reasoning. In: Ganzha, M., Maciaszek, L., Paprzycki, M. (eds.) Proceedings of the 2013 Federated Conference on Computer Science and Information Systems, FedCSIS 2013, pp. 1103–1110. Polskie Towarzystwo Informatyczne, IEEE Computer Society Press, Warsaw (2013)
13. Korczak, J., Dudycz, H., Dyczkowski, M.: Design of financial knowledge in dashboard for SME managers. In: Ganzha, M., Maciaszek, L., Paprzycki, M. (eds.) Proceedings of the 2013 Federated Conference on Computer Science and Information Systems, FedCSIS 2013, pp. 1111–1118. Polskie Towarzystwo Informatyczne, IEEE Computer Society Press, Warsaw (2013)
14. Kersten, G., Wachowicz, T.: On winners and losers in procurement auctions. In: Ganzha, M., Maciaszek, L., Paprzycki, M. (eds.) Proceedings of the 2014 Federated Conference on Computer Science and Information Systems, FedCSIS 2014, pp. 1163–1170. Polskie Towarzystwo Informatyczne, IEEE Computer Society Press, Warsaw (2014)
15. Paweloszek, I.: Approach to analysis and assessment of ERP system. A software vendor's perspective. In: Ganzha, M., Maciaszek, L., Paprzycki, M. (eds.) Proceedings of the 2015 Federated Conference on Computer Science and Information Systems, FedCSIS 2015, pp. 1415–1426. Polskie Towarzystwo Informatyczne, IEEE Computer Society Press, Warsaw, Los Alamitos (2015)
16. IDEF0, Integration definition for function modeling. National Institute of Standards and Technology, FIPS Publication (1993). http://www.idef.com/pdf/idef0.pdf
17. Gordijn, J., Akkermans, H.: Value based requirements engineering: exploring innovative e-commerce idea. Requirements Eng. J. **8**(2), 114–134 (2003)

Extension of Intelligence of Decision Support Systems: Manager Perspective

Jerzy Korczak[✉], Helena Dudycz, Bartłomiej Nita, Piotr Oleksyk,
and Adrian Kaźmierczak

Wrocław University of Economics,
Komandorska 118/120, 53-345 Wrocław, Poland
{jerzy.korczak, helena.dudycz, bartlomiej.nita,
piotr.oleksyk, adrian.kazmierczak}@ue.wroc.pl

Abstract. The article presents an approach to extend the functionality and knowledge of Decision Support Systems to answer the requirements of managers of small and medium-sized enterprises (SMEs). It concerns two major aspects of the system, i.e. the interface that takes into account the level of knowledge of the manager, and the interpretation of economic and financial information using the built-in domain ontologies. The project is related to the design of smart decision support systems based on financial ontology and on the model of manager knowledge created by eye-tracking analysis. An experiment was carried out on real financial data extracted from the database of BINOCLE system, developed by Bilander Co. To create a model of manager knowledge, a number of financial analysts, experts and economists were invited to analyze the pre-defined financial reports. Their tasks were observed and analyzed by the eye-tracking system StudioTM, Tobii. The logs of the system as well as the financial ontology have been used to develop the intelligent interface of a Decision Support System.

Keywords: Model of manager knowledge · Ontology · Financial analysis · Eye tracking · Decision support system

1 Introduction

Decision-making in small and medium-sized enterprises is an extremely difficult process. The most important problems of the functioning of such enterprises are operational continuity, ensuring the ongoing customer service and support, as well as technological aspects. Managing a business requires access to the appropriate information system that must always go hand in hand with the methods of financial analysis, allowing managers to monitor the changes in the environment, identify the different types of risk, choose appropriate forms of insurance against these risks, and follow appropriate scenarios of development. Each of the scenarios predicts future financial situations, using the methods and tools of financial analysis. Managers of small and medium-sized enterprises (SMEs), on the one hand, are usually confronted with the barriers and limits on information, and on the other hand are able more easily to control costs and expenses using an individual, simplified information processing system,

© Springer International Publishing AG 2017
E. Ziemba (Ed.): AITM 2016/ISM 2016, LNBIP 277, pp. 35–48, 2017.
DOI: 10.1007/978-3-319-53076-5_3

regardless of the requirements of accounting standards. It may be difficult for them to access prospective information allowing the evaluation of the anticipated environment changes.

In general, most existing managers of SMEs need solutions that support their decisions based on transactional data which, after being processed by the tools of financial analysis, allow them to prepare the decision draft. Today's information technology assures managers access to the multi-dimensional data stored in various databases and enables them to perform multi-criteria analysis. The problem appears, among others, to lie in the excessive numbers of reports which are generated by transactional and executive information systems. In the process of management, the information overload significantly reduces the ability to make the right decision.

In SMEs, financial forecasts needed to make good business decisions oriented towards improving financial efficiency and dynamic development are very often prepared in a cursory manner or simply ignored. This is mainly due to lack of time, and not to sufficient and limited managerial knowledge.

The aim of this article is to present an approach to modeling manager knowledge, using the ontology of Decision Support Systems and eye-tracking logs. Data from eye-tracking illustrates not only a manager's perception of the economic reports, but also makes it possible to discover schemes of data analysis. It facilitates also the establishment of a manager-knowledge profile and, consequently, creates a possibility of adapting the interface to an individual's skills. In the project, the whole process of analysis of financial data will be supported by built-in ontologies of economic and financial knowledge which is essential for SME managers. This will be possible thanks to research focusing on the development of an intelligent interface supporting the interpretation of economic information, which also is associated with the modelling of managerial knowledge. The described approach is a continuation of the construction of the intelligent cockpit for managers (InKoM project), whose main objective was to facilitate financial analysis and the evaluation of the economic status of the company in a competitive market [1].

The structure of the article is as follows. The next section focuses on the issues related to management-based analysis, particularly in relation to SMEs. The following section briefly refers to managerial analysis in the context of the Key Performance Indicators (KPI) used to build an ontology of economic and financial knowledge. The subsequent three sections are devoted to the modeling of managerial knowledge, together with a synthetic description of the eye-tracking results. The article concludes with a summary of work to date and future research.

2 Supporting of Managerial Analysis

Management of the SME is a very complex and difficult task. In such organizations, resources for wider financial and accounting services are usually limited. Often, these tasks are assigned to accountants who are excessively burdened with operational activities and supervision of the correct tax settlements. Managers of SMEs often have to focus on the technological problems related to the core business, which limits the possibility of financial projections associated with the preparation of the right decisions to ensure financial security and dynamic development based on improving financial efficiency.

Financial analysis allows the interpretation of the information necessary for the ongoing management of an enterprise[1]. Managers of SMEs are expected to find support in the following areas:

- assessment of the financial standing highlights the most important areas of a company's activity exposed to risk. The key problem is the analysis of liquidity and the sufficiency of cash available. The main goal of such analyses is to eliminate payment bottlenecks;
- assessment of cash flows – whether it is possible to repeat a generated surplus in subsequent periods or whether that will no longer occur in the future.

The main activities of the SMEs are focused on business operations. Information processing and related decisions concern the core activities of the company and are associated with its specificity and membership in a particular industry. An important element of operational management in SMEs is to control liquidity, while it should be emphasized that classical liquidity ratios used in large companies cannot always be directly applied to SMEs. In this view it is worth designing solutions that make use of analytical accounting records to project liquidity on a monthly basis. There is no doubt that this kind of analysis of liquidity, taking into account the size of the entity, the specificity of the industry, and the type of products or services offered, is not possible without expert knowledge. On the basis of empirical studies, we found that information requirements for short term management concern [2] information about liquidity, information on revenues generated by the company, and information on costs incurred. But for the long-term management area, information is needed: about the company's indebtedness, about the profitability of planned investments, and about the financial situation of the branch.

The process of decisions support made needs – firstly – the decomposition and the proper selection of management instruments. Managing medium-sized enterprises requires information about the possibility of gridlock preventing stable business in the near future. Secondly, there is a need to acquire information to generate the appropriate level of profit and a minimum level of margins in order to make the right choices. They are focused on obtaining information on opportunities to increase revenue or to carry out activities aimed at cost minimization.

Regarding long-term decisions, managers of small companies are not able to relate to the use of advanced solutions for e.g. capital budgeting. They need analytical models that enable them to identify signals indicative of the need for investment decisions and the level of resources involved. With regard to medium-sized enterprises, this type of analysis should be augmented by simulations on the effectiveness of individual organizational units (responsibility centers) and the profitability of equity involved.

---

[1] It should be emphasized that the selection of appropriate methods of analysis of the financial requirements of SME managers is necessary to determine the company's ability to continue its operations, and to define financial needs, budgets and capital resources of financing assets, signs of danger and risk of changes in the competitive position and trends in various business areas.

Acquisition of information to support such decisions is possible mainly through the use of patterns developed by experts in financial management. Unfortunately, it is impossible in this case to use the universal solutions – in this case it is necessary to dispose over an intelligent system that using expert knowledge provides ready-made decisions, taking into account the specific nature of the company[2].

Also important are analysis of the index of debt level and the use of static and dynamic methods of estimating the profitability of investment. For organizations with greater economic importance, the study should be completed by:

- the use of the Balanced Score Card and the early warning system,
- analysis of indicators of debt service, study of the cost of capital: domestic and foreign capital, the weighted average cost of capital,
- pro-forma financial statements - as information about the financial effects of planned long-term actions,
- evaluation of the company's profitability: return on sale ratios, return on assets and equity - to various cuts in the financial result,
- methods of budgeting process.

Generally, the support of decision-making is based on the generation of ready-made paths, together with projections of the effects of planned decisions. For example, in a Binocle system of the Bilander company which is classified as a category of DSS, there are many useful and powerful functionalities that make possible multivariate analysis of financial data. However, due to the limited resources of SMEs, it is necessary to develop ready-made reporting and decision paths for managers and owners of SMEs. These reports and patterns of decision-making should take into account inter alia the support for operational and financial planning, and risk analysis (in particular, the risk of bankruptcy). In addition, they may include support in investment decisions and measuring the effectiveness of the company as a whole and its individual organizational units.

In addition, to improve the decision-making processes in SMEs, three important issues should be taken into account:

- number of KPIs (key measures of achievement),
- methods of forecasting and simulation to facilitate taking corrective actions,
- standard indicators for SMEs needed for benchmarking.

Also crucial is a selection of available reports (option in the Binocle system) to present the most important information for the manager. If needed, these reports may be further detailed.

---

[2] The management of long-term financial analysis conducted by managers of small businesses should include: a preliminary analysis of financial statements, ratio analysis, information on liquidity ratios, evaluation of static measures of liquidity, turnover ratios of inventories, receivables and payables analysis, analysis of the operating cycle in terms of the efficiency of indicators of capital engagement, productivity of assets and equity, and information on current and future income and expenses.

3 KPI in Decision Support Systems

A Decision Support System (DSS) can be defined as "an interactive computer-based system or subsystem intended to help decision makers use communications technologies, data, documents, knowledge, and/or models to identify and solve problems, complete decision process tasks, and make decisions" [3, p. 16]. There are five types of DSS: (1) communications-driven, (2) data-driven, (3) document-driven, (4) knowledge-driven, and (5) model-driven systems [4]. Our approach can be assigned to the data-driven DSS, which provide access to large data stores and analytics to extract information and knowledge using data mining methods.

An important function of business-oriented DSS is the visualization of the calculated KPIs. These indicators are the basis of decision-making both at strategic as well as tactical and operational levels. The usefulness of indicators depends on the manager's understanding of the concepts, measures and structural links involved. The essence of the evaluation is the appropriate computing and use of indicators derived from different financial statements (including Balance sheet, Profit and Loss Statement etc.). According to the degree of data aggregation, the measures might be global or partial, where the indicators can be summed up, differentiated, multiplied or divided.

Indicator analysis used to assess the activities of the company has both advantages and disadvantages. Among the first are: the ease of measurement, the availability of source data, the ability to identify critical areas of economic activities, the universality of the indicators, allowing, among other things, the conduct of comparative analyses with other companies. While the disadvantages are: no indication of the reasons for unfavourable events, the risk of misinterpretation of measures, the lack of universal standard ratios. Analysing the semantic relationships between economic indicators can facilitate the evaluation of the data by finding the causes of adverse events and taking note of the positive factors.

A characteristic feature of the new generation of information systems for managers is the reliance on the ontology and semantic retrieval of information. In their architecture, there are new elements, such as ontology. The use of ontologies and visual information retrieval within analytical tools can be helpful to solve the following problems [5, p. 215]:

- definition of business rules in order to get proactive information and advice in the decision-making process,
- specification of semantic layer describing the relationships between different economic concepts,
- presentation of business information,
- the rapid modification of existing databases and data warehouses.

Development of information systems that support managers is progressing towards the use of visual information retrieval based on semantic models.

4 Ontological Foundation

Many research projects show that an ontology of economic and financial indicators is advantageous in decision making [5–11]. It is important to note that there is no single universal system of economic indicators that might be used in all organizations. Besides, a lot of companies use a number of assessment models of business based on the analysis of various indicators.

An ontological approach to modeling domain knowledge was proposed in our project "Intelligent dashboard for managers (InKoM)" (described in [1, 12]). The main objective of the project was to develop an intelligent cockpit for managers of small and medium-sized enterprises which facilitates analysis and interpretation of the economic situations of the company, and supports analysis of economic and financial data. Three new components of the cockpit were important: the financial ontology, the data mining algorithms, and the mechanism of deep retrieval on the Internet. The new system significantly extended the usefulness of the existing solution [13]. This solution has enabled adequate, expandable and adaptable definition of economic and financial knowledge, without having to modify the existing system of TETA BI.

Designing a new intelligent interface, the ontological approach was completed by eye-tracking methods. Available in the DSS, a visual presentation of knowledge and related data permits one quickly to assess the economic situation and take appropriate action. To discover a way of analysing financial reports and statements, the experiments were carried out with managers, financial analysts, and students of economics. The eye-tracking logs created during the reading of these documents were used to find the patterns of operations and to model the financial knowledge of each of the participants. The concepts and analytical operations performed by each manager were then matched with the financial ontology available in the system.

5 Case Study – Evaluation of a Company's Liquidity

Each company assesses various aspects of its business on an ongoing basis. The necessity for such assessment may result from the need to evaluate managers' performance. However, this evaluation aspect should not be perceived as a dominant factor in overall company assessment; much more important issues refer to the assessment of future prospects of a company.

As previously noted, the liquidity analysis is heavily based on estimating the ability of a company to pay its debt on time. While conducting liquidity analysis the proper cash management should be taken into consideration with regard to the phases of the key repayment obligations. It is also very important not to exceed the basic safety thresholds. Any analyses require examining current financial obligations, and may be based on different sources of information such as financial market news. Improving financial liquidity also refers to accounts receivable, which are converted into cash in a normal business cycle. According to the literature, the appropriate management of accounts receivable should be based on the following factors:

- reliable and continuous information regarding the current cash in-flows,
- fast identification of delayed accounts receivable along with the simulation of interest charges,
- efficient verification, reconciliation and collection of overdue payments from debtors,
- reports, analyzes, and statistics that support the process of debt management,
- evaluation of risk of errors associated with the identification of receivables.

Such receivables management solution can also be helpful in improving the liquidity of the company and providing additional information in the liquidity analysis.

The aim of our experiment was to - demonstrate the usefulness of liquidity indicators (namely current indicator, quick indicator, and cash indicator) in the analysis of corporate financial stability. The starting point of the experiment was a preliminary analysis of the internal managerial report containing all the necessary data to analyse liquidity. Participants' attention was focused on the ambiguous changes in current indicator and quick indicator in relation to cash indicator.

Liquidity management is not possible without a detailed information coming from the internal reporting system. A useful report is a Summary Statement indicating the status of liabilities. Such report includes information on: bank loans, trade credits, lease payments, guarantees and warranties. In addition, it is very useful to generate information on loans used in finance investment projects and information on liabilities overdue more than six months. This report provides information as to the amount of liabilities that hinder the repayment of loan instalments. Any remedial action is completed by the additional monthly and quarterly reports, which are as reliable as the financial statements.

Liquidity management requires detailed information on cash state, including information on cash surplus or cash deficit. It concerns concise information including cash in-flows and cash out-flows. This information is very useful for estimating future cash flows. It allows one to estimate the ability to compute cash excess in the various phases of the loan repayment.

Another important component is a report containing detailed information on the planned cash out-flows, broken down by individual business segments. This report complements the cost information in the Profit and Loss Statement. However, it is very useful because it contains current expenses as well as committed cash out-flows to be occurred in the future.

The last source of information is a report containing detailed data about cash in-flows broken down by strategic business units. This report serves as the supplement to the revenue information included in Profit and Loss Statement. This report also contains currently received in-flows as well as the amount of receivables that have not yet been gathered on a cash basis.

Due to the need for the proper interpretation of the liquidity risks, it was necessary to design an ontology describing the scope of liquidity management. This ontology is presented in Fig. 1.

Liquidity indicators are used not only in current cash management issues. They are often used to assist complex indicators for assessing the validity and usefulness of the planned development and restructuring projects. In the literature there are three basic liquidity indicators widely cited [14]:

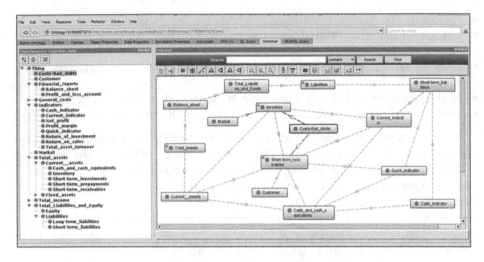

Fig. 1. Ontology: view of liquidity [Source: own elaboration based on Protégé 4]

$$Current\ indicator = \frac{inventory + accounts\ receivable + cash}{short\ term\ liabilites}$$

$$Quick\ indicator = \frac{accounts\ receivable + cash}{short\ term\ liabilites}$$

$$Cash\ indicator = \frac{cash}{short\ term\ liabilites}$$

The idea of the liquidity analysis is based on the assumption that inventories, reflected in the current indicator, are converted into cash in a short time, and accounts receivable are paid by all consumers on a regular basis.

In Polish enterprises, the liquidity analysis based on the cash indicator is the most frequently used. Usually the reason is the over-supply of products and services as well as a significant problem with money collection. Most trade contracts are signed for more than a three-month payment period, and unfortunately in practice they often are not paid on time. The correct way to analyze receivables should be carried out in accordance with the diagram shown in Fig. 2.

In liquidity analysis, it is necessary to take into consideration current information contained in internal reporting, unpaid invoices, which must be consistent with the data from the financial statements. During the experiment, the participants analyzed the financial statements of the company, in which the following changes were reported:

- an increase in liabilities,
- fast identification of delayed accounts receivable along with the simulation of interest charges,
- an increase in inventory,
- a significant increase in short-term receivables,
- negligible increase in cash.

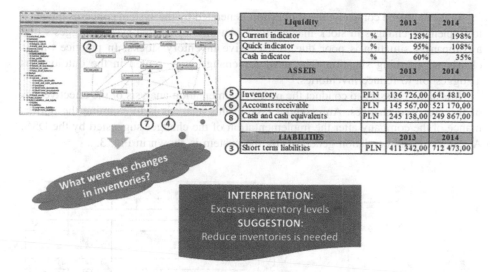

Liquidity		2013	2014
Current indicator	%	128%	198%
Quick indicator	%	95%	108%
Cash indicator	%	60%	35%
ASSETS		**2013**	**2014**
Inventory	PLN	136 726,00	641 481,00
Accounts receivable	PLN	145 567,00	521 170,00
Cash and cash equivalents	PLN	245 138,00	249 867,00
LIABILITIES		**2013**	**2014**
Short term liabilities	PLN	411 342,00	712 473,00

What were the changes in inventories?

INTERPRETATION:
Excessive inventory levels
SUGGESTION:
Reduce inventories is needed

Fig. 2. Supporting the proper interpretation of liquidity indicators: task 1

To examine the financial situation of the company, the following tasks should be done (see Fig. 2):

(1) an increase in liabilities,
(2) analysis of the ontology that describes in detail the problem of liquidity management,
(3) examining the changes in the short-term liabilities which link together all the liquidity indicators,
(4) analysis of the ontology focused on the differences among various liquidity indicators (current indicator, quick indicator, and cash indicator),
(5) verification of changes in inventory,
(6) verification of changes in trade receivables,
(7) identification of the most important factors affecting the financial stability,
(8) verification of changes in cash balance.

The described sequence of tasks should lead to the proper assessment of the performance achieved by a company. As a result, the managers should take a decision to change an internal stock management policy, for instance to produce less, to buy less material, to launch production processes only for contracted orders. However, proper interpretation of the company's performance is not an easy task. Managers are often focused on non-financial issues and external factors. They do not always distinguish between positive and negative symptoms of particular indicators. In these cases, financial ontologies can provide very useful aid.. The use of ontologies embedded in an intelligent decision support system allows managers to avoid problems with customer insolvency or payment backlogs in the future. In the case of ambiguous results, the intelligent system should indicate the most important threats. Simultaneously, the system has to eliminate less important elements of reporting (for instance information noise).

In the analyzed company, the suggestion generated by the system concerns the need to implement changes in stock management. An ontology-aided system suggests that a company's situation is poor due to excessive inventory stocks. In practice this is clearly an alarming situation. The need for change is presented in the ontology as a suggestion to reduce inventories.

It is also necessary to conduct the post-implementation analysis of the effectiveness of the proposed changes. An essential task in this analysis is to examine the performance of the company after the implementation of the changes suggested by the DSS. A sample recommendation generated by the system is shown in Fig. 3.

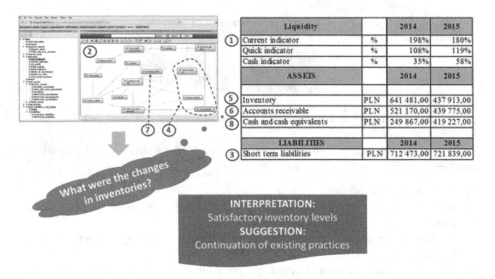

Liquidity		2014	2015
Current indicator	%	198%	180%
Quick indicator	%	108%	119%
Cash indicator	%	35%	58%
ASSETS		2014	2015
Inventory	PLN	641 481,00	437 913,00
Accounts receivable	PLN	521 170,00	439 775,00
Cash and cash equivalents	PLN	249 867,00	419 227,00
LIABILITIES		2014	2015
Short term liabilities	PLN	712 473,00	721 839,00

What were the changes in inventories?

INTERPRETATION:
Satisfactory inventory levels
SUGGESTION:
Continuation of existing practices

Fig. 3. Supporting the proper interpretation of liquidity indicators: task 2

Based on the ontology, the manager is able to verify the validity of the implemented changes. While performing the sequence of tasks indicated in Fig. 3, the manager acquires certainty about the effectiveness of the corrective recommendations.

The experiment clearly pointed out that the differences in the interpretation of the data depend on the level of the participants' experience. Interpretation of the information contained in the internal reporting varied depending on the qualifications of novices and experienced managers. Novices paid attention only to the increase in current liquidity indicator and quick indicator. They neglected the decline in the cash indicator. Most experienced managers focused their attention just on the cash indicator. The behavioral pattern of experienced managers confirmed the usefulness and comprehensiveness of the ontology. The inventory increases were a serious drawback that caused changes in the allocation of monetary sources. Neglecting the use of ontologies could be the reason for making a wrong decision, e.g. initiating purchases of new materials. Based on the ontology, the appropriate decisions with regard to inventory management may have to be taken.

An in-depth analysis of all the liquidity indicators, as well as changes in inventory, accounts receivables, cash balances, and accounts payable, is required in order to properly interpret the financial position of the company. The use of systematic knowledge in the form of ontology is helpful. The ontology can be considered as the essential component of the intelligent system to make the right decisions designed to prevent liquidity problems faced by the company.

6 Approach to Modelling of Managerial Knowledge

In the design of a new interface of DSS, an important role should be given to the manager profile, in particular to the identification of his or her financial and economic knowledge. There are a number of methods for modelling of a manager's knowledge and activities: crowdsourcing [15], testing of physiological brain activity [16], explorations of the observation of the manager's eye movements, otherwise called eye tracking. In the project, this last method was applied. In Fig. 4, the left part shows the areas of the manager's focus on the presented content. The colored areas indicate which parts of the document get attention and were examined more closely (colors close to red), and which ones were omitted. Green colors on the map show areas that drew less attention. The right part of the figure shows the sequence and depth of the search of the financial information by two persons (green and purple tracks) scanning the same document. The arrangement of fixations and saccades that is attained reveals the path of analysis, indicating the items of greatest attention. In this way, it is possible to show the difference in detail and the method of analysis of the presented case study.

The first results of sequence analysis have indicated that the level of the manager's knowledge determines the perception of the presented data and the manner of analysis. Novices focused their attention only on increases in two of the three liquidity indicators. They did not take into account the fact that the greatest threat was due to the

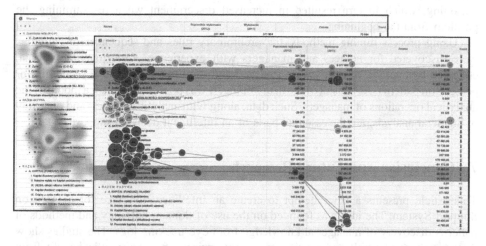

Fig. 4. Example heat map and the path of the scan along with defined areas of interest (AOI) (Color figure online)

significant decline in cash liquidity. Experienced managers effectively took advantage of the ontology and focused on any decrease in cash amounts. They understood that the growth of the current liquidity indicator and the quick liquidity indicator were associated with the increase of stock level and receivables. This was not a good symptom for the company's financial situation, because both stock and receivables cannot be not easily converted into cash. Experts using ontology have analysed various threats that were not noticed by the novices.

Saved in numerical form, eye movement data can be analyzed, processed, and used for different analytical reports. For instance, the log of the user operations provides detailed data about the perception of information on the screen, about the order of the perception of the content and the length of time of focus at any given area of the document. For example, we can define areas of interest (AOI), shown in the right part of Fig. 4. Each of the shaded areas indicates a separate AOI. With such data, one can generate different queries, statistics and measurements. For instance, the information about attraction of the manager's particular attention, and the scheduled time of observation. This information in conjunction with a scanning path made it possible to obtain information on how a manager has analyzed and understood the data in the report.

The results of the experiments raised three questions: (1) how and why does the experienced manager proceed; (2) how to identify the short-comings and errors committed by inexperienced managers, and (3) how to recognize a manager's fatigue and stress, which were identified after detailed analysis of the acquired data. The answers to these and other questions are essential to build patterns of schematic perception of economic information. For example, at this stage of the project it was not easy to uniquely identify which particular state affects the errors in analysis. It boiled down to difficulties in concentration, thereby generating a considerable amount of fixations with very short saccades. A similar result can be caused by the sudden detachment of sight, when the person's focus was drawn to the external environment; for example, if a door was opened or someone entered the room. Referring to the analysis of the financial statements, it was noticed that there were problems in coming back to deliberate reasoning, which in turn resulted in increased discernment when re-examining the problem from the beginning.

Using process mining methods, the preliminary rules and sequences of activities were discovered for novices and managers with experience. Raw quantitative data, collected by tracking software, were analysed and used in the process of searching for perception patterns. As a result of the data mining, it was possible to obtain a model of the analytical operations of managers. Such data, along with analytical models and ontology of financial analysis, are the essential parts of an intelligent decision support system.

7 Conclusion and Future Research

This article presents a new attempt to create an intelligent interface for a Decision Support System. The idea was founded on the use of domain ontology and methods of patterns discovery of managerial knowledge from eye-tracking logs. The studies show that managers of small and medium-sized enterprises often have little benefit from achievements in the field of broadly understood financial analysis and IT technology, to strengthen their competitive position on the market and maintain financial credibility. The problem is often caused by the lack of the knowledge required to correctly interpret the financial reports as well as economic indicators. Also, these studies have shown difficulties for the knowledgeable use of information systems that contain too many functions and tools that exceed the user's knowledge and skills. Usually, numerous ways of reporting, and the complex visualization tools, deepen the difficulties in the perception of the financial situation of an enterprise and its environment.

The use of improved visualization and access to semantic searches are primary characteristics of the DSS. One of the main artefacts in semantic networks is the ontology of business information. The experiments showed the usefulness of ontology where each concept and relationship can be considered in a multifaceted way. In the case studies, we have demonstrated that decision making without the use of ontology may lead to wrong conclusions, e.g. introducing sales promotion to increase sales growth. It should be pointed out that analysis of indicators alone without relation to other components of financial reporting can lead to the choice of improper interpretations. Ontology is therefore an essential element in the DSS that allows a manager to make correct business decisions oriented toward company prosperity and avoiding the threat of bankruptcy.

The use of eye-tracking allowed us to develop preliminary patterns of analysis of financial reports and the ways of interpreting the most important indicators. The sequences of actions discovered on the basis of the eye-tracking of experts makes it possible to define best practices to analyze financial data. However, these patterns are not sufficient to solve the problem. They must be associated with the financial ontology that helps to interpret the data and provide appropriate adequate recommendations.

Preliminary results of the experiments demonstrated large differences between the experienced managers and novices in the manner of data perception and a way of analysis of financial reports. To develop a user-oriented interface, further in-depth studies on identifying the level of manager knowledge are needed. The project will be continued, especially on the modeling of manager knowledge using eye-tracking.

Acknowledgements. The authors thank the staff and the companies Bilander and Tobii for their support in developing the prototype. Thanks go also to the financial experts: Wojciech Hasik, Mariola Kotłowska and Wojciech Ostojski, and students of the Faculty of Management, Informatics and Finance of Wrocław University of Economics.

References

1. Korczak, J., Dudycz, H., Dyczkowski, M.: Intelligent dashboard for SME managers. Architecture and functions. In: Ganzha, M., Maciaszek, L., Paprzycki, M. (eds.) Proceedings of the Federated Conference on Computer Science and Information Systems, pp. 1003–1007. Polskie Towarzystwo Informatyczne, IEEE Computer Society Press, Warsaw, Los Alamitos, (2012)
2. Samonas, M.: Financial Forecasting, Analysis and Modelling. Wiley, Chichester (2015)
3. Power, D.J.: Decision Support Basics. Business Expert Press, LLC (2009)

4. Power, D.J., Sharda, R., Burstein, F.: Decision Support System. Wiley Encyclopedia of Management, vol. 7. Management Information Systems (2015)
5. Dudycz, H.: The Topic Map as a Visual Representation of Economic Knowledge. Wrocław University of Economics, Wrocław (2013). (in Polish)
6. Aruldoss, M., Maladhy, D., Prasanna, Venkatesan V.: A framework for business intelligence application using ontological classification. Int. J. Eng. Sci. Technol. 3(2), 1213–1221 (2011)
7. Cheng, A., Lu, Y.-C., Sheu, C.: An ontology-based business intelligence application in financial knowledge management system. Expert Syst. Appl. 36(2), 3614–3622 (2009). part 2
8. Neumayr, B., Schrefl, M., Linner, K.: Semantic cockpit: an ontology-driven, interactive business intelligence tool for comparative data analysis. In: Troyer, O., Medeiros, C.B., Billen, R., Hallot, P., Simitsis, A., Mingroot, H. (eds.) ER 2011. LNCS, vol. 6999, pp. 55–64. Springer, Heidelberg (2011). doi:10.1007/978-3-642-24574-9_9
9. Pinto, F., Santos, M.F., Marques, A.: Ontology based data mining – a contribution to business intelligence. In: 10th WSEAS International Conference on Mathematics and Computers in Business and Economics (MCBE 2009), 23–25 March, Czech Republic, pp. 210–216, (2009)
10. Saggion, H., Funk, A., Maynard, D., Bontcheva, K.: Ontology-based information extraction for business intelligence. In: Aberer, K., et al. (eds.) ASWC/ISWC -2007. LNCS, vol. 4825, pp. 843–856. Springer, Heidelberg (2007). doi:10.1007/978-3-540-76298-0_61
11. Sell, D., da Silva, D.C., Beppler, F.D., Napoli, M., Ghisi, F.B., Pacheco, R., Todesco, J.L.: SBI: a semantic framework to support business intelligence. In: Proceeding of the First International Workshop on Ontology-supported Business Intelligence, Article no. 11. ACM, New York (2008)
12. Korczak, J., Dudycz, H., Dyczkowski, M.: Design of financial knowledge in dashboard for SME managers. In: Ganzha, M., Maciaszek, L., Paprzycki, M. (eds.) Proceedings of the 2013 Federated Conference on Computer Science and Information Systems. Annals of Computer Science and Information Systems, vol. 1, pp. 1111–1118. Polskie Towarzystwo Informatyczne, IEEE Computer Society Press, Warsaw, Los Alamitos (2013)
13. Dyczkowski, M., Korczak, J., Dudycz, H.: Multi-criteria evaluation of the intelligent dashboard for SME managers based on scorecard framework. In: Ganzha, M., Maciaszek, L., Paprzycki, M. (eds.) Proceedings of the 2014 Federated Conference on Computer Science and Information Systems. Annals of Computer Science and Information Systems, New York City, vol. 2, pp. 1147–1155 (2014). doi:10.15439/2014F388
14. Subramanyam, K.R., Wild, J.: Financial Statement Analysis. McGraw-Hill Education (2013)
15. Schenk, E., Guittard, C.: Towards a characterization of crowdsourcing practices. J. Innov. Econ. Manage. 7, 93–107 (2011)
16. Hwang, H.J., Kwon, K., Im, C.H.: Neurofeedback-based motor imagery training for brain-computer interface (BCI). J. Neurosci. Methods 179, 150–156 (2009). Republic of Korea

Use of Information and Communication Technologies for Knowledge Sharing by Polish and UK-Based Prosumers

Ewa Ziemba[1(✉)], Monika Eisenbardt[1], and Roisin Mullins[2]

[1] Faculty of Finance and Insurance, University of Economics in Katowice,
1 Maja 50, 40-287 Katowice, Poland
{ewa.ziemba,monika.eisenbardt}@ue.katowice.pl
[2] Faculty of Business and Management College Street,
University of Wales Trinity Saint David, Lampeter, Ceredigion, UK
r.mullins@uwtsd.ac.uk

Abstract. Information and communication technologies (ICTs) can enhance the knowledge sharing by lowering temporal and spatial barriers between prosumers and enterprises, and improving access to prosumers' knowledge for enterprises. A major challenge for enterprises involves investing in the appropriate ICTs that help facilitate prosumers' knowledge engagement and knowledge transfer. The purpose of the paper is to indicate which ICTs are currently used and expected to be used to enable knowledge sharing by Polish and UK-based prosumers. The reported outcomes are the result of a questionnaire survey that yielded responses from 783 Polish and 171 UK-based prosumers. The results indicate the primary ICTs choices for use and expected use by Poland and UK-based prosumers and reveals important differences between these countries. The mobile applications being favored amongst the UK respondents whereas the dedicated enterprise website is the favored ICT amongst Polish respondents. The results explore the choice and variety of ICTs available for prosumers that may be overlooked by enterprises as trends change. The variety of ICTs provided by enterprises may be too limiting to promote the type of knowledge sharing and communications expected to reassure the prosumers, and the ICT trends and customer culture have an affect the choice of ICT uptake for knowledge sharing with enterprises.

Keywords: Information and communication technologies · Knowledge · Prosumers · Knowledge sharing · Poland · United Kingdom

1 Introduction

Knowledge is currently viewed as a fundamental driver for the commercial success of enterprises and is crucial to their competitive advantage [1–4]. Moreover, customer knowledge becomes an essential intangible asset for every line of business [5], leads to better response and respect toward customers [6, 7], makes a contribution towards new and innovative products [8, 9], contributes to the improvement of business value [10], and enhances the competitiveness of businesses [11, 12].

© Springer International Publishing AG 2017
E. Ziemba (Ed.): AITM 2016/ISM 2016, LNBIP 277, pp. 49–73, 2017.
DOI: 10.1007/978-3-319-53076-5_4

Consumers who share their knowledge with enterprises with the aim of creating values and benefits for enterprises and their own consumption are known as "prosumers," whereas the process in which they share knowledge with enterprises is consistent with the notion of "prosumption" [13–18]. In general, prosumption refers to situations in which prosumers share knowledge not only with enterprises, but also with other prosumers to produce things of value for enterprises, and also for themselves. They can share knowledge voluntarily and do not expect any tangible benefits [19]. Other times they share knowledge under the condition of obtaining certain benefits in return, such as rewards or fulfilling personal goals [20].

Given that advances in ICTs have made it easier to share knowledge and these ICT developments have made the world increasingly interconnected, many enterprises recognise there are challenges to employ the appropriate ICTs to facilitate knowledge sharing with prosumers. In considering the complexity of prosumption, prosumers' knowledge sharing initiatives and the variety of ICTs, enterprise must often confront these challenging tasks in deciding what type of ICTs to deploy in support of their prosumption initiatives.

The existing studies mostly examine ICTs for knowledge management in enterprises [21–26]. Researchers argued that ICTs play an important role in acquiring, codifying, storing, creating, sharing and applying knowledge that can be crucial for effective decision making and control at all levels.

The authors of this paper, following an extensive review of the literature, did not unearth any insightful studies to interpret how ICTs support prosumers' knowledge sharing with enterprises. This reveals a need to study the ICTs that should be adopted and used by enterprises to better enable prosumers' knowledge sharing. Therefore, conducting research among prosumers and enterprises should contribute to greater understanding of the use of ICTs for prosumers' knowledge sharing and should help fill the gap in the existing body of knowledge.

In light of the above limitations, this paper focuses on investigating the choice of ICTs supporting prosumers' knowledge sharing in Poland and the UK. It presents extended and detailed analyses presented in the previous paper [27]. The aim of this paper is to indicate the ICTs that are currently used by prosumers in comparison with the preferred ICTs expected to be used by prosumers. The replies to a number of questions were presented and a number of hypothesis were tested.

The paper is structured as follows. Section 1 is an introduction to the subject. Section 2 states the theoretical background of ICTs for supporting prosumers' knowledge sharing and poses research questions and hypotheses. Section 3 describes the research methodology. Section 4 presents the research findings on ICTs used and expected to be used by prosumers to facilitate knowledge sharing. Section 5 presents the discussion of research findings. Section 6 provides the study's contributions and limitations, and implications for the findings and considerations for future investigative work.

2 Theoretical Background and Research Questions

2.1 Understanding Prosumers' Knowledge and Its Sharing with Enterprises

The concept of prosumption has emerged from consumption theory. It focuses on the role that can be played by pro-active consumers willing to cooperate with enterprises. Nonetheless, according to Ritzer [28], this concept still remains a niche concept in the literature and is largely unknown to most observers. In his opinion it is definitely because of the other hegemonic concepts – production and consumption – that are so omnipresent and powerful.

The term 'prosumer' was coined by Toffler [16]. According to him, selected enterprises' tasks (mainly manual tasks), previously performed by enterprises' employees, are increasingly performed by consumers in accordance with the do-it-yourself principle, and by implication consumers become co-creators of products and services. Indeed, the terms of prosumption and prosumer have evolved over the years [29, 30]. A significant role in the development of prosumption was played by the ICT progress. In addition, the direction of prosumption development was established by prosumers' willingness to collaborate with enterprises and employ ICTs for this purpose [31, 32]. As a result, modern approaches to prosumption differ greatly from Toffler's proposal. The modern approach to prosumption emphasizes the creativity of prosumers, as well as being connected to the value of prosumers' knowledge for enterprises. They could be perceived as outside experts who are able to perform some business tasks [33]. Enterprises can use their knowledge to attain business goals and, as a consequence, engage prosumers in business tasks.

Prosumers' knowledge is the most important asset for most sectors engaged in contemporary business and is one of the most important contributors in improving business value and enhancing business performance [6, 34–37]. It is usually categorized into three types [38, 39]:

- *Knowledge about prosumers* represents both prosumers' needs and requirements; it may encompass characteristics in prosumers' behavior, their demographics and previous purchasing patterns; it may allow an understanding of prosumers' motivation in order to adjust and personalize products' or services';
- *Knowledge for prosumers* is created to satisfy prosumers' needs; it may include knowledge about enterprises, products and services; it may support prosumers in their buying cycle, impact on prosumers' perception of enterprises and offers, and become the base of knowledge from prosumers; and
- *Knowledge from prosumers* is created through the prosumers' experience with enterprises; it may embrace ideas, thoughts, reviews, opinions, discussions, advice and rankings that enterprises receive from their prosumers and use them to enhance their products and services.

Additionally, some authors distinguished knowledge with prosumers, also called 'knowledge co-creation'. This knowledge is created through a prosumers' participation within a shared practice or community of practice. It means that prosumers, as environment partners, participate in the development of enterprise knowledge and new knowledge and innovations are created in a shared and intensive process [40, 41]. They suggest that the classification embracing three types of knowledge should be completed by adding this fourth type of knowledge. Xuelian, Chakpitak, and Yodmongkol [42] claimed that knowledge with prosumers will shape the future of business. Koniorczyk [43] indicated that an example of this type of knowledge is IKEA Innovation Labs.

The sharing of these various kinds of prosumers' knowledge between the prosumers and enterprises is critical in order to produce things that are of value not only for enterprises but also for prosumers. It could be characterized as a process in which prosumers' knowledge is exchanged among prosumers and enterprises. In this process prosumers share what they have learned and transfer what they know to enterprises that have a business interest in it and that have found this new knowledge to be useful for business improvement [44]. In this process the value of knowledge appreciates when it is shared [32].

In this study, the term "prosumers' knowledge sharing" means providing knowledge from prosumers (prosumers' ideas of products developments and creation, thoughts, reviews, opinions, discussions, advice and rankings) to enterprises and other prosumers. This approach is in line with the proposal of Wang and Noe, who distinguished knowledge sharing from knowledge exchange [45]. According to them, "knowledge exchange includes both knowledge sharing (or employees providing knowledge to others) and knowledge seeking (or employees searching for knowledge from others)." It should however be noted that "knowledge sharing" can be also used interchangeably with "knowledge exchange" [46].

2.2   ICTs Supporting Prosumers' Knowledge Sharing

Some studies show that ICTs, especially CRM systems [47], Business Intelligence systems [48], and social media [49–54] can be used for knowledge management or can affect decisions of potential consumers and thus enterprises activities [55]. Other studies indicate that mobiles technologies (both mobile devices and mobile applications) can be used for prosumers and enterprises innovations [56, 57].

Additionally, researchers have examined ICT-tools for knowledge sharing [22, 58]. Jiebing, Bin, and Yongjiang [59] provided a conceptual framework to explore the linking mechanisms between customer knowledge management and ICT-based business model innovation. Studies concerned with the role of ICTs in knowledge sharing enlist such primary technologies as blogs, e-mail systems, e-collaborative systems, e-forums, knowledge repository, instant messaging, audio conferencing, podcasts, video conferencing, and wiki in the context of challenges faced by the practitioners in distributed projects [60] or in the context of Nonaka and Takeuchi's SECI model [61]. The focus of the SECI model on knowledge creation explores the cycle of generating tacit knowledge through to explicit knowledge and recreating tacit knowledge. The knowledge change in the SECI model is summarised as tacit to tacit (Socialization), tacit to explicit (Externalization), explicit to explicit (Combination), explicit to tacit (Internalization) [61, 62].

Only a few of the studies explore the application of social media for sharing customer knowledge. For example Chua and Banerjee [50] presented how Starbucks redefined the roles of its customers through the use of social media by transforming them from passive recipients of beverages to active contributors of innovation. Wijaya, Spruit, Scheper, and Versendaal [63], who examined the influence of web 2.0 concept in the webstrategy formulation for organizations, claimed that consumers would like to use web applications from multiple devices and even they would not have been able to share knowledge if the software was only accessible through one device. Jalonen [64] explored the interplay between knowledge and emotion in the organisational knowledge creation process in the context of social media. Okazaki et al. [65] found a clear connection among customer engagement, prosumption, and Web 2.0 in a context of service-dominant logic. Moreover, they identified social networks created by prosumers. Yang and Li [66] examined the popularity of consumer-generated content of online co-creation communities which share and exchange product-related knowledge. They confirmed that social capital between customers, particularly the norm of reciprocity, was a strong driver of popularity of consumer-generated content. Based on the literature review, Zembik [67] explored various types of social media and their role as source of knowledge about, for, and from customers. Ziemba and Mullins [39] proposed the conceptual customer stratification framework which explains the stages required by a business to observe customers social media discussions.

2.3 Research Questions and Hypotheses

After extensively searching through the literature, it was observed that there is a research gap in the existing body of knowledge related to ICTs used currently by prosumers and expected to be used by them to support prosumers' knowledge sharing. Also there is no research focusing on comparative analysis between less developed countries (like Poland) and better developed (like the UK) in the above mentioned area.

In order to bridge the gap this study examines ICTs facilitating Polish and UK-based prosumers' knowledge sharing and focuses on addressing the following research question:

Q1: What ICTs are used for knowledge sharing by Polish and UK-based prosumers combined?

Q2: Are there statistically significant differences between Polish and UK-based prosumers in ICTs used for knowledge sharing?

Q3: What ICTs are expected to be used for knowledge sharing by Polish and UK-based prosumers combined?

Q4: Are there statistically significant differences between Polish and UK-based prosumers in ICTs expected to be used for knowledge sharing?

Q5: Are there statistically significant differences between ICTs used and expected to be used for knowledge sharing by Polish and UK-based prosumers combined?

Q6: What ICTs are used for knowledge sharing by Polish prosumers?

Q7: What ICTs are expected to be used for knowledge sharing by Polish prosumers?

Q8: Are there statistically significant differences between ICTs used and expected to be used for knowledge sharing by Polish prosumers?

Q9: What ICTs are used for knowledge sharing by UK-based prosumers?

Q10: What ICTs are expected to be used for knowledge sharing by UK-based prosumers?

Q11: Are there statistically significant differences between ICTs used and expected to be used for knowledge sharing by UK-based prosumers?

Taking into account the above considerations and above research questions, five research hypotheses were formulated:

H1: There are statistically significant differences between Polish and UK-based prosumers in ICTs used for knowledge sharing.

H2: There are statistically significant differences between Polish and UK-based prosumers in ICTs expected to be used for knowledge sharing.

H3: There are statistically significant differences between ICTs used and expected to be used for knowledge sharing by Polish and UK-based prosumers combined.

H4: There are statistically significant differences between ICTs used and expected to be used for knowledge sharing by Polish prosumers.

H5: There are statistically significant differences between ICTs used and expected to be used for knowledge sharing by UK-based prosumers.

3 Research Methodology

Research methods included a critical review of the literature, logical deduction, case studies, a survey questionnaire, and statistical analysis. The research process followed the following steps:

1. The critical review of existing studies related to "prosumption," "prosumer," "customer," "consumer," "knowledge," "knowledge sharing," "ICT," "information technology" enabled to examine some ICTs supporting prosumers' knowledge sharing. The review embraces five bibliographic databases: Ebsco, ProQuest, Emerald Management, Scopus and ISI Web of Knowledge.
2. Interpretation of the case studies reporting prosumers' knowledge sharing informed the identification of the ICTs that are used by prosumers to share knowledge with enterprises.
3. An initial pilot survey questionnaire was designed. The questionnaire was divided into two parts. After a few demographics questions all participants were obliged to answer the question: *Have you ever assessed or commented on products or companies, proposed products improvements to the companies or designed new products?* This question enabled the division of respondents into consumers (not active in this area) and prosumers (active ones). The questionnaire contained questions concerning specified ICTs employed by enterprises to support prosumers' knowledge sharing. The questions were: (1) Which ICTs offered by enterprises have you used to share your knowledge, ideas and proposals about products or enterprises? (2) If you could in a free and unlimited way share your knowledge about

products or enterprises, propose ideas of products developments or design new products – please indicate which ICTs would you like to use? The former question was directed only to prosumers. The latter was directed to both – prosumers and consumers. Various kinds of ICTs were listed for those questions. For each listed ICTs the respondents could choose one of five responses, according to a 5-point Likert scale: (1) definitely not (never), (2) probably not, (3) I don't know (no answer), (4) probably yes, (5) definitely yes (many times).

4. In November 2014 the more in-depth pilot survey was conducted in Poland. The purpose was substantive and methodological scrutiny of the questionnaire. To conduct reliability analysis, Cronbach's coefficient alpha was used. Cronbach's alpha for 16 analyzed items was 0.881. Hinton et al. [68] suggested four different ranges of reliability, i.e. the excellent range (0.90 and above), the high (0.70–0.90), the high moderate (0.50–0.70) and the low (0.50 and below). Thus, it can be concluded that the scale had high reliability and it could be used in the research process. Moreover, substantive scrutiny of the questionnaire enabled the researchers to perform minor changes in order to improve the quality of the questionnaire.

5. Applying the CAWI (Computer-Assisted Web Interview) method and employing the Polish platform Ankietka.pl, and the English platform Bristol Online Survey (BOS), hosted at the University of Bristol, the survey questionnaires was uploaded to the websites. Data collection took place between the end of December 2014 and March 2015 in Poland, and between February and April 2016 in the United Kingdom. In Poland, the designed sample size was 2.500 people, comprising people of different age, gender, and ICT skills. In the UK the online survey letter and URL was initially posted to 1000 individuals comprising people of different age, gender, and ICT skills, and presented to a random sample of the target population. Using online tools permits contact with an accessible audience as the survey appears on search engine lists due to metatags and appropriate placing of keywords. After screening the responses and excluding outliers, there was a final research sample of 783 usable, correct and complete questionnaires from Poland and 171 from the United Kingdom. The data was stored in Microsoft Excel format. The demographic analysis of the research sample is presented in Table 1.

6. As the process of collecting data was completed the reliability was calculated. The Cronbach's alpha coefficient with all 16 items confirmed a high internal consistency (0.882). Additionally, the values of Cronbach's alpha for each item, with the assumption that a given item was deleted, were calculated. The Cronbach's alpha values for the items were between 0.883 and 0.845. The results showed that the removal of some items would not lead to the improvement of internal consistency among items on the scale. Overall, the original alpha scores with all 16 items show a strong internal consistency and reliability.

7. In order to answer the research questions and conform the research hypotheses, the statistical analysis was employed. Firstly, the descriptive analysis was employed to describe ICTs used and expected to be used by prosumers. The following statistics were calculated: mean, median (MDN), first quartile (Q25), third quartile (Q75), mode, variance (VAR), standard deviation (SD), coefficient of variation (CV), skewness (SK), and coefficient of kurtosis (CK). Secondly, the Mann-Whitney U test was applied in order to identify differences between Polish and UK-based

Table 1. Demographics analysis of the research sample

Demographic profile	Poland		United Kingdom	
	Number of respondents	Percentage of respondents	Number of respondents	Percentage of respondents
Gender				
Female	599	76.5%	98	57.3%
Male	184	23.5%	73	42.7%
Age				
Builders generation – over 65 years old	14	1.8%	8	4.68%
Baby-Boomers generation – 51–65 years old	35	4.5%	25	14.62%
X generation – 36–50 years old	108	13.8%	67	39.18%
Y generation – 21–35 years old	369	47.1%	68	39.77%
Z generation – less than 21 years old	257	32.8%	3	1.75%
Level of education				
Higher education	217	27.7%	89	52.05%
Secondary education	559	71.4%	75	43.86%
Less than secondary education	7	0.9%	7	4.09%
Place of residence				
City with a population of more than 100.000	419	53.5%	96	56.14%
City with a population of less than 100.000	244	31.2%	53	30.99%
Rural area	120	15.3%	22	12.87%

prosumers, and between ICTs used and excepted to be used by prosumers. This test was selected because it does not assume any assumptions related to the distribution, and it is used to test whether two independent samples of observations are drawn from the same or identical distribution. The nine ICTs were analyzed, i.e. e-mails (E-ma), Internet forums (InFo), enterprises' websites (EnWe), information websites (InWe), industry specialized portals (InPo), mobile applications (MoAp), enterprises' specialized applications (EnAp), Facebook fanpages (FaFa), online surveys (OnSu). These ICTs were identified as crucial for prosumers in order to knowledge sharing with enterprises [27].

4   Research Findings

In order to analyze ICTs supporting prosumers' knowledge sharing, we examined which ICTs facilitating prosumers' knowledge sharing are currently used and expected to be used by prosumers in Poland and the UK. ICTs used by prosumers reflect these ICTs which currently are used by prosumers to share their knowledge. Whereas, ICTs expected to be used by prosumers reflect these ICTs which are needed by prosumers to share their knowledge. Additionally, the analyses were made in the context of Poland and UK combined, as well as separately in Poland and the UK.

4.1 ICTs Used and Expected to Be Used for Knowledge Sharing by Polish and UK-Based Prosumers Combined

The following research questions and hypothesis were posed and relate to the combined results regarding ICTs used by prosumers in Poland and the UK:

Q1: What ICTs are used for knowledge sharing by Polish and UK-based prosumers combined?

Q2: Are there statistically significant differences between Polish and UK-based prosumers in ICTs used for knowledge sharing?

H1: There are statistically significant differences between Polish and UK-based prosumers in ICTs used for knowledge sharing.

In order to answer the research question Q1, detailed analysis concerning ICTs used by Polish and UK-based prosumers to share their knowledge, was made. The results are presented in Table 2. It is found that prosumers mainly used five kinds of ICTs for knowledge sharing, i.e. enterprises' websites, e-mails, Internet forums, Facebook fanpages and online surveys. Other ICTs were used by prosumers but very rarely.

Table 2. ICTs used for knowledge sharing by Polish and UK-based prosumers combined

Code	Mean	Q25	MDN	Q75	Mode	VAR	SD	CV	SK	CK
EnWe	3.69	3	4	5	4	1.47	1.21	0.33	−0.26	−0.24
E-ma	3.49	2	4	4	4	1.70	1.30	0.37	−0.39	−0.93
InFo	3.39	2	4	4	4	1.78	1.33	0.39	−0.46	−1.02
FaFa	3.22	2	4	4	4	2.05	1.43	0.44	−0.54	−1.29
OnSu	3.13	2	4	4	4	1.81	1.35	0.43	−0.65	−1.21
InPo	2.94	2	3	4	4	1.9	1.38	0.47	−0.77	−1.35
MoAp	2.80	1	3	4	4	1.9	1.38	0.49	−0.87	−1.42
InWe	2.74	2	2	4	2	1.74	1.32	0.48	0.56	−1.24
EnAp	2.59	1	2	4	1	1.83	1.35	0.52	1.18	−1.27

In order to answer the research question Q2 about significant differences between Polish and UK-based prosumers in ICTs used for knowledge sharing, the Mann-Whitney U test was used. The test results presented in Table 3 did not show any significant differences between Polish and UK-based prosumers in such ICTs like e-mails, Internet forums, and online surveys. Whereas, there were significant differences in ICTs like: enterprises' websites, information websites, industry specialized portals, mobile applications, enterprises' specialized applications, and Facebook fanpages.

The detailed analysis (Appendix 1) shows that:

- Enterprises' websites were more likely used by Polish prosumers (Mean = 3.71; MDN = 4; Mode = 4) than UK-based prosumers (Mean = 3.52; MDN = 4; Mode = 4);

Table 3. The Mann-Whitney test results for ICTs used for knowledge sharing by Polish and UK-based prosumers combined

ICT	E-ma	InFo	EnWe	InWe	InPo	MoAp	EnAp	FaFa	OnSu
Z	1.48	0.99	2.11	2.58	−2.18	−8.11	−6.79	−3.42	1.00
p value	0.14	0.32	0.03	0.01	0.03	0.00	0.00	0.00	0.31

- Information websites were more likely used by Polish prosumers (Mean = 2.85; MDN = 3; Mode = 4) than UK-based prosumers (Mean = 2.33; MDN = 2; Mode = 2);
- Industry specialized portals were more likely used by UK-based prosumers (Mean = 3.26; MDN = 4; Mode = 4) than Polish prosumers (Mean = 2.87; MDN = 3; Mode = 4);
- Mobile applications were more likely used by UK-based prosumers (Mean = 4.01; MDN = 4; Mode = 4) than Polish prosumers (Mean = 2.56; MDN = 2; Mode = 1);
- Enterprises' specialized applications were more likely used by UK-based prosumers (Mean = 3.59; MDN = 4; Mode = 4) than Polish prosumers (Mean = 2.38; MDN = 2; Mode = 1); and
- Facebook fanpages were more likely used UK by based prosumers (Mean = 3.78; MDN = 4; Mode = 4) than Polish prosumers (Mean = 3.11; MDN = 4; Mode = 4).

The following research questions and hypothesis related to ICTs expected to be used by prosumers in Poland and UK combined were posed:

Q3: What ICTs are expected to be used for knowledge sharing by Polish and UK-based prosumers?
Q4: Are there statistically significant differences between Polish and UK-based prosumers in ICTs expected to be used for knowledge sharing?
H2: There are statistically significant differences between Polish and UK-based prosumers in ICTs expected to be used for knowledge sharing.

In order to answer the research question Q3, detailed analysis concerning ICTs expected to be used by Polish and UK-based prosumers, to share knowledge, was made. The results are presented in Table 4. It is found that most prosumers expected to use enterprises' websites and e-mails. The mean values are 3.91 and 3.68 respectively, the median and mode values are 4.00.

In order to answer the research question Q4 about significant differences between Polish and UK-based prosumers in ICTs expected to be used for knowledge sharing, the Mann-Whitney U test was used. The test results presented in Table 5 did not show any significant differences between Polish and UK-based prosumers in such ICTs like enterprises' specialized applications and Facebook fanpages. Whereas, there were significant differences in ICTs like: e-mails, Internet forums, enterprises' websites, information websites, industry specialized portals, mobile applications, and online surveys.

Table 4. ICTs expected to be used for knowledge sharing by Polish and UK-based prosumers combined

Code	Mean	Q25	MDN	Q75	Mode	VAR	SD	CV	SK	CK
EnWe	3.91	4	4	5	4	1.01	1.01	0.26	−0.09	0.80
E-ma	3.68	3	4	5	4	1.42	1.19	0.32	−0.27	−0.47
InPo	3.51	3	4	4	4	1.39	1.18	0.34	−0.41	−0.64
InFo	3.47	2	4	4	4	1.44	1.20	0.35	−0.44	−0.84
FaFa	3.40	2	4	4	4	1.74	1.32	0.39	−0.45	−1
EnAp	3.39	2	4	4	4	1.50	1.23	0.36	−0.50	−0.83
MoAp	3.36	2	4	4	4	1.55	1.24	0.37	−0.51	−0.90
InWe	3.27	2	4	4	4	1.58	1.26	0.38	−0.58	−1.16
OnSu	3.06	2	3	4	4	1.61	1.27	0.41	−0.74	−0.71

Table 5. The Mann-Whitney test results for ICTs expected to be used for knowledge sharing by Polish and UK-based prosumers combined

ICT	E-ma	InFo	EnWe	InWe	InPo	MoAp	EnAp	FaFa	OnSu
Z	5.05	3.61	5.43	8.33	3.15	−4.26	1.67	−0.89	2.07
p value	0.00	0.00	0.00	0.00	0.00	0.00	0.10	0.37	0.04

The detailed analysis (Appendix 1) shows that:

- E-mails are more likely expected to be used by Polish prosumers (Mean = 3.77; MDN = 4; Mode = 4) than UK-based prosumers (Mean = 3.29; MDN = 4; Mode = 4);
- Internet forums are more likely expected to be used by Polish prosumers (Mean = 3.54; MDN = 4; Mode = 4) than UK-based prosumers (Mean = 3.18; MDN = 4; Mode = 4);
- Enterprises' websites are more likely expected to be used by Polish prosumers (Mean = 4.00; MDN = 4; Mode = 4) than UK-based prosumers (Mean = 3.53; MDN = 4; Mode = 4);
- Information websites are more likely expected to be used by Polish prosumers (Mean = 3.44; MDN = 4; Mode = 4) than UK-based prosumers (Mean = 2.53; MDN = 2; Mode = 2);
- Industry specialized portals are more likely expected to be used by Polish prosumers (Mean = 3.57; MDN = 4; Mode = 4) than UK-based prosumers (Mean = 3.25; MDN = 4; Mode = 4);
- Mobile applications are more likely expected to be used by UK-based prosumers (Mean = 3.74; MDN = 4; Mode = 4) than Polish prosumers (Mean = 3.28; MDN = 4; Mode = 4); and
- Online surveys are more likely expected to be used Polish prosumers (Mean = 3.10; MDN = 3; Mode = 4) than UK-based prosumers (Mean = 2.89; MDN = 2; Mode = 2).

The following research question and hypothesis were posed related to a comparison between ICTs used and ICTs expected to be used to support knowledge sharing by prosumers in Poland and the UK:

Q5: Are there statistically significant differences between ICTs used and expected to be used for knowledge sharing by Polish and UK-based prosumers combined?
H3: There are statistically significant differences between ICTs used and expected to be used for knowledge sharing by Polish and UK-based prosumers combined.

In order to answer the research question Q5 about significant differences between ICTs used and expected to be used by Polish and UK-based prosumers for knowledge sharing, the Mann-Whitney U test was used. The test results presented in Table 6 did not show any significant differences between Polish and UK-based prosumers in such ICTs like Internet forums and online surveys. Whereas, there were significant differences in ICTs used and expected to be used like: e-mails, enterprises' websites, information websites, industry specialized portals, mobile applications, enterprises' specialized applications, and Facebook fanpages.

Table 6. The Mann-Whitney test results for ICTs used and expected to be used by Polish and UK-based prosumers for knowledge sharing

ICT	E-ma	InFo	EnWe	InWe	InPo	MoAp	EnAp	FaFa	OnSu
Z	−2.26	−0.50	−2.51	−6.91	−7.17	−6.98	−10.10	−2.00	1.19
p value	0.02	0.62	0.01	0.00	0.00	0.00	0.00	0.05	0.23

The detailed analysis (Appendix 1) shows that:

- Enterprises' specialized applications are more likely expected to be used by Polish and UK-prosumers (Mean = 3.39; MDN = 4; Mode = 4) than they are currently used by them (Mean = 2.59; MDN = 2; Mode = 1);
- Industry specialized portals are more likely expected to be used by Polish and UK-prosumers (Mean = 3.51; MDN = 4; Mode = 4) than are currently used by them (Mean = 2.94; MDN = 2; Mode = 2);
- Mobile applications are more likely expected to be used by Polish and UK-prosumers (Mean = 3.36; MDN = 4; Mode = 4) than are currently used by them (Mean = 2.80; MDN = 3; Mode = 4);
- Information websites are more likely expected to be used by Polish and UK-prosumers (Mean = 3.27; MDN = 4; Mode = 4) than are currently used them (Mean = 2.74; MDN = 2; Mode = 2);
- Enterprises' websites are more likely expected to be used by Polish and UK-prosumers (Mean = 3.91; MDN = 4; Mode = 4) than are currently used (Mean = 3.69; MDN = 4; Mode = 4);
- E-mails are more likely expected to be used by Polish and UK-prosumers (Mean = 3.68; MDN = 4; Mode = 4) than are currently used by them (Mean = 3.49; MDN = 4; Mode = 4); and

- Facebook fanpages are more likely expected to be used by Polish and UK-prosumers (Mean = 3.40; MDN = 4; Mode = 4) than are currently used by them (Mean = 3.22; MDN = 3; Mode = 4).

4.2 ICTs Used and Expected to Be Used for Knowledge Sharing by Polish Prosumers

The following research questions and hypothesis related to a comparison between ICTs used and ICTs expected to be used to support knowledge sharing by prosumers in Poland were posed:

Q6: What ICTs are used for knowledge sharing by Polish prosumers?

Q7: What ICTs are expected to be used for knowledge sharing by Polish prosumers?

Q8: Are there statistically significant differences between ICTs used and expected to be used for knowledge sharing by Polish prosumers?

H4: There are statistically significant differences between ICTs used and expected to be used for knowledge sharing by Polish prosumers.

In order to answer the research questions Q6 and Q7, detailed analysis concerning ICTs used and expected to be used by Polish prosumers to share their knowledge, was made. The results are presented in Table 7 (ordered by mean values of ICTs expected to be used). It is found that Polish prosumers mainly used five kinds of ICTs for knowledge sharing, i.e. enterprises' websites, e-mails, Internet forums, Facebook fanpages, and online surveys. However, all ICTs were more expected to be used by Polish prosumers, especially enterprises' websites, e-mails, industry specialized portals, Internet forums, and information websites.

In order to answer the research question Q8 about significant differences between ICTs used and expected to be used by Polish prosumers, the Mann-Whitney U test was used. The test results presented in Table 8 did not show any significant differences between ICTs used and expected to be used by Polish prosumers in such ICTs like

Table 7. ICTs used and expected to be used by Polish prosumers for knowledge sharing

Code	ICTs used						ICTs expected to be used					
	Mean	Q25	MDN	Q75	CV	SK	Mean	Q25	MDN	Q75	CV	SK
EnWe	3.72	3	4	5	0.34	−0.22	4.00	4	4	5	0.25	−0.01
E-ma	3.52	2	4	5	0.38	−0.36	3.77	3	4	5	0.32	−0.18
InPo	2.87	2	3	4	0.49	−0.80	3.57	3	4	4	0.33	−0.36
InFo	3.40	2	4	4	0.40	−0.43	3.54	3	4	4	0.34	−0.38
FaFa	2.82	2	3	4	0.48	−0.86	3.44	2	4	4	0.36	−0.45
EnAp	2.40	1	2	4	0.54	1.07	3.43	3	4	4	0.36	−0.47
MoAp	3.11	2	4	4	0.47	−0.61	3.38	2	4	4	0.40	−0.46
InWe	2.56	1	2	4	0.51	1.19	3.28	2	4	4	0.38	−0.57
OnSu	3.16	2	4	4	0.44	−0.61	3.10	2	3	4	0.41	−0.72

Table 8. The Mann-Whitney test results for ICTs used and expected to be used by Polish prosumers for knowledge sharing

ICT	E-ma	InFo	EnWe	InWe	InPo	MoAp	EnAp	FaFa	OnSu
Z	−2.63	−0.91	−2.69	−7.01	−7.84	−8.35	−11.81	−2.78	1.02
p value	0.01	0.36	0.01	0.00	0.00	0.00	0.00	0.01	0.31

Internet forums and online survey. Whereas, there were significant differences between ICTs used and expected to be used like: e-mails, enterprises' websites, information websites, industry specialized portals, mobile applications, enterprises' specialized applications, and Facebook fanpages.

The detailed analysis (Appendix 1) shows that:

- E-mail are more likely expected to be used by Polish prosumers (Mean = 3.77; MDN = 4; Mode = 4) than they are currently used by Polish prosumers (Mean = 3.52; MDN = 4; Mode = 4);
- Enterprises' websites are more likely expected to be used by Polish prosumers (Mean = 4.00; MDN = 4; Mode = 4) than they are currently used by Polish prosumers (Mean = 3.72; MDN = 4; Mode = 4);
- Information websites are more likely expected to be used by Polish prosumers (Mean = 3.44; MDN = 4; Mode = 4) than they are currently used by Polish prosumers (Mean = 2.82; MDN = 3; Mode = 4);
- Industry specialized portals are more likely expected to be used by Polish prosumers (Mean = 3.57; MDN = 4; Mode = 4) than they are currently used by Polish prosumers (Mean = 2.87; MDN = 3; Mode = 4);
- Mobile applications are more likely expected to be used by Polish prosumers (Mean = 3.28; MDN = 4; Mode = 4) than they are currently used by Polish prosumers (Mean = 2.56; MDN = 2; Mode = 1);
- Enterprises' specialized applications are more likely expected to be used by Polish prosumers (Mean = 3.43; MDN = 4; Mode = 4) than they are currently used by Polish prosumers (Mean = 2.40; MDN = 2; Mode = 1); and
- Facebook fanpages are more likely expected to be used by Polish prosumers (Mean = 3.38; MDN = 4; Mode = 4) than they are currently used by Polish prosumers (Mean = 3.11; MDN = 4; Mode = 4).

4.3 ICTs Used and Expected to Be Used for Knowledge Sharing by UK-Based Prosumers

The following research questions and hypothesis related to a comparison between ICTs used and ICTs expected to be used to support knowledge sharing by prosumers in the UK were posed:

Q9: What ICTs are used for knowledge sharing by UK-based prosumers?
Q10: What ICTs are expected to be used for knowledge sharing by UK-based prosumers?

Q11: Are there statistically significant differences between ICTs used and expected to be used for knowledge sharing by UK-based prosumers?

H5: There are statistically significant differences between ICTs used and expected to be used for knowledge sharing by UK-based prosumers.

In order to answer the research questions Q9 and Q10, detailed analysis concerning ICTs used and expected to be used by UK-based prosumers to share their knowledge, was made. The results are presented in Table 9 (ordered by mean values of ICTs expected to be used). It is found that UK-based prosumers mainly used and also expected to use seven kinds of ICTs, i.e. mobile applications, enterprises' websites, Facebook fanpages, e-mails, industry specialized portals, enterprises' specialized applications, Internet forums. The mean values for these ICTs are above 3.00, the median values are 4.

Table 9. ICTs used and expected to be used by UK-based prosumers for knowledge sharing

Code	ICTs used						ICTs expected to be used					
	Mean	Q25	MDN	Q75	CV	SK	Mean	Q25	MDN	Q75	CV	SK
MoAp	4.01	4	4	5	0.25	0.01	3.74	4	4	4	0.29	−0.24
EnWe	3.53	3	4	4	0.28	−0.48	3.53	2	4	4	0.29	−0.47
FaFa	3.78	3.75	4	5	0.30	−0.20	3.53	2	4	4	0.33	−0.41
E-ma	3.34	2	4	4	0.34	−0.58	3.29	2	4	4	0.34	−0.64
InPo	3.26	2	4	4	0.37	−0.61	3.25	2	4	4	0.35	−0.65
EnAp	3.59	2.75	4	4	0.32	−0.35	3.25	2	4	4	0.37	−0.62
InFo	3.33	2	4	4	0.33	−0.61	3.18	2	4	4	0.35	−0.73
OnSu	2.99	2	2.5	4	0.40	0.83	2.89	2	2	4	0.44	0.70
InWe	2.33	2	2	2	0.41	0.35	2.53	2	2	3	0.40	0.52

In order to answer the research question Q11 about significant differences between ICTs used and expected to be used by UK-based prosumers, the Mann-Whitney U test was used. The test results presented in Table 10 did not show any significant differences between ICTs used and expected to be used by UK-based prosumers for knowledge sharing.

Table 10. The Mann-Whitney test results for ICTs used and expected to be used by UK-based prosumers for knowledge sharing

ICT	E-ma	InFo	EnWe	InWe	InPo	MoAp	EnAp	FaFa	OnSu
Z	0.35	0.89	−0.07	−1.21	0.14	1.89	1.90	1.61	0.70
p value	0.73	0.37	0.94	0.23	0.89	0.06	0.06	0.11	0.48

5 Discussion of Research Findings

5.1 Respondents Characteristics

The findings indicate the different use and expected use of ICTs for knowledge sharing with enterprises by Poland and UK respondents. The demographics for the Polish and UK-based respondents are consistent with other studies [69] where females are more inclined to respond to surveys. In categorizing the participants in the age categories, the builders generation presented a low response from Poland and the UK, and would not be unexpected given the training and technical competences of this generation and their culture of communicating more face-to-face rather than through online questionnaires. With generation Y the response rate from Poland and the UK were similarly high and are consistent with research from authors [70, 71], as this age category expect to use devices to communicate online and are comfortable with this mode of communication.

There were differences in the responses from Generation X and Z in Poland and the UK. Responses from Poland was 13.8% while UK was 39.18% and this is a marked difference in responses indicating a possible culture of more accepted online communication in the UK for this age range. Finally generation Z responses in Poland was 32.8% whereas UK responses was only 1.75%, a marked difference in responses and this needs further research to determine if the survey was more visible to this age range in Poland where their use of technology is embedded in their everyday social interactions particularly to enhance the opportunities of financial benefits or merits for the household [70, 71].

There was few responses from both countries from those who are less educated, showing educational attainment may be an indicator for participating in knowledge sharing.

The respondent's place of residence was equally captured for both countries with half of the respondents from both countries living in a city with a population of more than 100.000, and this is interesting as the greater the chances to communicate offline in larger population centers the more likely the respondents are to use time for online communication, and this is a cultural communication shift noted in other recent studies.

5.2 ICTs for Current and Future Prosumers Knowledge Sharing

The uncertain business environment places pressure on businesses to recognise opportunities for change and implement ICTs as part of the business offer to engage with consumers. The survey responses lead to five research hypotheses formulated and statistically tested and the results summarised in Table 11. Using the data for Mann-Whitney U test we were able to accept or reject the hypotheses.

The spread of web-based ICTs provides opportunities for business to improve understanding of their customers [72]. This study supports the need for business to recognize the ICTs in use and expected to be used by prosumers to ensure improved knowledge sharing capabilities. In addition, we found that (Table 11):

Table 11. Summary of hypotheses testing

Hypothesis	Results
H1: There are statistically significant differences between Polish and UK-based prosumers in ICTs used for knowledge sharing	Supported
H2: There are statistically significant differences between Polish and UK-based prosumers in ICTs expected to be used for knowledge sharing	Supported
H3: There are statistically significant differences between ICTs used and expected to be used for knowledge sharing by Polish and UK-based prosumers combined	Supported
H4: There are statistically significant differences between ICTs used and expected to be used for knowledge sharing by Polish prosumers	Supported
H5: There are statistically significant differences between ICTs used and expected to be used for knowledge sharing by UK-based prosumers	Not supported

- The results for Q1 and Q2 indicated there were no significant differences between Polish and UK-based prosumers in their use of standard ICTs, such as e-mails, Internet forums, and websites of enterprises. However, Polish prosumers were more likely to use enterprises' websites and information websites, compared to UK prosumers preference in their use of industry specialized portals, mobile applications, enterprises' specialized applications and Facebook fanpages. This suggests UK prosumers willingness to widely switch between the formal industry channels to the less formal generic sharing channels such as Facebook. The hypothesis is supported.
- Results for Q3 and Q4 did not show any significant differences between Polish and UK-based prosumers in using enterprises' specialized applications and Facebook fanpages. Whereas, there were significant differences in ICTs expected to be used by Polish prosumers including e-mails, Internet forums, enterprises' websites, information websites, industry specialized portals, and online surveys. Whereas UK prosumers expect to use mobile applications, and this is consistent with research to support the prolific use of responsive technologies such as mobile as an enabler of knowledge sharing. The hypothesis is supported.
- The combined results for Q5 did not show any significant differences between Polish and UK-based prosumers in using Internet forums and online surveys. Whereas, there were significant differences in ICTs used and expected to be used including: e-mails, enterprises' websites, information websites, industry specialized portals, mobile applications, enterprises' specialized applications, and Facebook fanpages. The combined results indicate the different choices made by the respondents in the countries suggesting cultural and behavioral leanings being followed. The hypothesis is supported.
- Interestingly, results from Q6, Q7 and Q8 indicated five ICTs expected to be used by Polish prosumers for supporting knowledge sharing, i.e. enterprises' websites, e-mails, Internet forums, Facebook fanpages, and online surveys. However, there were significant differences between ICTs used and expected to be used like: e-mails, enterprises' websites, information websites, industry specialized portals, mobile applications, enterprises' specialized applications, and Facebook fanpages.

This suggests a considered move by prosumers in Poland to mobile, e-mail and Facebook and matches the current trends in the UK. The hypothesis is supported.

- It is found that UK-based prosumers mainly used and also expected to use seven kinds of ICTs, but there was no significant difference between ICTs used and expected to be used by UK-based prosumers for knowledge sharing. i.e. mobile applications, enterprises' websites, Facebook fanpages, e-mails, industry special-ized portals, enterprises' specialized applications, Internet forums. The hypothesis is not supported. An existing study [73] suggests there are numerous barriers to knowledge sharing which deny knowledge being 'accessible and usable within or between chosen organizations' and in exploring the relationships between the prosumers and business it is likely that the hypothesis is not supported may well be due to the businesses not having adopted the required communication method for interoperability and timely responsive engagement with the customer.

The most substantial difference in the ICTs used and expected by prosumers relates to mobile applications – the mean value is 2.56 for Poland, whereas it is 4.01 for UK.

The overall analysis of ICTs used shows that UK-based prosumers use ICTs for knowledge sharing more frequently than Polish respondents and this may be associated with levels of education achieved as there was almost twice as many UK (52.05%) responses than Polish respondents (27.7%) with higher education attainment.

The findings also show that mobile applications are the 'expected ICTs' needed by UK-based prosumers to share knowledge, followed by the use of Facebook fanpages and enterprises' websites. Whereas, Polish prosumers mainly expect to engage in use of enterprises' websites, followed by e-mails and industry specialized portals.

The results outline the choice and variety of ICTs available for prosumers that may be overlooked by enterprises. There is a paradox observed in that the 'information richness' [74] is perceived to be low when the communication is impersonal and the tasks become more routine when ICTs are used in a communication process yet the channel of communication is rich because it encourages unpredicted dialog that may be dispersed and disparate and determine the perceived value of the enterprise offer. Further studies by Hermanrund, and Oddvar-Soernes [75] in investigating knowledge sharing networks in distributed organizations clarify that 'people sometimes like to be asked a question via one channel and then answer it via another channel'. This suggests that the choice of ICTs in use and expected to be used by prosumers to engage with enterprises requires further investigation.

A recommendation is that the enterprises need to take consideration of the culture of contemporary communication choices associated with the wide age ranges of pro-sumers. Finally the enterprises need to embed a comprehensive choice of ICT's par-ticular to their prosumers needs to actively encourage knowledge sharing.

The survey results point to the recognition of the use and expected use of ICTs for future business. In this case the role of these ICTs are viewed as complementary and follow trends to shift to current ICTs for communications and knowledge sharing

6 Conclusions

6.1 Research Contribution

This work contributes to existing research on prosumption, especially prosumers' knowledge sharing with the use of ICTs by:

- indicating the ICTs currently used by prosumers to promote knowledge sharing with enterprises; and
- indicating the ICTs expected to be used by prosumers to stimulate knowledge sharing with enterprises.

Firstly, this study indicates that mobile application use is expected to a greater degree by UK-based prosumers. However, it is clear that the prosumer chooses the ICTs based on their own suitability as the results indicate they also expect to use the enterprise websites and Facebook fanpages indicating the diverse expectations and somewhat divergent needs of UK-based prosumers and the opportunities this presents to enterprises.

Secondly, the outcomes show that ICTs which are currently offered to UK-based prosumers by enterprises meet their current expectations but these may not necessarily be expected to be used in future engagement. However, the prosumers usage and expectations of ICTs for knowledge sharing are significantly different in Poland suggesting that the enterprises do not meet their expectation, and this may result in less engagement in knowledge sharing.

6.2 Implications for Research and Practice

This study is useful for researchers as it raises questions about ICTs implemented that encourage prosumer knowledge sharing and engagement. Researchers may use this methodology to undertake similar analyses with different sample groups in Poland, United Kingdom, and other countries; additionally many comparisons between different groups and countries can be made. Moreover, the methodology constitutes a very comprehensive basis for identifying ICTs to support knowledge sharing, both, about prosumers, as well as for and from prosumers, but researchers may develop, verify and improve this methodology and its implementation. In addition, researchers may use these research findings and employ them in studies of enterprises. Their goal could be the analysis of ICTs and the possibilities of adjusting them to the expectations of prosumers.

Moreover, for practitioners, the results of this study can be used to improve activities aimed at prosumption adoption, especially helping them understand which ICTs should be used to support prosumers' knowledge sharing.

6.3 Limitations and Future Works

As with many other studies, this study has its limitations. The first one was the selection of the survey respondents in Poland. Most of the respondents were young people below 35 years old. It is advisable to extend future research to elderly persons, inter alia prosumers 50+.

The second limitation was the relatively low number of respondents from the United Kingdom in comparison with the number of respondents from Poland. Resulting from the low UK responses and timing of the survey the research will continue in the UK to ensure a higher response rate for deeper analysis and additional statistical tests. Since the initial results reveal interesting findings the research will continue so to generate a higher response rate, and for this reason this paper is rather preliminary, and recognizes the analysis are not to be generalized. Therefore the research will be extended with detailed analysis in further works.

A third limitation, it is possible to specify a methodological limitation. The research sample embraced only prosumers, not enterprises. It is advisable to extend the research to enterprises as interesting indications have emerged from ICT trends associated with the Polish and UK respondents.

A fourth limitation is that the study did not explore use of ICTs in relation to the frequency of interaction with the enterprise. Frequent sharing versus irregular or one-off exchanges may determine a different complement of ICT choices and it would be useful to categorize these in an ICT use perspective.

All these above issues should be carefully considered and assimilated in future works.

Appendix 1: Descriptive Statistics

Code	U/E	Cou.	Mean	Q25	MDN	Q75	VAR	SD	CV	SK	CK	Mode
E-ma	U	UK	3.34	2	4	4	1.27	1.17	0.33	−0.58	−1.22	4
	U	PL	3.52	2	4	5	1.78	1.33	0.38	−0.36	−0.89	4
	E	UK	3.29	2	4	4	1.23	1.11	0.33	−0.64	−1.39	4
	E	PL	3.77	3	4	5	1.43	1.19	0.31	−0.19	−0.14	4
InFo	U	UK	3.33	2	4	4	1.21	1.10	0.33	−0.61	−0.92	4
	U	PL	3.40	2	4	4	1.89	1.37	0.40	−0.43	−1.06	4
	E	UK	3.18	2	4	4	1.26	1.12	0.35	−0.73	−1.41	4
	E	PL	3.54	3	4	4	1.46	1.21	0.34	−0.38	−0.68	4
EnWe	U	UK	3.53	3	4	4	0.97	0.97	0.28	−0.48	−0.15	4
	U	PL	3.72	3	4	5	1.56	1.25	0.33	−0.22	−0.26	4
	E	UK	3.53	2	4	4	1.03	1.01	0.28	−0.46	−0.74	4
	E	PL	4.00	4	4	5	0.96	0.98	0.24	−0.00	1.41	4
InWe	U	UK	2.33	2	2	2	0.89	0.94	0.40	0.34	0.78	2
	U	PL	2.82	2	3	4	1.87	1.37	0.48	−0.85	−1.33	4
	E	UK	2.53	2	2	3	1.05	1.02	0.40	0.51	−0.07	2
	E	PL	3.44	2	4	4	1.55	1.24	0.36	−0.45	−0.83	4
InPo	U	UK	3.26	2	4	4	1.47	1.21	0.37	−0.61	−0.90	4

(*continued*)

(*continued*)

Code	U/E	Cou.	Mean	Q25	MDN	Q75	VAR	SD	CV	SK	CK	Mode
	U	PL	2.87	2	3	4	1.96	1.40	0.48	−0.80	−1.34	4
	E	UK	3.25	2	4	4	1.30	1.14	0.35	−0.65	−1.15	4
	E	PL	3.57	3	4	4	1.39	1.17	0.33	−0.36	−0.51	4
MoAp	U	UK	4.01	4	4	5	1.02	1.01	0.25	0.01	3.29	4
	U	PL	2.56	1	2	4	1.73	1.31	0.51	1.19	−1.32	1
	E	UK	3.74	4	4	4	1.16	1.08	0.28	−0.24	0.25	4
	E	PL	3.28	2	4	4	1.59	1.26	0.38	−0.57	−0.99	4
EnAp	U	UK	3.59	2.75	4	4	1.33	1.15	0.32	−0.35	−0.43	4
	U	PL	2.40	1	2	4	1.69	1.30	0.54	1.07	−1.02	1
	E	UK	3.25	2	4	4	1.48	1.21	0.37	−0.62	−1.39	4
	E	PL	3.43	3	4	4	1.50	1.22	0.35	−0.47	−0.68	4
FaFa	U	UK	3.78	3.75	4	5	1.29	1.13	0.30	−0.19	0.18	4
	U	PL	3.11	2	4	4	2.12	1.45	0.46	−0.61	−1.40	4
	E	UK	3.53	2	4	4	1.34	1.16	0.32	−0.41	−0.50	4
	E	PL	3.38	2	4	4	1.82	1.34	0.39	−0.46	−1.08	4
OnSu	U	UK	2.99	2	3	4	1.40	1.18	0.39	0.83	−1.46	2
	U	PL	3.16	2	4	4	1.89	1.37	0.43	−0.61	−1.17	4
	E	UK	2.89	2	2	4	1.63	1.27	0.44	0.70	1.43	2
	E	PL	3.10	2	3	4	1.59	1.26	0.40	−0.71	−1.08	4

Abbreviations: U – ICTs used by prosumers, E – ICTs expected to be used by prosumers, Cou. – Country: PL – Poland, UK – United Kingdom.

References

1. Jaki, A., Mikuła, B. (eds.): Knowledge – Economy – Society. Managing Organizations: Concepts and Their Applications (in Polish). University of Economics, Cracow (2014)
2. Kisielnicki, J.: Zarządzanie i informatyka (in Polish). Placet, Warsaw (2014)
3. Kowalczyk, A., Nogalski, B.: Zarządzanie wiedzą: koncepcje i narzędzia (in Polish). Difin, Warsaw (2007)
4. Omotayo, F.P.: Knowledge management as an important tool in organisational management: a review of literature. Libr. Philosophy and Practice (e-j.), Paper 1238 (2015). http://digitalcommons.unl.edu/libphilprac/1238/
5. Rowley, J.: Eight questions for customer knowledge management in e-business. J. Knowl. Manag. **6**(5), 500–511 (2002). doi:10.1108/13673270210450441
6. Aghamirian, B., Dorri, B., Aghamirian, B.: Effects of customer knowledge management's eight factors in e-commerce. Manag. Sci. Eng. **7**(4), 1–11 (2013)
7. Tseng, S.-M.: The effect of knowledge management capability and customer knowledge gaps on corporate performance. J. Enterpr. Inf. Manag. **29**(1), 51–71 (2016). doi:10.1108/JEIM-03-2015-0021
8. Brabham, D.C.: Motivations for participation in a crowdsourcing application to improve public engagement in transit planning. J. Appl. Commun. Res. **40**(3), 307–328 (2012). doi:10.1080/00909882.2012.693940

9. Tsai, W., Tsai, M., Li, S., Lin, C.: Harmonizing firms' knowledge and strategies with organizational capabilities. J. Comp. Inf. Sys. **53**(1), 23–32 (2012)

10. Croteau, A.-M., Li, P.: Critical success factors of CRM technological initiatives. Canad. J. of Admin. Sci. **20**(1), 21–34 (2003). doi:10.1111/j.1936-4490.2003.tb00303.x

11. Song, E.-J., Kang, M.-S.: A study on the platform of knowledge integration for customer feedback in B2C service industry. Int. J. Inf. Commun. Tech. **8**(1), 26–36 (2016). doi:10.1504/ijict.2016.073637

12. Wiechoczek, J.: Creating value for customer in business networks of high-tech goods manufacturers. J. Econ. Manag. **23**(1), 76–90 (2016). http://www.ue.katowice.pl/en/units/journal-of-economics-and-management/journal-issues.html

13. Fuchs, C.: Web 2.0, Prosumption, and surveillance. Surve. Soc. **8**(3), 288–309 (2011)

14. Ritzer, G., Jurgenson, N.: Production, consumption, prosumption: the nature of capitalism in the age of the digital 'prosumer'. J. Cons. Cult. **10**(1), 13–36 (2010). doi:10.1177/1469540509354673

15. Tapscott, D., Williams, A.S.: Wikinomics: How Mass Collaboration Changes Everything. Penguin Group, New York (2006)

16. Toffler, A.: The Third Wave. Bantam Books, New York (1980)

17. Xie, C., Bagozzi, R.P., Troye, S.V.: Trying to prosume: toward a theory of consumers as co-creators of value. J. Acad. Mark. Sci. **36**, 109–122 (2008)

18. Ziemba, E.: Conceptual model of information technology support for prosumption. In: Proceedings of International Conference on Management, Leadership and Governance. ICMLG 2013, pp. 355–363. Bangkok University, 07–08 February 2013

19. Yuan, D., Lin, Z., Zhuo, R.: What drives consumer knowledge sharing in online travel communities? Personal attributes or e-service factors? Comp. Hum. Behav. **63**, 68–74 (2016)

20. Ziemba, E., Eisenbardt, M.: Incentives encouraging prosumers to knowledge sharing - framework based on polish study. Online J. Appl. Knowl. Manag. **4**(2), 40–58 (2016)

21. Osuszek, Ł., Stanek, S.: Knowledge management and decision support in adaptive case management platforms. In: Proceedings of the 2015 Federated Conference on Computer Science and Information Systems 2015, vol. 5, pp. 1539–1549 (2015). doi:10.15439/2015f60

22. Bayram, Ö.G., Demirtel, H.: Effect of ICT on information sharing in enterprises: the case of ministry of development. In: Proceedings of European Conference on Knowledge Management ECKM, Academic Conferences International Limited, pp. 94–101. Kidmore End (2014)

23. Chen, Y.-Y., Huang, H.-L.: Strategic orientation of knowledge management and information technology and their effects on performance. In: Proceedings of Pacific Asia Conference on Information Systems, Paper 166, PACIS 2014, Chengdu (2014)

24. García-Álvarez, M.T.: Analysis of the effects of ICTs in knowledge management and innovation: the case of Zara Group. Comp. Hum. Behav. **51**, 994–1002 (2015). doi:10.1016/j.chb.2014.10.007

25. Piraquive, F.N.D., García, V.H.M., Crespo, R.G., Liberona, D.: Knowledge management, innovation and efficiency of service enterprises through ICTs appropriation and usage. In: Uden, L., Fuenzaliza Oshee, D., Ting, I.-H., Liberona, D. (eds.) KMO 2014. LNBIP, vol. 185, pp. 300–310. Springer, Heidelberg (2014). doi:10.1007/978-3-319-08618-7_29

26. Subashini, R., Rita, S., Vivek, M.: The role of ICTs in knowledge management (KM) for organizational effectiveness. Commu. Comp. Inf. Sci. **270**, 542–549 (2012). doi:10.1007/978-3-642-29216-3_59

27. Ziemba, E., Eisenbardt, M., Mullins, R.: Information and communication technologies for supporting prosumers' knowledge sharing – evidence from Poland and United Kingdom. In: Proceedings of the 2016 Federated Conference on Computer Science and Information Systems, pp. 1273–1282. Gdańsk University of Technology. doi:10.15439/2016F285. https://fedcsis.org/proceedings/2016/pliks/285.pdf

28. Ritzer, G.: Prosumption: evolution, revolution, or eternal return of the same? J. Cons. Cult. **14**(1), 3–24 (2014). doi:10.1177/1469540513509641

29. Izvercianu, M., Seran, S., Buciuman, C.F.: Changing marketing tools and principles in prosumer innovation management. In: European Conference on Managment, Leadership & Governance, Kidmore End, pp. 246–255 (2012)

30. Jelonek, D., Stępniak, C., Turek, T.: Prosumpcja w regionalnych społecznościach elektronicznych dla potrzeb przedsięwzięć miejskich (in Polish). In: Gołuchowski, J., Frączkiewicz-Wronka, A. (eds.) Zeszyty Naukowe Uniwersytetu Ekonomicznego in Katowice, vol. 243, pp. 151–164. University of Economics Press, Katowice (2015)

31. Rayna, T., Striukova, L.: Involving consumers: the role of digital technologies in promoting 'prosumption' and user innovation. J. Knowl. Econ. 1–20 (2016). Open Access, doi:10. 1007/s13132-016-0390-8

32. Ziemba, E., Eisenbardt, M.: Prosumers' eagerness for knowledge sharing with enterprises – a Polish study. Online J. Appl. Knowl. Manag. **2**(1), 40–58 (2014)

33. Martín, D., Alcarria, R., Robles, T., Sánchez-Picot, A.: Prosumer framework for knowledge management based on prosumer service patterns. Int. J. Soft. Eng. Knowl. Eng. **26**(07), 1145–1173 (2016)

34. Cui, A.S., Wu, F.: Utilizing customer knowledge in innovation: antecedents and impact of customer involvement on new product performance. J. Acad. Mark. Sci. 1–23 (2015). doi:10.1007/s11747-015-0433-x

35. Panni, M.F.A.K.: CKM and its influence on organizational marketing performance: proposing an integrated conceptual framework. In: Kaufman, H.R., Panni, M.F.A.K. (eds.) Customer-centric marketing strategies: Tools for building organizational performance, pp. 103–125. IGI Global, Hershey (2015). doi:10.4018/978-1-4666-2524-2.ch006

36. Shihab, M.R., Lestari, A.A.: The impact of customer knowledge acquisition to knowledge management benefits: a case study in Indonesian banking and insurance industries. In: Proceedings of 2014 International Conference on Advanced Computer Science and Information Systems, pp. 301–306 (2014). doi:10.1109/icacsis.2014.7065867

37. Taherparvar, N., Esmaeilpour, R., Dostar, M.: Customer knowledge management, innovation capability, and business performance: a case study of the banking industry. J. Knowl. Manag. **3**(18), 591–610 (2014). doi:10.1108/jkm-11-2013-0446

38. Chan, J.O.: Big data customer knowledge management. Commun. IIMA **14**(3) (2014). Article 5, http://scholarworks.lib.csusb.edu/ciima/vol14/iss3/5

39. Ziemba, E., Mullins, R.: Identifying more about customers: the phenomenon of the switch to the knowledge exchange. J. Appl. Knowl. Manag. **4**(1), 165–179 (2016)

40. Smith, H.A., McKeen, J.D.: Developments in practice XVIII-customer knowledge management: Adding value for our customers. Commun. Assoc. Inf. Sys. **16** (2005). Article 36. http://aisel.aisnet.org/cais/vol16/iss1/36

41. Gibbert, M., Leibold, M., Probst, G.: Five styles of customer knowledge management, and how smart companies use them to create value. Eur. Manag. J. **20**(5), 459–469 (2002). doi:10.1016/S0263-2373(02)00101-9

42. Xuelian, L., Chakpitak, N., Yodmongkol, P.: A novel two-dimension' customer knowledge analysis model. Asian Soc. Sci. **11**(16), 257–266 (2015). doi:10.5539/ass.v11n16p257

43. Koniorczyk, G.: Customer knowledge in (co)creation of product. a case study of IKEA. J. Econ. Manag. **22**(4), 107–120 (2015). http://www.ue.katowice.pl/en/units/journal-of-economics-and-management/journal-issues.html
44. Cheng, M.Y., Ho, J.S.Y., Lau, P.M.: Knowledge sharing in academic institutions: a study of multimedia university Malaysia. Electr. J. Knowl. Manag. **3**(7), 313–324 (2009)
45. Wang, S., Noe, R.A.: Knowledge sharing: a review and directions for future research. Hum. Res. Manag. Rev. **20**, 115–131 (2010)
46. Lin, H.-G.: Knowledge sharing and firm innovation capability: an empirical study. Int. J. Manpower **28**(3/4), 315–332 (2007)
47. Bagheri, S., Kusters, R.J., Trieneken, J.: Business-IT alignment in PSS value networks – linking customer knowledge management to social customer relationship management. In: Proceedings of 17th International Conference on Enterprise Information Systems ICEIS, Barcelona, Spain, pp. 249–257 (2015). doi:10.5220/0005370002490257
48. Lee, M.C.: Business Intelligence, knowledge management and customer relationship management – Technological support in enterprise competitive competence. Bus. Intell. Concepts Methodol. Tools Appl. 216–23 (2015). doi:10.4018/978-1-4666-9562-7.ch011
49. Bharati, P., Zhang, W., Chaudhury, A.: Better knowledge with social media? Exploring the roles of social capital and organizational knowledge management. J. Knowl. Manag. **19**(3), 456–475 (2015). doi:10.1108/jkm-11-2014-0467
50. Chua, A.Y.K., Banerjee, S.: Customer knowledge management via social media: the case of Starbucks. J. Knowl. Manag. **17**(2), 237–249 (2013). doi:10.1108/13673271311315196
51. Ford, D.P., Mason, R.M.: A multilevel perspective of tensions between knowledge management and social media. J. Organiz. Comp. Electr. Commerce **23**(1–2), 7–33 (2013). doi:10.1080/10919392.2013.748604
52. Heller-Baird, C., Parasnis, G.: From social media to social customer relationship management. Strat. Leadersh. **39**(5), 30–37 (2011). doi:10.1108/10878571111161507
53. Levy, M.: WEB 2.0 implications on knowledge management. J. Knowl. Manag. **13**(1), 120–134 (2009). doi:10.1108/13673270910931215
54. Zhang, Z.: Customer knowledge management and the strategies of social software. Bus. Process Manag. J. **17**(1), 82–106 (2011). doi:10.1108/14637151111105599
55. Gafni, R., Golan, O.T.: The influence of negative consumer reviews in social networks. Online J. Appl. Knowl. Manag. **4**(2), 44–58 (2016)
56. Simon, J.P.: User generated content – users, community of users and firms: toward new sources of co-innovation? Info **18**(6), 4–25 (2016). doi:10.1108/info-04-2016-0015
57. Zborowski, M., Chmielarz, W.: Aspects of mobility in e-marketing from the perspective of a customer. In: Ganzha, M., Maciaszek, L., Paprzycki, M. (eds.) Proceedings of the 2016 Federated Conference on Computer Science and Information Systems, ACSIS, vol. 8, pp. 1329–1333 (2016). doi:10.15439/2016F112
58. Fast-Berglund, Å., Blom, E.: Evaluating ICT-tools for knowledge sharing and assembly support. In: Ahram, T., Karwowski, W., Marek, T. (eds.) Proceedings of the 5th International Conference on Applied Human Factors and Ergonomics AHFE, Krakow, Poland, pp. 2734–2742 (2014)
59. Jiebing, W., Bin, G., Yongjiang, S.: Customer knowledge management and IT-enabled business model innovation: a conceptual framework and a case study from China. Eur. Manag. J. **31**(4), 359–372 (2013). doi:10.1016/j.emj.2013.02.001
60. Razzak, M.A., Ahmed, R.: Knowledge sharing in distributed agile projects: techniques, strategies and challenges. In: Proceedings of the 2014 Federated Conference on Computer Science and Information Systems, pp. 1431–1440 (2014). doi:10.15439/2014f280
61. Lee, S.C., Kelkar, R.S.: ICT and knowledge management: perspectives from SECI model. Electr. Libr. **31**(2), 226–243 (2013). http://dx.doi.org/10.1108/02640471311312401

62. Nonaka, I.: Dynamic theory of organizational knowledge creation. Organ. Sci. 5(1), 14–37 (1994). doi:10.1287/orsc.5.1.14

63. Wijaya, S., Spruit, M., Scheper, W., Versendaal, J.: Web 2.0-based webstrategies for three different types of organizations. Comp. Hum. Behav. 27, 1399–1407 (2011)

64. Jalonen, H.: Social media and emotions in organisational knowledge creation. In: Proceedings of the 2014 Federated Conference on Computer Science and Information Systems, pp. 1371–1379 (2014). doi:10.15439/2014f39

65. Okazaki, S., Díaz-Martín, A.M., Rozano, M., Menéndez-Benito, H.D.: Using Twitter to engage with customers: a data mining approach. Internet Res. 25(3), 416–434 (2015). doi:10.1108/intr-11-2013-0249

66. Yang, X., Li, G.: Factors influencing the popularity of customer-generated content in a company-hosted online co-creation community: a social capital perspective. Comp. Hum. Behav. 64, 760–768 (2016). doi:10.1016/j.chb.2016.08.002

67. Zembik, M.: Social media as a source of knowledge for customers and enterprises. J. Appl. Knowl. Manag. 2(2), 132–148 (2014)

68. Hinton, P.R., Brownlow, C., McMurvay, I., Cozens, B.: SPSS Explained. Routledge, East Sussex (2004)

69. Smith, G.: Does gender influence online survey participation? A record-linkage analysis of university faculty online survey response behavior. ERIC Doc. Reproduction Service, ED 501717 (2008). http://eric.ed.gov/?id=ED501717

70. Ziemba, E. (ed.): Czynniki sukcesu i poziom wykorzystania technologii informacyjno-komunikacyjnych w Polsce (in Polish). CeDeWu, Warsaw (2015)

71. Ziemba, E.: Factors affecting the adoption and usage of ICTs within Polish households. Interdisc. J. Inf. Knowl. Manag. 11, 89–113 (2016)

72. Lee, M.K.O., Cheung, C., Lim, K.H., Sia, C.: Understanding customer knowledge sharing in web-based discussion boards: an exploratory study. Internet Res. 16(3), 289–303 (2006)

73. Paulin, D., Suneson, K.: Knowledge transfer, knowledge sharing and knowledge barriers – three blurry terms in KM. Electr. J. Knowl. Manag. 10(1), 81–91 (2012)

74. Lengel, R.H., Daft, R.L.: The selection of communication media as an executive skill. Acad. Manag. Executive 2(3), 225–232 (1988)

75. Hermanrund, I., Oddvar-Soernes, J.: ICT use and network relations: Exploring knowledge-sharing networks in distributed organizations. Inf. Sci. Inf. Tech. 6, 25–44 (2009)

Information Technology and Systems for Business Transformation

Analysis of Predispositions of E-gamers and Its Relevance in the Use of Computer Games Didactic Process

Witold Chmielarz[(✉)] and Oskar Szumski

Faculty of Management, University of Warsaw,
ul. Szturmowa 3, 02-678 Warsaw, Poland
{witold.chmielarz,oskar.szumski}@uw.edu.pl

Abstract. The main aim of this article is to show the characteristics of individuals playing computer games (e-gamers), their styles and predispositions of
play and possibilities of their application in the plays for didactic process. In
order to present the relevant data, the authors limited the study sample to a
selected group of individual users. In this paper the authors presented the
commonalities of gamers, their approach towards participation in games, the
awareness of potential changes or improvements in the area, psychological
results of games and ability to use them in the games used in didactic process.
Authors also held discussions concerning the obtained solutions and drew
conclusions based on the present stage of research.

Keywords: E-gamers · Computer games · Didactic process

1 Introduction

The main aim of this work is to analyze the use of computer games as one of the
alternative forms of entertainment in the selected group of users under the circumstances of a dynamic development of devices and mobile applications running on them.
The aim of this article is to analyze the situation where computer games are used by
people who treat them not only as a form of entertainment but also as a kind of sport.
The popularity and specific universal nature of the access to computer games facilitates
a fast development of information technologies. A broadly defined concept of mobility
also impacts the use of computer games, moving the focus from using PCs to the use of
smartphones and tablets.

According to the statistics of Newzoo [1] service, in Poland in 2013 the number of
gamers amounted to 13.4 million, out of which 98% used their PCs to play computer
games (together with other platforms). We take the second position in Europe among
the examined countries. The market of computer games in Poland is growing every
year – in the end of 2014 it was worth about 280 million dollars and it will be growing
by 3.8% a year, thus increasing the value of the entire market to 437 million dollars at
the end of 2016 [2]. Hence, undoubtedly the subject matter is worthy of attention.

Unfortunately, the phenomenon itself is difficult to define and examine taking into
account the formalized scientific analyses. Firstly, there is no clear definition of

© Springer International Publishing AG 2017
E. Ziemba (Ed.): AITM 2016/ISM 2016, LNBIP 277, pp. 77–102, 2017.
DOI: 10.1007/978-3-319-53076-5_5

computer games [3–9]. In its narrow sense, this concept is treated literally as games in the form of software running only on traditional hardware such as (desktop, micro-computers, laptops or palmtops). In its broad, historical approach, the group encompasses also games running on devices such as a console, TV, gaming machines, smartphones and tablets (which are in fact communication and application computers). As the games running on all kinds of devices were being developed in parallel, and, in fact, there are PC equivalents of all kinds of games, we sometimes use this term in its broad meaning. Thus, for the needs of this study, the authors assumed that computer games are a generic term (hypernym) encapsulating the whole class of all kinds of games presented as a homogenous phenomenon. Secondly, there is no one generally accepted definition of a person playing computer games (e-gamer). Thus, in the narrow sense of the word, an e-gamer is a person who plays computer games every day or a few times a week, individually or taking part in a multi-player game. Sometimes, the scope of this term is limited to include only those players who treat MMO (Massively Multiplayer Online games) class games as a sport, and they try to play them professionally. However, we observe a more and more common tendency to expand the term to include also any individuals who play any kind of game from time to time, perceiving it as just one more alternative kind of entertainment. This article treats the concept of e-gamers in such a way. Thirdly, there is no (specific or clear) classification of computer games: there are a number of typologies based on various criteria, most frequently taking into account the type of activity required from the e-gamer playing games (e.g. logic, strategic, arcade, RPG (role-playing games), MMO (Massively Multiplayer Online games) etc., with a number of varying kinds and versions.

The phenomenon of computer games has been examined in numerous studies, in numerous countries and social groups [e.g. 10–14], including large-scale studies [e.g. 15–17]; nevertheless, they were carried out before the recent period of extreme popularity and growth in the number of applications running on smartphones and tablets. And the second point is – that they are concentrated on statistics of the players (with their features) or social field of problem rather then on IT development. The authors hoped to establish certain implications of the new phenomena with regard to the direction of computer games development. Therefore, the authors have undertaken the studies whose main aim is to analyze the use of such applications among users. The findings presented in this article constitute a brief report on the first stage of the research conducted among the gamers in Poland in 2015 and 2016.

The main target of this research is to identify a pattern of e-gaming related to a particular group of people who play various kinds of games, using different kind of hardware and software, with a varying level of skills and expectations concerning the organizational and technical aspects of playing games from the perspective of frequency and personal engagement in computer gaming.

The research analyses the frequency of playing of e-games to create the addiction to games, to create different patterns of e-gamer behavior including gaming related emotions. The result of a high engagement of respondents in computer gaming authors decided to analyze the computer gaming to be the source of additional benefits for universities, including tools and devices to develop and expand didactic process. Research shows interesting implications for the development of mobile information technologies towards new development trends of the use of this kind of software as a source of entertainment and learning.

2 The Assumptions of Research Methodology and Population Sample

Due to limited and fragmentary research concerning the area of internet computer games and e-gamers, both from the point of view of an individual client and a group of customers, in Polish and foreign literature, the studies have been based on the authors' own approach [18], quite different from surveys in Poland [14, 17] and some different from research in the other countries [19, 20], consisting of the following steps:

- analysis of a selected group of players on the basis of a quantitative and qualitative survey, divided into the following parts:
  - characteristics of a computer player and identifying his or her preferences in computer games,
  - identification of potential effects and consequences of playing computer games for e-gamers,
  - specification of predispositions of e-gamers, and its relevance in the use of computer games in didactic process,
- placing an internet version of a survey on the servers of the Faculty of Management of the University of Warsaw, conducting functionality test and its verification,
- carrying out the survey among the users, analysis and discussion of the findings,
- drawing conclusions from the obtained results concerning the current situation and possible directions of the future development of internet computer games on the basis of the users' opinions.

The article concentrates on the results of the analysis of the first and the third part of the completed survey. It allowed for identifying a particular group of people who play various kinds of games, using different kind of hardware and software, with a varying level of skills and expectations concerning the organizational and technical aspects of playing games. Only after the selecting the group of best, "professional" players, we may proceed to specify the implications and psychophysical effects of their involvement in individual and multi-player games. The latter aspect was examined in the second, sequentially conducted, stage of the survey, whose results and conclusions will be presented in subsequent publications [21]. In the third part we identify good and bad features of e-gamers useful in didactic process and try to specify which kind of games may be suitable for the most common course son university faculties of economics and management.

The questionnaire surveys were conducted near the end of December 2015. The selection of the study sample was not accidental: it belonged to the category of convenience sampling, the respondents were mainly students of selected universities in Warsaw (University of Warsaw and Vistula University (Akademia Finansów i Biznesu Vistula), of full-time and part-time BA, BSc and MA studies. The survey was also completed by two members of university staff who declared playing computer games. The surveys were circulated electronically, and the response rate did not exceed 70%.

Students are particularly open to all kinds of innovation, especially if it concerns their private life or entertainment [22].

A specific limitation concerning this particular sample was an anticipated high percentage of smartphone, tablet, laptop and mobile phone users, devices of lower quality but with a longer durability. An additional argument for conducting research in this social group was the demand from company cooperating with us on the design and construction of specific game platforms. The company depended on the wide market recognition of students as the main customer of such a platform.

The survey was completed by 274 people, out of which 254 participants submitted correctly completed questionnaires (which constitutes 92.70% of the sample). Among the respondents there were 59.45% of women and 40.16% of men; 0.39% respondents did not answer this question. An average age of the respondent was 20.62 years, and the medium value was 19 years. The age is typical of students of the first years of BA and BSc students and the first years of the studies of the second cycle – the group asked to complete the questionnaires. The oldest person taking part in the survey (member of the university staff) was 37. Among the survey participants there were 63.39% of students, 35.83% working students and 0.79% employees. 70.87% indicated secondary level education and 20.08% post-secondary education – the survey was primarily conducted among the students of BA studies. 8.66% declared holding a BA degree or a certificate of completion of studies, only one person indicated having a PhD degree.

Over 45% of survey participants indicated that they are inhabitants of cities with over 500,000 residents, over 14% came from cities with 100,000–500,000 of inhabitants, over 21% from towns with 10,000–100,000 residents, almost 5% from towns up to 10,000 residents, and 12.6% declared that they come from rural areas. The simplicity of the survey did not cause many distortions during its completion; few respondents (17) completed also additional sections of the survey.

3 Analysis of the Findings and Discussion

Respondents provided answers to sixty-eight substantive questions, out of which responses to first twenty-one questions and last twenty seven questions concerned the issues which are the aim of this article. The first group of questions concerned the characteristics of e-gamers and their use of computer games. The second one – possibility of using abilities of players and different types of games in teaching at the university level.

Nearly 40% of respondents provided positive answers to the question concerning frequent use of computer games, i.e. every day (20%) and a few times a week (over 19%). This is the score which is 10% points lower than rare use of e-games, which amounts to more than 49%. After preliminary interviews with respondents it seemed that the interest in computer games will be higher. The high score of a reasonable way of playing computer games (a few times a month) – 22% showed that the games are just one of many alternative kinds of entertainment available today. Figure 1 illustrates the findings of the research.

Taking into account the technical aspects concerning platforms which e-gamers use, in the last 12 months we observe a specific shift towards mobile devices,

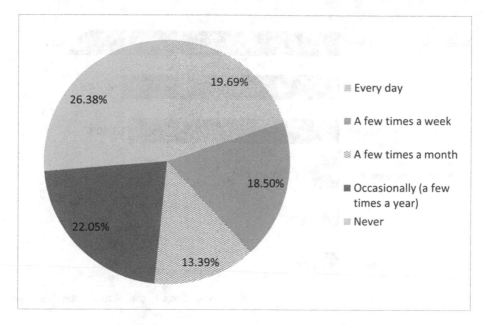

Fig. 1. The frequency of playing computer games

smartphones in particular. Thus, over 35% of e-gamers (80.75% including other platforms) used mobile platforms (mainly Android) last year. The second place was taken by PC platform – 28.31% (65.24% including other devices), and the third position was occupied by the console (e.g. Xbox, PS) with the score of 27.38 (63.10% – respectively). Smart TV platform received the lowest scores in this ranking – 2.09% (4.81).

In the perception of particular platforms among the e-gamers, we notice considerable discrepancies, amounting to 33% points. The greatest number of respondents simultaneously use smartphones and PCs as platforms for games. Here, the dispersion of the results reaches almost 76% points. The observed tendencies are presented in Fig. 2.

On the other hand, it probably stems from the fact that the majority of e-gamers 59.87% (including other kinds of game access – 97.33%) use the games installed on a device (a PC or a smartphone). The second position of Steam, Origin etc. platforms amounting to 26.32% (respectively 42.78%) is a rather interesting phenomenon. The two main sources of games together constitute over 86% of "places" where e-gamers used the possibility of playing games in the last year. The remaining places where games were downloaded e.g. Facebook (6.25%) and low score of browsers (e.g. Quake Live) – 7.57% seem to be of marginal importance in this relation. The Fig. 3 illustrates the scores.

The responses to the question concerning the age of e-gamers at the moment when they started to play games brought about very interesting results. The age which was most frequently indicated by respondents (almost 50% of responses) was within the

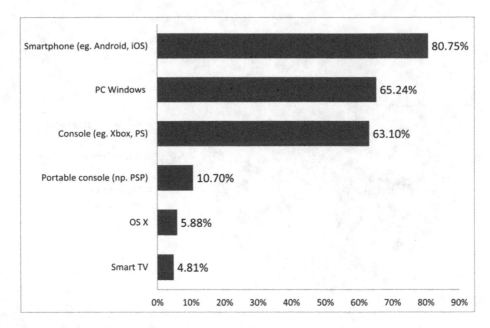

Fig. 2. The platforms which were most frequently used as e-games platforms in the last year

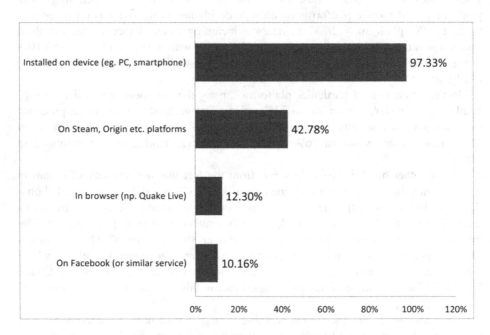

Fig. 3. Places where e-gamers installed games

range of 6–9 years (median of 6–7 years). If we add a group of people aged 10–11, we have more than two thirds of all gamers! It is also significant that 17.11% of e-gamers declare that they started being interested in games at the age of 5. A marginal number (1.07%) admits starting playing games at the age of 20–25 (and the group that indicated the age of 16–25 amounted to 2.76%). This indicates the very early age when people become interested in computer games and treating the games as an alternative kind of entertainment in relation to films, TV, games or outdoor activities. Unfortunately, the limitation of the research was the fact that the authors did not examine children and young people from this age group. Nevertheless, the obtained results explain where – among others – the interest in computer games later in life comes from. The responses of survey participants were presented in Fig. 4.

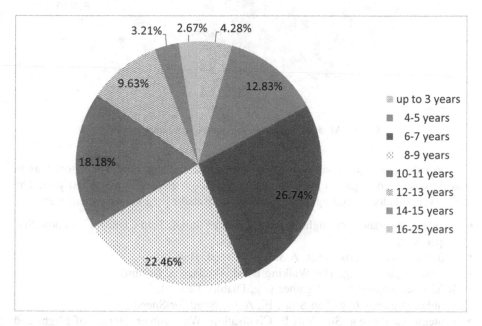

Fig. 4. The age when respondents started playing computer games

Subsequently, the authors examined also the amounts of money which e-gamers spend monthly at playing computer games. The vast majority of them – 79.14% - use free applications installed on smartphones or free (or, as some people claim, illegally downloaded from the Internet) PC games. The remaining 18.18% of respondents are willing to pay up to PLN 80 monthly, and only 2.67% from PLN 81–300. From the commercial point of view, the last group (in particular 2.14% of survey participants who are willing to pay between PLN 151–300) is most interesting to examine because it includes mainly hobbyists, enthusiasts and fanatics – as it seems – professional e-gamers. The representatives of this group are interested in sport, which in this case is realized by means of various electronic tools (PC, smartphone or tablet, console, etc.). The study results are presented in Fig. 5.

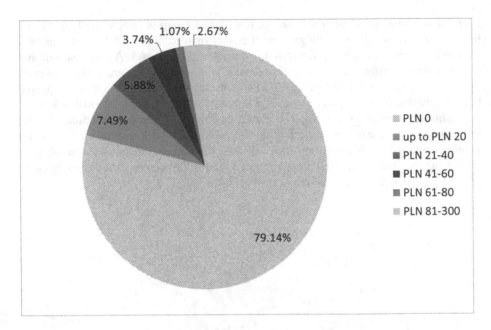

Fig. 5. Monthly payments for playing computer games

The subsequent questions were used to evaluate the situation. Their goal was to indicate what kind of games the e-gamers played most frequently in the last year. The games were divided according to the typology indicated by the most frequent e-gamers:

- arcade games (shooting, fighting) (e.g. Counter Strike, Tom Clancy's Rainbow Six, Super Mario),
- action-adventure games (e.g. Assassin's Creed, Half-Life),
- adventure games (e.g. The Walking Dead, Wallace & Gromit),
- RPG (role-playing games) games (e.g. Diablo, Fallout),
- simulation games (e.g. The Sims, FIFA 16, Need for Speed),
- strategic games (e.g. StarCraft II, Civilisation, Warhammer, Heroes of Might and Magic),
- survival horror games – (e.g. Resident Evil),
- Massively Multiplayer Online games –MMO and their variants (e.g. World of Warcraft, Lord of the Rings Online).

Subsequently, the respondents answered the questions related to whether they played a particular kind of game in the period of last year. The questions formulated in such a way seemed to allow for more accurate responses that the ones which referred to the type of games they played most frequently. The authors worried that the responses concerning the last few months would dominate in the survey. They did not examine the recent trends in the market, the influence of newly published books and films related to particular themes, etc. The greatest number of positive responses, 80.75%, was indicated in the case of the simplest type of games – e.g. simulation games.

The group of simple games also includes arcade games (57.75%) and action-adventure games (50.27%), where the number of positive responses exceeded 50%. In general, the greater complexity, the more complex relations, or the duration and additional limitations, the smaller the percentage of e-gamers admitting that they play a particular kind of game. The external factors, such as the history (the game was on the market "since I remember"), the popularity of a hero or a heroine or a plot constructed and popularized in films, books, board games, etc. contribute to the preeminence of the game. The games where the gamer needs to be more involved and stay in one place are less popular. The results of this part of the study are presented in Fig. 6.

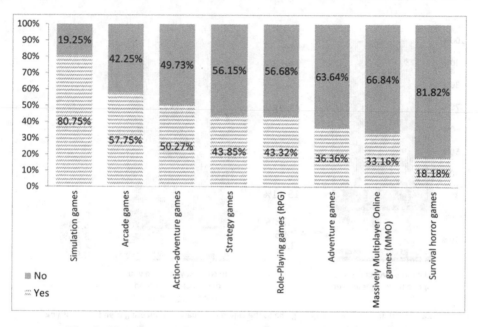

Fig. 6. The most popular and most frequently played kinds of games

A good indication of the level of the engagement of the player is his or her willingness to choose to spend time in a game over other kinds of entertainment. The respondents were asked two questions if they (1) ever or (2) within the period of last year have chosen to spend time in a game over other, alternative forms of entertainment, such as:

- going to the cinema,
- meeting friends,
- going on a date,
- going for a trip with friends,
- going to a party,
- no such case.

It turned out that computer games are not enjoyable enough for players to give up anything in the past (61.78%) or in the last year (77.40%). If the respondents are willing to resign from something, it is mainly a meeting with friends 15.11% and a party 9.78%. In case of giving up anything in the last year in favor of a computer game, the results were similar. The respondents indicated a social meeting – 8.17% and a party – 6.73%. In reality, the difference indicated in the percentage of people who are willing to give up other forms of entertainment amounts to 17.32% points, and decreases the actual numbers of indications in particular categories – the greatest with regard to social meetings – nearly 7% points and parties – over 3% points. The detailed scores are illustrated in Fig. 7.

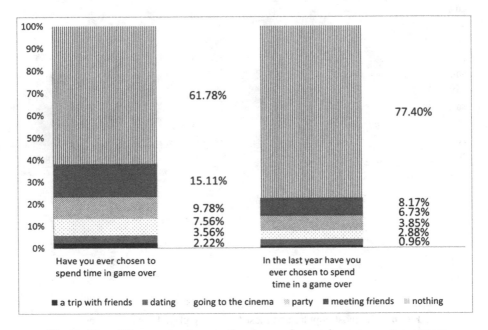

Fig. 7. The willingness to give up other forms of entertainment among e-gamers

In the respondents' views, the quality of computer games meets all or most expectations of players in 70% (Fig. 8). The response that the game fulfills e-gamers' expectations to a moderate and limited degree is indicated only by 28% of respondents. A fraction of the sample evaluated the games as not enjoyable enough to consider giving up other activities in favor of spending time in the game. Probably, it is one of the reasons why games are still so popular.

The vast majority of interviewed e-gamers (64%) are not interested in being leaders in games (provided that games offer such an opportunity). The remaining options are rather evenly distributed: 11% – clan leader, 7% – officer, 6% – advisor, 4% – higher-ranked officer and 8% – playing other roles (Fig. 9).

Most e-gamers (54%) complete one game, take a break and only later start to play another computer game. Nearly 32% play a few games simultaneously. Only 14%

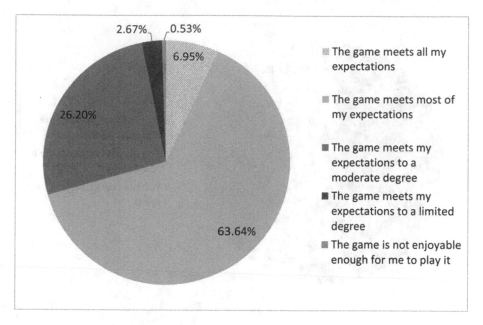

Fig. 8. The quality of computer games in e-gamers' opinions

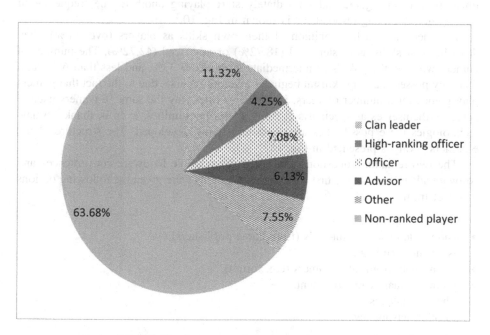

Fig. 9. The frequency of playing computer games

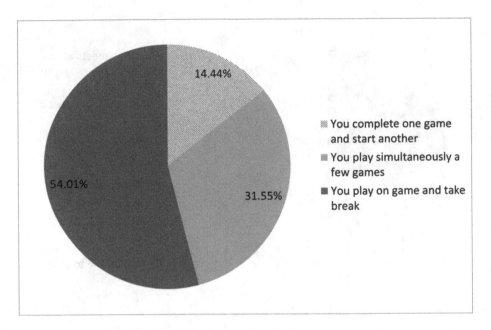

Fig. 10. The willingness to be a leader among e-gamers

finish playing one game and immediately start playing another. The frequency of playing games among respondents is shown in Fig. 10.

E-gamers have a high opinion of their own skills as players (over 60%): they describe their skills as master level (18.72%) or advanced (42.72%). The number of gamers who see their skills as intermediate amounts to 33%, and less than 6% claim that they possess gaming skills at beginner level. Of course, due to the fact that gamers play games for a number of years, and general rules stay the same, e-gamers usually perceive themselves as specialists at using such opportunities, even if, thanks to new technologies these possibilities are constantly being developed. The structure of the e-gamers' skills is presented in Fig. 11.

The two remaining questions concerned the possible hardware conveniences and software advantages. In the first case, the respondents were given the following options to select from:

- obtaining mentor's help,
- using video and text tutorials (from game publishers),
- using in-game help,
- getting help from other gamers (e.g. forum),
- getting virtual or real payment,
- other advantages,
- no other advantages.

Almost 30% of gamers do not expect any advantages in this regard. They focus on the game they are currently playing, and they are satisfied with the game itself (passive

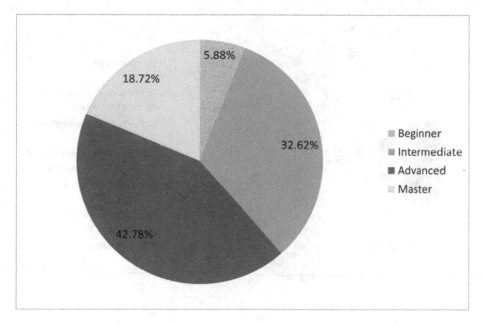

Fig. 11. The structure of e-gamers' skills

players). Undoubtedly, the other e-gamers would be more satisfied if they could get help from other game users e.g. forum (22.14%), use text and video tutorials (12.55%) or in-game help (12.18%). Their satisfaction (18.08% of respondents) would increase if they received bonuses (additional options, game paths, etc.) or even actual reward (payment); yet, they have unrealistic or vague expectations concerning the latter. They do not pay attention to other conveniences or advantages of such kind. The results of this query are presented in Fig. 12.

With regard to the technical conveniences, e-gamers were asked about the following, potential possibilities of changes concerning:

- computer hardware (e.g. graphic card) or a better tablet,
- armchair/seat,
- accessories (e.g. professional mouse, keyboard, earphones),
- better monitor/VR goggles,
- other,
- I don't want to change anything.

In this case the responses were completely different than in the previous rankings. First of all, the structure of their responses was not evenly distributed. Nevertheless, almost one fourth (23.53%) of respondents are not satisfied with the hardware they own that they use to play a game, and they would like to change it. The distribution of the potential changes or lack thereof, was actually similar in relation to the remaining elements: better monitor or goggles – 18.53%, better armchair/seat – 21.76%, better accessories – 16.76% or no change at all – 16.47%.

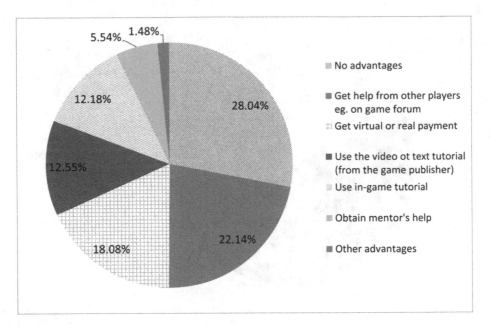

5.54%   1.48%

12.18%

28.04%

12.55%

18.08%   22.14%

No advantages

Get help from other players eg. on game forum

Get virtual or real payment

Use the video ot text tutorial (from the game publisher)

Use in-game tutorial

Obtain mentor's help

Other advantages

Fig. 12. Non-technical conveniences for e-gamers

Similarly to the previous case, basically e-gamers do not notice any potential for changes – less than 3% provided positive responses to this question, and there were no significant indications which we could relate to (e.g. additional lighting, additional monitors, etc.). The results are presented in Fig. 13.

The next phase of the research was dedicated to psychological predispositions of e-gamers and the usefulness of those abilities in the educational process supported by computer games on the faculties of economy and/or management.

Influence of computer games is present in life of each e-gamer, whether they want this or not. Despite, its optimistic to find that 81.5% of the respondents declare that they prefer the real social life over the virtual reality. Only 2.5% respondents replayed that they prefer the virtual life. 16% of respondents treats equally real and virtual life. All the respondents are aware of the influence of games on their life. First of all its related to different forms of addiction. According to 74% of all answers, addiction to games states for the highest impact on person's life, and considering also responses "rather yes" – it makes all together 95% of all answers (Fig. 14).

The addiction to game is manifested mostly by continuous play in the game without any breaks (22%), playing in every life situation (17%), and also selective deafness – where player is not able to hear what others say to him (16%). Less important are such factors as confusion between reality and virtual life (11%), continuous attempt to reach higher levels (11%), lack of reaction on any stimuli (10%).

Even lesser are such factors as starting another game just after finishing one and changing played game's difficulty level to harder. Among other symptoms of addiction, respondents list also forgetting about physiological needs, gambit nights, spending

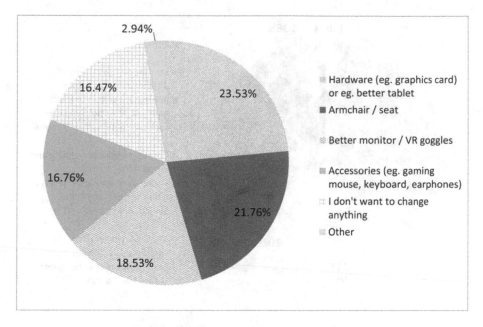

Fig. 13. Technical conveniences for e-gamers

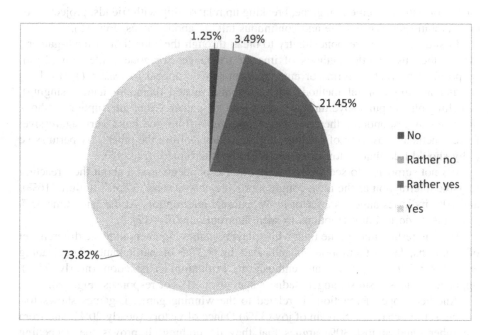

Fig. 14. Possibility of e-gamer's addiction to a game

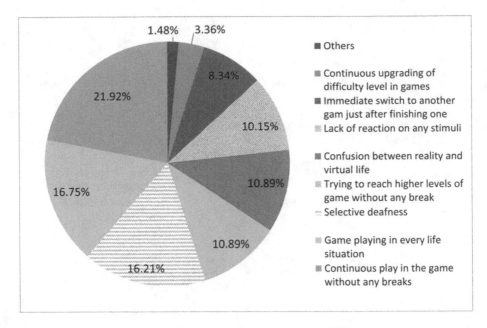

Fig. 15. Symptoms of computer game addition

money on extra movement in game, breaking up relationship with friends, projection of ones ambitions to virtual life and continuous talking about games (Fig. 15).

In situation, when respondents try to break through the addiction of the e-gamers, mostly they use gentle methods of impact: try to get someone's attention (29%), proposal of alternative forms of entertainment (24%), appeal to reason (17%). Less popular are more brutal methods such as sound related (clapping hands, singing), switching off computer, overturning a chair with a e-gamer. Other interruption methods indicated by respondents there are very opposing – from one hand very aggressive, forced methods (covering of monitor, hitting e-gamer), from the other very permissive (why should I do that, I don't like myself to be interrupted) (Fig. 16).

It's not surprising to see the last response. Respondents asked about their reaction to game interruption as the most common provide nervousness (37.5%), failure (16%), and 10% indicates anger as a factor to the external interruption. At the same time 31% respondents do feel any emotions to such interruptions (Fig. 17).

It is interesting that all the time while playing games e-gamers indicate different set of emotions, lack of emotions is indicated by 3.37% of participants. The leading emotions related to games are enthusiasm, exultation, satisfaction (nearly 75%). opposite feelings – stress, anger, sadness state over 21% of responses (Fig. 18).

Another scope of reactions is related to the winning game. E-games shows following set of behaviors. Scream of joy (33%) Dance of victory (nearly 20%), and from the other hand almost 30% argues that they do nothing. It proves the deepening dichotomy between gamers playing computer games for pleasure and enthusiasts or even professional gamers, sometimes – as statistics shows – addicted to games. Among

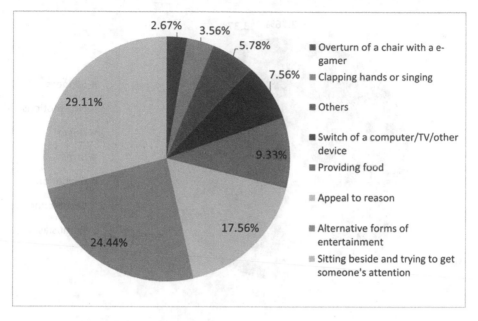

Fig. 16. Methods of breaking of a e-gamer's addiction to games

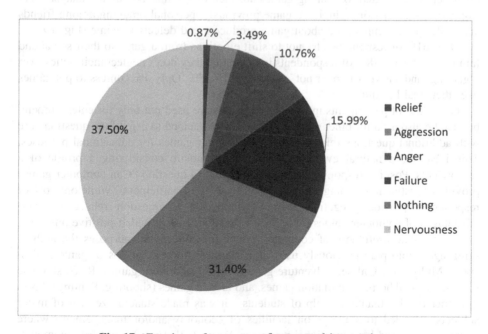

Fig. 17. Emotions of a e-gamer after external interruptions

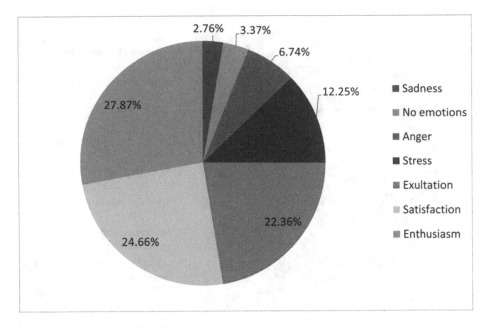

Fig. 18. Emotions related to a computer game

other behaviors related to winning games are mentioned: mistake/failure analysis, that stopped a e-gamer from winning a game previously, personal bragging among friends and colleagues, complaining about game producers and defects in game (Fig. 19).

Over 61% of respondents try not to shift emotions from a game to their social and family life. Nearly 48% of respondents indicate that they don't neglect their duties over e-gaming, and answer of "rater not" was given by 38%. Only 4% confess to put games over their real life duties.

Over 75% of participants indicated that games are used not only for entertainment, but can be also used for other purposes, the authors decided to extend the questionnaire with additional questions related to use of computer games for educational purposes. This idea was a natural evolution of the questionnaire considering a profile of a respondents. Positive response (yes and rather yes) to question "Can computer games provide educational advantages?" was given by 94% of participants, while only 6% of respondents provided negative answer. Comparing to question related to sport advantages of computer games, only 59% of respondents provided positive answer.

To evaluate usefulness of computer games for educational purposes the authors bring again into play previously used division into different groups of games: Massively Multiplayer Online, Adventure games, action-adventure games, RPG, strategic games, survival horror, simulation games, and arcade games (shooting, fighting). From the other hand – thanks to help of students - it was made standardized set of major subjects provided to students on faculties of economy and/or management, where games can be used for educational processes. Subjects that can benefit from computer gaming as part of educational process are: economics, information technology, foreign

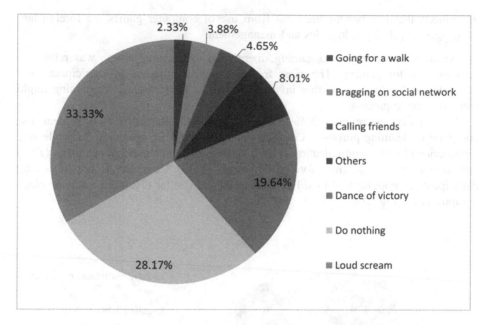

Fig. 19. Behaviors of e-gamers after a winning game

languages, logistics, marketing, mathematics, negotiations, law, psychology, accounting, sociology, management.

According to provided answers, following results were gathered:

- the most frequent answer was indicating possibility to learn foreign languages via gaming of following games: first rank – Massively Multiplayer Online (32% of all responses), second rank – adventure games – 23%, third rank action-adventure games – 19%, forth rank arcade games (shooting, fighting) – 18% and RPG – 16%,
- the most suitable for management teaching are strategy games (29%) and simulation games (23%),
- the most suitable to support psychology are games type horror survival (39%),
- to support educational process of economics – similarly as for management (although in smaller scope) are strategic games (13%) and simulation games (12%),
- as research shows also logistics can be supported by games, where the most suitable are strategic (24%) and action adventure games (16%),
- sociology can benefit from simulation games (12%) and adventure games (10%),
- negotiations can be best supported by Massive Multiplayer Online (12%),
- according to the respondents, in a very low scope, mathematics, information technology, accounting, law and marketing are not seem as a good target for game support in the educational process (responses ranged between 0–7%),
- the whole research shown that according to participants of the research, the most suitable to support didactic process are games of type Massively Multiplayer Online (31%) and strategic games (23%) the less suitable are games of type RPG,

- subjects that can benefit the most from use of computer games are foreign languages, psychology, logistics and management.

Another aspect related to gaming, mentioned in previous article was related to devices used for gaming. The most frequent device indicated by participants is a computer, and it leads to further investigations how devices used for gaming might support didactic process.

Based on current research 96% (response "Yes" and "Rather Yes") of students use computer for learning purposes. Computer is used mainly for searching and collecting information (19%), communication (17%), viewing of source materials and data (17%) and to translate to and from foreign languages (16%). Computer is not treated by participants as popular tool to solve math tasks and similar (7%) and to create bibliography (9%) (Fig. 20).

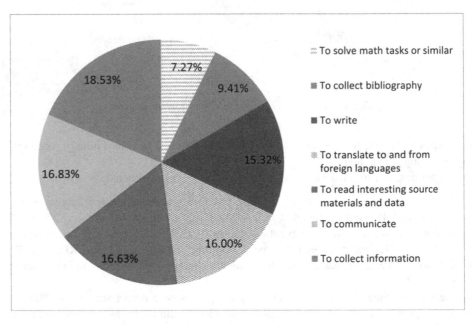

Fig. 20. Scientific domains where computer can be used

At the same time students express their belief that computer games are not suitable for collecting literature used for lectures, seminars and final papers. 63% respondents answers are "Not suitable" or "Rather not suitable". Participants represent similar opinion in relation to influence of computer games to extend one's interest in lectures at the university. Over 70% respondents indicated that they don't see such an influence, although playing games has its effect in better memorizing of content of lectures (74%). Also 94% of participants believes that computer gaming improves creative thinking and also other positive features, mostly associated with logical thinking (19%), faster reflex and better efficiency in foreign language (18%). The substantial part of these characteristics are ability to solve problems and issues (13%), better concentration (13%). All together with better mood (15%) those characteristics might help didactic process from the psychological side of learning. In particular as further research proves in learning foreign languages (18%), management (15%), logistics (9%), and psychology (8%). Over 71% students indicate that computer games can verify information gathered during lectures (Fig. 21).

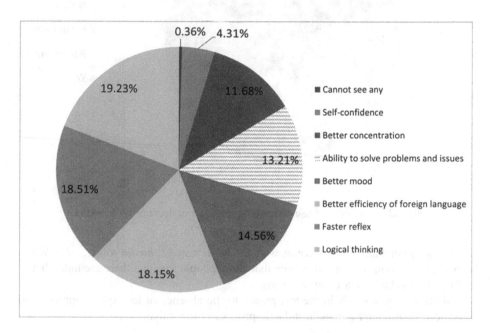

Fig. 21. Positive features extended by computer games

In respondents' view (19%), lecturers should use computer games during their lectures. Over 40% of respondents answered "Rather yes" to questions related to possibility of use games during lectures. Only 8% of participants don't see such a need (Fig. 22).

At the end of the questionnaire participants had possibility to express own opinions regarding suitability of computer games in educational process. Respondents provided wide spectrum of statements, where majority of views had positive note pointing general role of computer games in shaping personality and positive characterological traits (... *it develops personality at many layers... We can benefit from every type of computer games...*, it [game] *can teach new skills and logical thinking...*). Also opinions reasonably positive were present highlighting the need for creation of dedicated games used especially for didactic purposes, specified to support particular subjects. (*...properly defined games might positively influence educational process...*, ... *I am not aware of dedicated educational games, I believe those should be yet created....*) In opposition to those positive views many negative statements were raised highlighting detrimental effect of computer games leading to addictions, and living

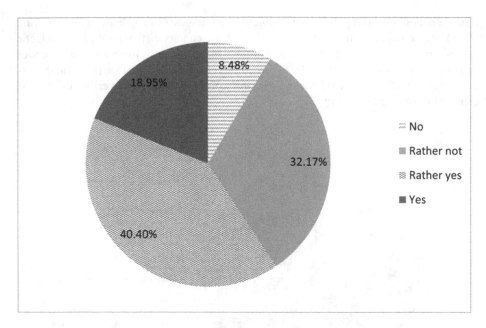

Fig. 22. Possibility of use computer games during lectures by lecturers

virtual life rather than reality (*…games might be dangerous media tool…, should not be used at universities…*). Furthermore that some people say, that there are much better methods of teaching than computer games.

All above testifies, within the test group, to the absence of an explicit approach to utilisation of computer games in didactic process at the university.

4 Conclusions

The research conducted and presented so far points to the following conclusions:

- almost all respondents (over 99% of the sample) in the current study were students, which was reflected in the obtained scores. The older the students, the weaker interest in completing the questionnaire or its findings. It is caused by the increasing number of tasks connected with studies as well as the heavy workload connected with regular or temporary work (nearly 36% of working students). The latter is confirmed in the scores of other surveys [17, 23–25], despite the fact that, in total, fewer than 25–16% students participated in the study (even though it was always the largest group of players),
- among people who completed questionnaires there were markedly more women (almost 60%) than in other survey studies (around 43–48%) [14], conducted two or three years ago. Thus, we may conclude that there occurs a specific change with regard to the number of women playing computer games. Naturally, we should also be aware of the fact that the present study examined mainly the responses of

students of economic faculties, and in this case the general number of female students in these faculties is greater than men. Still, the survey included also the option I don't play computer games, which the women could indicate,

- the frequency of playing the game (every day, up to a few times a week) in the examined sample was 20% points smaller than in the case of other studies (39%, as compared to 62–63%). It should also be considered that in the other studies authors took into consideration also another, the second largest group of potential gamers – pupils - who have more free time than students, especially senior students.
- All in all, majority of players – 54% of the interviewees, after completing one game, take a break before they start playing another game, and only 14% immediately start to play another game,
- the vast majority of players use their smartphone to play computer games (over 80%, mainly Android system – a large number of free games), which does not exclude also simultaneous use of other devices, mainly PC (over 65%) and a console, a regular (63%) or mobile one (11%). Smartphones and tablets started to take a role of a PC. Two or three years ago the proportions were more or less reversed; approximately 90% of respondents [2, 24, 25] used mainly personal computer, and only half of them a smartphone or a tablet. The devices allow for occasional use of many kinds of generally simple games at any place or time (not just during a break at work using your PC), killing the time while waiting for something else to take place,
- 97% of gamers use the games installed on a smartphone or a PC, with a surprisingly low percentage (10%) of people using Facebook games,
- due to the dynamic development of the use of smartphones and tablets in the last two years it occurred that the greatest number of people play simple simulation games (over 80%) and arcade games (58%) and action-adventure games (50%) which are becoming popular again. When we compare the present research with the earlier studies related to this area [2, 24, 25], the RPG games lost its popularity due to the increasing importance of mobile devices use (here: 44%, 65% – in other studies),
- notably, however, the early age when children start playing computer games, a shift towards younger and younger children (3–4 years younger since 2013) contributes to further development of computer games. More and more frequently it is caused by the fact that the first device with access to games is a smartphone, not a PC, and the fact that smartphones offer a greater number of free game applications,
- in general, the respondents (almost 80%) are not willing to pay for this kind of entertainment, and, as a vast majority, they use free smartphone applications and computer games which they received for their PC free of charge. It is reflected in the studies concerning the use of smartphones [18, 26] and a low tendency among students to spend their earnings on this purpose,
- it also explains the unwillingness to give up other kinds of entertainment, social life or rest to spend one's time in a game: almost 62% are not interested in choosing a game over any other kind of entertainment, and over 77% declared that they did not give up any activity in favor of a game last year,

- it appears that the fact that over 70% respondents claim that the level and quality of computer games fulfill all or almost all their expectations does not impact the situation,
- they have no expectations concerning taking leadership in a game (64%), they treat the games as a simple, not overly complex, form of entertainment. In general, they play games individually, and they are not interested – at least to a considerable degree – in multiplayer games,
- e-gamers have high opinions about their gaming skills – over 60% of participants claim that their skills are at least at an advanced level, and only 6% that they are beginners. On the one hand, it may be caused by the length of time of playing computer games (experience); on the other, it may result from the simplicity of most games that they play,
- the above said phenomenon is the reason why they do not expect too many advantages (none – 28%). If they were to choose, they would get help from other users (22%) or they would try harder to succeed in the game (18%) if they had a chance to obtain a reward or virtual bonus for winning the game,
- the case of technical conveniences is somewhat different. 23% would like to change their hardware hoping that this way they would have better chances to participate in the existing games and a greater possibility to participate in games of higher technical requirements. They pay attention to better accessories. Less than 3% would not improve anything as far as technical conditions of gaming are concerned,
- e-gamers and people from their surroundings notice problems related to potential addiction to computer games and try to counteract, even though people that prefer virtual reality state for only 2.5% of tested e-gamers,
- people that play computer games are divided into two groups. First group consist of engaged players, that strongly feel emotions related to winning and losing of games, second group – are represented by people who treat gaming as one form of entertainment, and don't show emotions that may accompany gaming,
- gamers are convinced, that computer games can support with success didactic process, especially to support learning of foreign languages at faculties of economics and/or management. Those faculties can also benefit from computer games to support also psychology, logistics, management and economics,
- according to the research the most suitable to support didactic process are games of type Massively Multiplayer Online and simulation games,
- students pointed out need for creation of dedicated games used to support didactic process, also they highlighted the need for lecturers to lead the initiative to create such games,
- student community represents high level of opinion differentiation related to games and possibility to use computer games to support didactic process. There is awareness of both advantages and disadvantages of positive characteristics influenced by games in people life and in didactic process, as well as negative ones, leading to addiction.

The conclusions from this stage of the research constitute good basis for further studies and expanding their offer, their consequences and impact of using games from the point of view of players. However, the present results already show interesting implications for the development of mobile information technologies towards new development trends of the use of this kind of software as a source of entertainment.

The further research – after preparing discussion and conclusions about sociological and psychological aspects of the gaming (include discussion of perceived positive and negative aspects of being a gamer or attempt to identify of the subcultures of players (the first attempt see [21]) – will focus on the market for suppliers of computer games and video games, in particular delivered to for mobile devices.

Results of a survey may be used not only by researchers in the field of computer games but by computer firms which want to make one step ahead in the development of this phenomenon.

References

1. GRYOnline.pl (2016). http://www.gry-online.pl/S013.asp?ID=82806
2. Platforma e-learningowa Ministerstwo Skarbu Państwa (2016). http://akcjonariatobywatelski.pl/pl/centrum-edukacyjne/gospodarka/1033,Polski-rynek-gier-komputerowych-na-tle-rynku-swiatowego.html
3. Homo Ludens 1/(2), Polskie Towarzystwo Badania Gier (2010)
4. Słownik IT (2016). http://it-pomoc.pl/komputer/gra-komputerowa
5. Wiedza i Edukacja (2016). http://wiedzaiedukacja.eu/archives/tag/analiza-gier
6. GRYOnline.pl (2016). http://www.gry-online.pl/S018.asp?ID=208&STR=2
7. Krajowa Izba Producentów Audiowizualnych (2016). http://www.kipa.pl/index.php/promocja-filmu/gry-komputerowe/definicje-gier-komputerowych
8. Wikipedia (2016). https://pl.wikipedia.org/wiki/Gra_komputerowa
9. Zając, J.: Jestem graczem w social media (2016). http://blog.sotrender.com/pl/2014/12/jestem-graczem-w-social-media
10. Duggan, M.: Gaming and gamers (2015). http://www.pewinternet.org/2015/12/15/gaming-and-gamers
11. Fang, X., Chan, S., Nair, C.: An online survey system on computer game enjoyment and personality. In: Jacko, J.A. (ed.) HCI 2009. LNCS, vol. 5613, pp. 304–314. Springer, Heidelberg (2009). doi:10.1007/978-3-642-02583-9_34
12. Fromme, J.: Computer games as a part of children's culture. Int. Comput. Game Res. 3(1) (2003). http://www.gamestudies.org/0301/fromme/
13. Mijal, M., Szumski, O.: Zastosowania gier FPS w organizacji. In: Chmielarz, W., Kisielnicki, J., Parys, T. (eds.) Informatyka @ przyszłości, pp. 165–176. Wydawnictwo Naukowe WZ UW, Warsaw (2013)
14. Żywiczyńska, E.: Co tak naprawdę wiemy o graczach (2014). http://zgranarodzina.edu.pl/2014/10/12/co-tak-naprawde-wiemy-o-graczach
15. Essential facts about computer and video games industry. ESA Entertainment Software Association (2015). http://www.theesa.com/wp-content/uploads/2015/04/ESA-Essential-Facts-2015.pdf
16. Lofgren, K.: Video game statistics & trends; who's playing what & why? (2015). http://www.bigfishgames.com/blog/2015-global-video-game-stats-whos-playing-what-and-why
17. Żywiczyńska, E.: Optymizm czy myślenie życzeniowe. Zaskakujące wyniki badania #je-stemgraczem (2014). http://zgranarodzina.edu.pl/2014/12/20/optymizm-czy-myslenie-zyczeniowe-zaskakujace-wyniki-badania-jestemgraczem

18. Chmielarz, W.: Study of smartphones usage from the customer's point of view. Procedia Computer Science **65**, 1085–1094 (2015). doi:10.1016/j.procs.09.045
19. SurveyMonkey Inc. (2016). https://www.surveymonkey.com/r/2WCW3K9
20. Survio (2016). http://www.survio.com/survey/d/D8Q9F2M7N4E0W5F0P
21. Chmielarz, W., Szumski, O.: Analiza wykorzystania gier komputerowych (Computer games application analysis). In: Chmielarz, W. (ed.) Mobilne aspekty technologii informacyjnych (Mobile aspects of IT), pp. 81–106. Wydawnictwo Naukowe WZ UW, Warsaw (2016). doi:10.7172/978-83-65402-25-7.2016.wwz.7
22. Świerczyńska-Kaczor, U., Wachowicz, J.: Student response to educational games – an empirical study. In: Proceedings of 2013 FedCSIS, pp. 1293–1299 (2013). https://fedcsis.org/proceedings/2013/plics/55.pdf
23. JestemGraczem (2016). http://www.jestemgraczem.com/wyniki
24. Marketing przy kawie (2016). http://www.marketing-news.pl/message.php?art=43734
25. Newzoo (2016). http://www.newzoo.com/product/global-games-market-report-premium
26. Chmielarz, W.: Porównanie wykorzystania sklepów internetowych z aplikacjami mobilnymi w Polsce z punktu widzenia klienta indywidualnego (Comparison of the use of mobile applications websites in poland from the point of view of individual client). In: Knosala, R. (ed.) Innowacje w zarządzaniu i inżynierii produkcji, vol. II, Part IX Inżynieria jakości produkcji i usług, pp. 234–245. Oficyna Wydawnicza Polskiego Towarzystwa Zarządzania Produkcją, Opole (2015)

Assessing the IT and Software Landscapes of Industry 4.0-Enterprises: The Maturity Model SIMMI 4.0

Christian Leyh[1(✉)], Thomas Schäffer[2], Katja Bley[1],
and Sven Forstenhäusler[2]

[1] Technische Universität Dresden Chair of Information Systems,
esp. IS in Manufacturing and Commerce, Helmholtzstr. 10,
01069 Dresden, Germany
{Christian.Leyh,Katja.Bley}@tu-dresden.de
[2] Faculty of Business Administration, University of Applied Sciences,
Max-Planck-Str. 39, 74081 Heilbronn, Germany
Thomas.Schaeffer@hs-heilbronn.de,
Sforsten@stud.hs-heilbronn.de

Abstract. The increasing digitalization of business and society leads to drastic changes within companies. Nearly all enterprises have to face enormous challenges when dealing with topics such as Industry 4.0/Industrial Internet. One of these challenges represents the realistic classification of the company's own IT infrastructure. In this paper we present a maturity model (SIMMI 4.0 – System Integration Maturity Model Industry 4.0) that enables a company to classify its IT system landscape with focus on Industry 4.0 requirements. SIMMI 4.0 consists of 5 stages. Each describes several characteristics of digitization, which allows a company to assess itself. Additionally, recommended activities are presented for each stage of digitization, which can enable a company to reach the next stage of maturity. Due to the large number of possible characteristics concerning Industry 4.0 and digitization, we also present several possible topics for future research to improve and refine the developed maturity model.

Keywords: Maturity model · Industry 4.0 · Industrial Internet · Digital transformation · Digitization

1 Motivation

One of the most important challenges that companies currently face is the digitization of business processes and of the enterprise itself. They have to join in global digital networking, improve automation of individual or even all business processes, and reengineer existing business models to gain momentum in digital innovation. Meanwhile, the progressive and steady digitization of society, with associated changes, has also arrived in the everyday life of enterprises. It has never been more important for enterprises to be able to rely on IT-enabled capabilities, as well as to count on a deep understanding of information technology in general and in digital innovation in particular. These changes and challenges are enormous and are no longer restricted solely

© Springer International Publishing AG 2017
E. Ziemba (Ed.): AITM 2016/ISM 2016, LNBIP 277, pp. 103–119, 2017.
DOI: 10.1007/978-3-319-53076-5_6

to industry sectors, which depend on or have to use innovative technologies for creating and selling their products or services. Without a doubt, nearly all enterprises have to undergo an increasing digital transformation to remain competitive in global markets. The areas affected by these changes are diverse: e.g., the use of enterprise resource planning (ERP) or similar company-wide enterprise systems to achieve holistic support and planning of business activities throughout the company and across the company's borders [1–4], or the increasing interconnectedness of classical horizontal value chains to a complex value network [1, 5]. Digitization offers many approaches for automating workflows, reducing transaction costs, and increasing flexibility in dealing with customers and business partners. In these efforts, the specific challenge for companies is to realize the increasing integration of virtual, digital programs with real objects or products in their everyday business in order to subsequently adapt, enhance, or optimize the processes [6].

For a while, trends such as Industry 4.0/Industrial Internet, Big Data, and Cloud Computing affected mainly large companies, especially since small- and medium-sized enterprises (SMEs) often judged those topics as too complex and expensive and partially classified them as not relevant. However, digitization is no longer limited to large companies and does not only concern separate functional areas such as the IT department. Rather, it takes place throughout the entire value chain of all companies [7]. The advantages are also relevant for SMEs (e.g., a profitable growth through new products, new services, and innovative business models). With digital technology, costs are reduced and the company can be more efficient in its daily business activities [8].

Realizing these advantages, SMEs open themselves for the complex topic of Industry 4.0 and try to reshape their business processes and business models in this direction by an increased usage of Information and Communication Technology (ICT). However, it is obvious that the increasing transformation of everyday business, in addition to the opportunities, is not without risks for existing business models. Such profound changes to the corporate structure require large investments and can lead to temporary shortfalls of individual departments during the restructuring process. However, this implementation seems inevitable regarding increasing national and international competition. For example, currently SMEs mainly use advanced ICT for handling production and business processes. E-mail and the internet as the main communication mediums are constantly increasing in importance; computerized programs specify production and enterprise systems support all kinds of daily business operations. Overall, together with this increasing digitalization of companies, the definitions of value-adding and supportive processes become vague, whereby the traditional supply chain of a company with its downstream processes develops into a holistic supply/value network.

To face up to this development the use of adequate ICT is essential. However, what is missing at this point is the companies' level of knowledge concerning their own digitization. A number of studies already exist applying to this topic (e.g., [9–12]). By using various interrogation techniques, the authors figure out which information and enterprise systems are used in business (especially in SMEs) and in what shape the IT-infrastructure of the company appears. There is, however, the question of how an IT landscape must be designed so that a company can "move" in the field of Industry 4.0.

Recognizing and evaluating what systems are needed, and in which way and for what purpose, still embodies a challenge for companies.

This is where the present paper comes in. As extended paper of Leyh et al. [13] we present a tool (a maturity model) that enables companies to classify their own provided IT system landscape in the needs of an Industry 4.0 system landscape. This results in the main research question for our research:

What should a maturity model look like to assess a company's IT system landscape in the context of Industry 4.0?

In order to answer this question the paper is composed of four sections. Following this motivation, Sect. 2 gives brief insight into the field of Industry 4.0, as well as in the field of existing maturity models, whereas Sect. 3 summarizes the development of our maturity model "SIMMI 4.0" (System Integration Maturity Model Industry 4.0). Sect. 4 represents the core of our paper. In this chapter, the components (dimensions and stages) of SIMMI 4.0 necessary to fulfill the requirements of an Industry 4.0 environment are described. The paper finishes with a short summary and an outlook for future research in this field.

2   Conceptual Background

As already mentioned in the motivation section, the topic "Industry 4.0" has gained more and more importance and has spread with all its diversity in enterprises. Industry 4.0, as the fourth stage of the industrial revolution is entitled, consists of an increasing digitization of products and systems, together with their interconnectedness. Thereby, the physical world is connected to the virtual world. The focus lies on an enhancement of the automation, flexibility, and individualization of the products, the production, and the connected business processes [14, 15].

The characteristics of Industry 4.0 are: e.g., horizontal integration across whole value networks, strong vertical integration within the company, and a digital transparency of the engineering across the entire value chain [14]. However, a universal definition for the term "Industry 4.0" does not exist. Despite this, from the aforementioned descriptions and further characteristics of Industry 4.0 we deduce a working definition as the foundation for our research:

Industry 4.0 describes the transition from centralized production towards one that is very flexible and self-controlled. Within this production the products and all affected systems, as well as all process steps of the engineering, are digitized and interconnected to share and pass information and to distribute this along the vertical and the horizontal value chains, and even beyond that in extensive value networks.

In addition to the organizational challenges, the question of the right business model, and the adjustments of the existing business models faced by companies that want to align themselves more towards Industry 4.0, the enterprise's IT department is also confronted with an integration challenge of further/additional IT systems. Through the development of the last few years (especially in the field of digitization), the homogeneous IT system landscape of the 1990s and 2000s is now divided into smaller heterogeneous systems. This change results from the requirements used when companies want to foster activities in the field of Industry 4.0, since those requirements often cannot be covered by one "large, all-encompassing" IT system. From this point of view, the need arises that the companies must be able to classify their IT system landscape regarding Industry 4.0 requirements. They have to be able to analyze their landscapes to identify whether or not it is sufficient and provides a stable foundation for Industry 4.0 activities. A tool is needed for this purpose (for example, a maturity model) that enables the company to classify its IT system landscape and also the landscapes of its business partners.

Therefore, to get an insight in the existing literature regarding maturity models, here with a focus on Industry 4.0 and its requirements, we conducted a systematic literature review. This analysis was done in three steps:

- **Step 1:** Development of a classification scheme for systematically assessing and evaluating maturity models. Here, we oriented our scheme on the classification scheme of Wendler [16] and enhanced this scheme with further criteria since Wendler [16] evaluates the papers and not the maturity models described within them. In the Appendix our classification and its assessment is provided by conducting one example evaluation of the maturity model of Benguria and Santos [17].
- **Step 2:** Conducting the systematic literature review. We used the approach suggested by vom Brocke et al. [18] to identify relevant articles. In addition, we used the paper of Wendler [15], which provides a valuable overview of maturity model papers.
- **Step 3:** Classification, assessment, and evaluation of the identified papers and maturity models. The identified articles (53 papers focusing maturity models) were analyzed and classified according to the scheme in the Appendix. The list and classification of all analyzed papers, and therefore of the maturity models, will not be part of this article, but will be provided by the authors upon request.

The analysis of the identified articles and maturity showed that the models have an average of five stages and numerically very different dimension characteristics per stage. Furthermore, not all maturity models follow a concrete process model in their development, and most of them lack a thorough evaluation especially with regard to their usage in practice. Mostly, the identified papers represent an initial proposal of a model and somehow the development process is described more or less extensively.

Summing up the results of our literature review, it became evident that there are a couple of maturity models for classifying the IT system or software landscape of enterprises (e.g., LISI: [19]; OIMM: [17]; SIMM: [20]; SPICE: [21]). However, we could not identify a maturity model that deals with or that has an explicit focus on the requirements of Industry 4.0 in combination with the IT system landscape of an enterprise and of its partners in the value chain. However, some of the analyzed maturity models contain in part some related and relevant approaches, but these mostly do not cover the required functionality and content of a highly integrative and organization-wide digitization for the model-application in the field of Industry 4.0. Hence, in combination with the statements from the motivation section, the need to develop a more capable and matching maturity model for the context of Industry 4.0 is given.

3 Research Methodology – Development of SIMMI 4.0

Since Industry 4.0 is an enterprise-wide and even an inter-corporate topic, the IT system landscape should also have an inter-corporate nature by using the potential of current technologies and approaches. To take this into account, the development of SIMMI 4.0 follows a detailed development strategy (described below) and is thus based on the derivation or modification of existing maturity models. For this purpose we especially used maturity models that are related to the topic of IT system landscape, e.g., CMM(I) [22–24] and SOAMM [25]. Several components of those models were combined and adjusted according to the requirements of Industry 4.0.

In general, maturity models can be regarded as artifacts, and, therefore, the principles of design-oriented research are applicable. For example, the development of a maturity model generally follows, according to those principles, three phases: problem identification, designing the artifact, and evaluation of the artifact [26].

As a process model for developing maturity models, de Bruin et al. [27] developed a generic phase model based on the findings of the analysis of the development process of the Business Process Maturity Model (BPMM) and the Knowledge Management Capability Assessment (KMCA). They suggest six steps for this process model: scope, design, populate, test, deploy, and maintain.

Whereas, Becker et al. [26] apply the seven guidelines (1–Design as an Artifact; 2–Problem Relevance; 3–Design Evaluation; 4–Research Contributions; 5–Research Rigor; 6–Design as a Search Process; 7–Communication of Research) of the Design Science framework from Hevner et al. [28] for the development process of maturity models. They suggest eight phases for the development process: (1) problem definition; (2) comparison of existing maturity models; (3) defining the development strategy; (4) iterative maturity model development; (5) conceptual design for the transfer and evaluation of the maturity model; (6) implementation of transfer approaches; (7) conducting the evaluation; and, if necessary, (8) discarding the maturity model [26].

Therefore, due to the iterative procedure, the full-scale documentation guide of the development process also assesses the validity and reliability of the model for the scientific discourse of the process model of Becker et al. [26]. In addition, due to the already successfully developed maturity models following the process model (e.g. [29, 30]), we decided to follow this process model for the development of SIMMI 4.0 (System Integration Maturity Model Industry 4.0).

Following this process model, SIMMI 4.0 is currently in phase 4 (iterative maturity model development). We identified an existing problem enterprises face within the field of Industry 4.0 (phase 1), and we compared existing maturity models (phase 2) by conducting a systematic literature review (see Sects. 1 and 2). However, we cannot describe the development process of SIMMI 4.0 to a full extent within this paper. Therefore, this process is described in Leyh et al. [31].

In phase 4, SIMMI 4.0 is in its first iteration. The findings from the analysis of the literature about the general structure of maturity models were combined with the requirements for an IT system landscape of a company that wants to operate entirely in the context of Industry 4.0. Thus, in the following section we present SIMMI 4.0 in detail to provide an understanding of how a company could/should evaluate its IT system landscape with focus on Industry 4.0.

4 SIMMI 4.0 – System Integration Maturity Model Industry 4.0

As a starting point for model development, a further literature analysis was conducted. Contrary to the literature analysis of Sect. 2, the aim of this analysis was to gain an understanding about the existing level of knowledge about Industry 4.0, and, therefore, to deduce the essential requirements for IT systems in the context of Industry 4.0. Several databases (e.g., EBSCO, ScienceDirect, SpringerLink, and Google Scholar) were searched using the following terms and combinations of these terms: Information systems, Industry 4.0, Maturity models, Integration, Digitization, Internet of things and services, Cyber-physical systems, Value networks, IT systems, Enterprise systems, and Business information systems. Some of the resulting requirements from this literature analysis are presented as follows.

4.1 Requirements for IT-Systems in the Context of Industry 4.0

In their final report about Industry 4.0, Kagermann et al. [14] highlighted three key requirements fostered by Industry 4.0 and thus should be supported by the enterprise application system landscape:

Vertical Integration along the hierarchical levels of a company: While the different enterprise systems support their own tasks very well, the data of the respective systems, such as Enterprise Resource Planning (ERP) systems, Supply Chain Management (SCM) systems, Management Information Systems (MIS), Product Life cycle Management (PLM) systems, etc., is often stored in separate databases (sometimes data interfaces are provided) and partly stored in different formats. This sub-optimal level of integration must be improved for implementing Industry 4.0 business processes and activities.

Horizontal Integration across value networks: For the implementation and use of different enterprise systems, failures and leakages throughout the flow of information must be avoided. In fact, the information must be accessible and useable at the right time in the right "place" along the entire supply chain and therefore for all business partners. Furthermore, the exchange of such information flows must be (completely) automatized.

Digital Continuity of engineering: This means supporting a product's engineering consistently and continuously along the entire supply chain by using adequate and appropriate enterprise systems and includes the production system development process as well.

Also, stemming from the literature review (especially from analyzed study results), cross-sectional technologies were identifiable as an important part of the enterprise systems. These technologies are defined below and their relevance to Industry 4.0 will be explained:

Service-Oriented Architecture: For example, the project "Platform Industry 4.0" has published a whitepaper that names the development of a reference architecture based on a Service-oriented architecture (SOA) as an important prerequisite for the implementation of Industry 4.0 [32].

Cloud Computing: Industry 4.0 not only leads to a digitization of separate production facilities, but also that of the enterprise's information technology at the production plant(s) as well as all companies digitally interconnected along the supply chain. Considering cloud computing, these aspects are provided as different services; therefore, this could help enterprises operate in the field of Industry 4.0 effectively and efficiently.

Information Aggregation and Processing: In this context, aggregation of information implies that data can be easily identified from various integrated enterprise systems through different ways of treatment, such as clustering, filtering, and correlation. In a next step, this data is made available to every user or machine that needs it. This illustrates not only that the data of the production floor/of the production systems (e.g., various interconnected machines, (semi-) products, sensors etc.) is aggregated and transferred towards the company's higher levels and enterprise systems (e.g., ERP systems, SCM systems), but also that the data needs to be transferred in the opposite direction to the production floor [33].

IT Security: In Industry 4.0, the company will be connected with/to the internet not just at an operational or higher level. As part of the Internet of things and services, the production level/production floor, maybe even the control level of several machines themselves, as well as all levels up to the strategic level of companies will be connected through a continuous link to the internet. For this reason, IT security will be a major challenge for establishing different kinds of IT systems. Here, IT security is defined as adequate protection of all information available in form of electronic data. In addition, it must be ensured that the IT systems themselves and their services are available at all times for the users and work properly [34, 35].

4.2   Components of SIMMI 4.0

Depending on its aims and strategic positions as well as on its arrangements in terms of Industry 4.0, not every company needs to fully implement all the dimensions of SIMMI 4.0. There are several gradations per dimension, which in turn result in different stages within the maturity model. These dimensions can have different characteristics in terms of scope and intensity for each company. Therefore, Table 2 in the Appendix gives a summary of our proposal for SIMMI 4.0. In the following chapters, the dimensions and stages of SIMMI 4.0 are described in detail.

Dimensions of SIMMI 4.0

Several dimensions of the development of SIMMI 4.0 are deduced from the requirements from our literature analysis. With these dimensions, SIMMI 4.0 can enable a company to assess its IT system landscape.

Dimension – Vertical Integration: This dimension focuses on the components of the lowest level of an enterprise, where different physical things ((semi-) products, machines, etc.) need to exchange information throughout the level itself and with the levels above. The most important criterion here is that this exchange is possible in both directions.

Dimension – Horizontal Integration: Industry 4.0 requires horizontal integration across the different value networks. Accordingly, an essential criterion has emerged from the requirements above. An automated and integrated information flow is necessary along the horizontal enterprise level as well as beyond the enterprise borders. Without this information flow, a business-wide value network is not realizable, meaning that the various enterprise systems of the different partners in the supply chain and in the value networks require interoperability at the data level. Therefore, a continuous and consistent information flow is needed [36, 37].

Dimension – Digital Product Development: For the engineering's digital continuity it is especially important that each process step is represented digitally. For this purpose, at least one enterprise system should be integrated into each respective process step. In addition, the resulting data and information of each step must be forwarded to the next and previous step/enterprise system.

Dimension – Cross-Sectional Technology Criteria: This dimension focuses on assessing the extent to which technologies are used across all different fields of Industry 4.0. Based on the requirements, the respective fields are: Service-oriented architecture, Cloud computing, Big Data, and IT Security. In addition, the level of support that enterprise systems can provide for these fields should be evaluated in this dimension.

Stages of SIMMI 4.0

SIMMI 4.0 is divided into five stages. This five-stage division is justified by the fact that in the middle of this stage-model, in the third stage, the implementation of an intelligent factory (Smart factory) is completed. This foundation for Industry 4.0 should be and must be implemented in each company before stable, robust, and versatile value networks can be realized. By implementing an intelligent factory, a company can gain operating experience and test technology before the company and its systems are connected to other companies [36]. Key activities for each stage, which must be conducted in order to be able to achieve a higher stage, are briefly specified.

Stage 1 – Basic Digitization Level: The company has not addressed Industry 4.0. Requirements are not or only partially met.

The enterprise systems along the enterprise's value chain support only their respective fields of activity. When integration is achieved, it is with specially implemented and complex interfaces. In addition, the processes are not or are only partially digitized. Product prototypes are designed in a costly way because of product development activities are not digitized. The company does not pursue service-oriented and cloud-based approaches.

The data of the enterprise systems are aggregated only for strategic decisions. In addition, the confidentiality of the data is not provided. The company's data is not protected against industrial espionage for example, incurring enormous damage annually. Anytime and continuous availability of data is not ensured. Sometimes, users cannot receive the data when they request it or access is not provided.

Activities:

- Start of engagement with focus on Industry 4.0
- First explorations of service-oriented approaches

Stage 2 – Cross-Departmental Digitization: The company is actively engaged with Industry 4.0 topics. Digitization has been implemented across departments, and the first Industry 4.0 requirements have been implemented throughout the company.

Information can be (partially) exchanged automatically among different departments and business areas. This level of integration no longer contains data islands within the company. In addition, several production plants are connected but instead through cloud solutions they are connected through the exchange of information in other ways (paper-based, email, FTP, etc.).

Production and product development is supported by several enterprise systems. However, data and information exchange is not automatized. Therefore, the previous and following steps are not optimized. The company starts to implement an SOA. Legacy systems are broken down, and their functionalities are encapsulated into services. New systems are implemented directly following the SOA principles. Thus, initial processes can be built as services. In addition, an enterprise service bus (ESB) is implemented to replace enterprise application integration principles and to enable direct connection between new systems.

Activities:

- Implementing an SOA
- Achieving cross-departmental integration
- First approaches for an IT security model
- First developments of mobile applications

Stage 3 – Horizontal and Vertical Digitization: The company is horizontally and vertically digitized. The requirements of Industry 4.0 have been implemented within the company, and information flows have been automated. The product development is consistently supported by enterprise systems. Information from the respective process steps can be forwarded to the next or previous process step.

The company has established an SOA. All the functionalities of the integrated systems are provided as services. The (semi-) products are part of this SOA and provide services themselves.

To exchange information within the enterprise, cloud principles are applied. Services are available company-wide and can be accessed anywhere. Employees are able to retrieve information everywhere through mobile devices. In addition, machines and (semi-) products are displayed on the mobile devices as soon as they come into the device's range. With this feature, the devices can display additional information about the machines (e.g., current processing step, maintenance status, etc.).

Various data from the production plants will be aggregated and processed together. Using this data and information gained from production, production itself can be optimized in real time and can be adapted to prevailing or changing conditions when necessary.

IT security is increased through the use of an advanced security model. Access to data is continuously protected, and data is transmitted in an encrypted state within the enterprise. The data's confidentiality, availability, and integrity are completely guaranteed.

Activities:

- Connection with other companies to build value networks
- Development of a cloud-based platform to offer services across the company borders

Stage 4 – Full Digitization: The company has been completely digitized, even beyond corporate borders, and integrated into value networks. Industry 4.0 approaches are actively followed and anchored within the corporate strategy.

Consequently, the level of integration can be described as enterprise-wide and cross-corporate horizontal and vertical integration. In order to optimize processes, the product development steps automatically pass information to previous and following production steps.

The company has established a service-oriented and cloud-based platform that offers services in the value network in order to exchange information along the supply chain in real time. Machines can be maintained globally, regardless of their location (in terms of their software). Data is aggregated and processed company-wide as well as provided via entire value networks. The production floor in general is at a highly optimized level.

In addition to enterprise-wide data encryption, encryption is also used within the value networks. Users can access data anywhere by using established authentication measures.

Activities:

- Beginning collaborations with companies within the value networks for end-to-end solutions and the optimization of information flows

Stage 5 – Optimized Full Digitization: The company is a showcase for Industry 4.0 activities. It collaborates strongly with its business partners and therefore optimizes its value networks. Through these collaborations, new business models and new end-to-end solutions are developed and enabled. During this development process each step inside and outside the company is digitized.

Within the value networks physical value and information flows can also be represented digitally, so the entire added value can be simulated in real time. Thus, it is possible to automatically perform necessary adjustments for all companies of the value network.

Furthermore, the IT security adjusts promptly to new risks. Occurring security problems are immediately solved. Encryption is optimized in cooperation with the partners the along the value networks.

5   Summary and Future Aspects

The aim of this paper was to develop a maturity model for the classification of a company's IT system landscape in the context of the Industry 4.0 requirements. Through a systematic literature review, we could demonstrate that no maturity model currently exists that meets the needs of Industry 4.0 in terms of a company-wide and even a cross-corporate IT system landscape. However, due to the drastic changes produced by the digitalization of businesses and society itself, it becomes necessary for enterprises to assess their IT system landscape in a realistic way. Therefore, an easy-to-handle tool could provide adequate support for assessment.

With this in mind, we designed a new maturity model (SIMMI 4.0 – System Integration Maturity Model Industry 4.0) for assessing the readiness of a company's IT system landscape in terms of Industry 4.0. Therefore, we derived several Industry 4.0 requirements based on a second literature review and combined them with the results of our first literature review with a focus on existing maturity models. In general, our design process was conducted with reference to suggested procedure model of Becker et al. [26]. However, this design process is not described in detail in this paper but can be found in Leyh et al. [31].

Therefore, this paper presents the first version of our maturity model SIMMI 4.0. According to the procedure model of Becker et al. [26], the development of SIMMI 4.0 is currently in phase 4 (iterative model development). Thus, the model's development is not yet fully complete. The next iterations in phase 4 include:

- Conducting several expert interviews and model adjustments based on the interviews if necessary (2nd iteration);
- Group interviews with companies to test the model's practicability (3rd iteration).

After phase 4 is completed, evaluation of the maturity model will follow. These steps should be based on the concrete application of the model within several companies. The resulting design decisions based on the iteration steps, the transfer and evaluation in terms of the model's dimensions and stages, more detailed evaluation steps, and the model's scientific as well as practical contributions will be addressed in subsequent papers.

Beyond the development of SIMMI 4.0 (here primarily based on the literature review in Sect. 2, the comparison of existing maturity models), we identified additional links and needs for further research For example, some maturity models already exist for the field of Industry 4.0 that deal with organizational aspects [38] or system-specific aspects in detail [39]. A mapping of these maturity models would be necessary to combine their different points of view. For example, different maturity level assignments and dimensions between these models should be developed to enable companies to fully classify themselves in terms of Industry 4.0 requirements in all levels of their enterprise. With this work, companies would be able to determine their overall maturity in the field of Industry 4.0.

A further aspect to investigate in the future is the data quality within various enterprise systems along the supply chain. Since companies in an Industry 4.0 environment must exchange data in large amounts and on an automated basis, a certain data quality is necessary to ensure efficient company-wide and cross-corporate business processes. Therefore, those companies should implement adequate master data management and data quality management. On this topic, two questions arise: (1) What design elements and components should be part of master data management and data quality management in the context of Industry 4.0? (2) How can master data management be integrated in maturity models addressing the IT systems landscape of Industry 4.0 companies? We will address those two questions in further research projects.

To conclude this contribution, some limitations must be recognized. Currently, SIMMI 4.0 has not been evaluated or tested. It is a maturity model that was derived from the literature by combining aspects of IT-related maturity models with Industry 4.0 requirements. In this respect, the development process of SIMMI 4.0 must continue. In the next iteration steps, we will clarify and review the model's components based on expert and company assessment. Additionally, SIMMI 4.0 must prove its practicability and usefulness in an enterprise environment. Therefore, we will address both aspects of the model's limitations in our research project's future steps focusing the field of Industry 4.0.

Appendix

Tables 1 and 2.

Table 1. Example of a categorized maturity model (see [17]) according to our classification scheme

#	Attribute	Description
A1	**Paper title**	**SME Maturity, Requirement for Interoperability**
A2	**Year of publication**	2008
A3	**Country**	Spain
A4	**Summary**	The paper presents an implementation strategy for interoperability in the SME context (small and medium-sized enterprises). The strategy consists of: (a) an improvement cycle for establishing and for ensuring an interoperable state; (b) a maturity model for the classification of interoperability based on best practices; (c) an evaluation method to measure interoperability.

(continued)

Table 1. (*continued*)

#	Attribute	Description
A5	**Name of the maturity model**	No name specified
A6	**Industry sector/Field of application**	Spanning various classes of business
A7	**Company size**	Small and medium-sized enterprises (SMEs) → up to 250 employees and up to 50 million Euro turnaround per year
A8	**Artifacts**	Improvement cycle, Interoperability maturity model, Assessment method
A9	**Stages of maturity**	5 Stages: (1) Initial; (2) Performed; (3) Modeled; (4) Integrated; (5) Interoperable
A10	**Relevance and definition of the problem**	Development of a practicable and useable maturity model for SMEs
A11	**Comparison of existing maturity models**	• Capability Maturity Model Integration (CMMI); • Software Process Improvement and Capability Determination (SPICE); • Service-Oriented Architecture Maturity Model (SOA MM); Extended Enterprise Architecture Maturity Model; • Organizational Interoperability Maturity Model; • Levels of Information Systems Interoperability; • European Interoperability Framework; • Malcolm Baldridge National Quality Award (MBNQA); • European Foundation for Quality Management (EFQM); • ISO 9000; • Six Sigma
A12	**Defining the development strategy**	Combining multiple models to one maturity model
A13	**Iterative maturity model development**	One improvement cycle was performed
A14	**Evaluation**	An evaluation was conducted as case study within a medium-sized door manufacturer. Objectives of the case study: Testing the maturity model, its application and its classification approach, especially with an SME focus Getting know to interoperability limits regarding IT systems, technical aspects and organizational issues between customers and suppliers
A15	**Further research needs**	No information provided

Table 2. Overview of SIMMI 4.0

Dimension vertical integration	Dimension horizontal integration	Dimension digital product development	Dimension cross-sectional technology criteria
Stage 5 – Optimized full digitization			
The company is a showcase for Industry 4.0 activities. It collaborates strongly with its business partners and therefore optimizes its value networks			
Continuous cross-corporate integration that is constantly optimized	Continuous cross-corporate integration and collaboration in value networks	Product development is processed digitally inside and outside the company (digitized end-to-end solution)	Simulation and optimization of value and information flows in real-time within the value network. IT security adjusts promptly to new risks. Occurring security problems are immediately solved. Encryption is optimized along the value networks
Stage 4 – Full digitization			
The company is completely digitized even beyond corporate borders and integrated into value networks. Industry 4.0 approaches are actively followed and anchored within the corporate strategy			
Continuous cross-corporate integration	Continuous cross-corporate integration in value networks	Product development information are digitally forwarded	Service-oriented cloud-based platform. Services are offered for the partners in the value networks. Information and data are exchanged in real-time along the supply chain. Optimization of the entire production through Big Data solutions. Access to data is protected. Cross-corporate encryption of data and authentication for global access
Stage 3 – Horizontal and vertical digitization			
The company is horizontally and vertically digitized. Requirements of Industry 4.0 have been implemented within the company, and information flows have been automated			
Complete internal/enterprise-wide integration of all enterprise systems and machines	Complete internal/enterprise-wide integration of all enterprise systems and machines	Product development is continuously digitally supported	SOA has been established. All functions are provided as services. (Semi-) products and their functionalities are available as services. To exchange information within the enterprise, cloud principles are applied. Production is adjusted and optimized in real-time. IT security is increased through the use of an advanced security model. Access to data is continuously protected, and data is transmitted in an encrypted state within the enterprise

(*continued*)

Table 2. (*continued*)

Dimension vertical integration	Dimension horizontal integration	Dimension digital product development	Dimension cross-sectional technology criteria
Stage 2 – Cross-departmental digitization The company is actively engaged with Industry 4.0 topics. Digitization is implemented across departments and first Industry 4.0 requirements are implemented throughout the company			
Cross-departmental integration	Cross-departmental integration	Production and product development is supported by several enterprise systems. Data and information exchange is not automatized	Implementation of first services (SOA with an enterprise service bus (ESB)). First experience with Big Data and its applications. Development of the first IT security models
Stage 1 – Basic digitization level The company has not addressed Industry 4.0. Requirements are not or only partially met			
Integration of enterprise systems only departmental-specific. The enterprise systems along the enterprise's value chain support only their respective fields of activity	Integration of enterprise systems only departmental-specific. The enterprise systems along the enterprise's value chain support only their respective fields of activity	Product development is not digitally supported	No service-oriented or cloud-based approaches. Data and information flows are not used for product improvement/optimization. Confidentiality, availability and integrity of the data are not guaranteed

References

1. Pagani, M.: Digital business strategy and value creation: framing the dynamic cycle of control points. MIS Q. **37**(2), 617–632 (2013)
2. Sambamurthy, V., Bharadwaj, A., Grover, V.: Shaping agility throug digital options: reconceptualizing the role of information technology in contemporary firms. MIS Q. **27**(2), 237–263 (2003)
3. Straub, D., Watson, R.: Transformational issues in researching is and net-enabled organizations. Inf. Syst. Res. **12**(4), 337–345 (2001)
4. Wheeler, B.: NEBIC: a dynamic capabilities theory for assessing net-enablement. Inf. Syst. Res. **13**(2), 125–146 (2002)
5. Bitran, G.R., Gurumurthi, S., Sam, S.L.: The need for third-party coordination in supply chain governance. MIT Sloan Manag. Rev. **48**(3), 30–37 (2007)
6. Schlick, J., Stephan, P., Loskyll, M., Lappe, D.: Industrie 4.0 in der praktischen Anwendung. In: Bauernhansl, T., ten Hompel, M., Vogel-Heuser, B. (eds.) Industrie 4.0 in der Produktion, Automatisierung und Logistik, pp. 56–84. Springer, Wiesbaden (2014)
7. El Sawy, O.A., Malhotra, A., Park, Y., Pavlou, P.A.: Seeking the configurations of digital ecodynamics: it takes three to tango. Inf. Syst. Res. **21**(4), 835–848 (2010)
8. Keen, P., Williams, R.: Value architectures for digital business: beyond the business model. MIS Q. **37**(2), 643–647 (2013)
9. Beckmann, H., Schäffer, T.: ERP-Studie. Erfolgsfaktoren für die Integration von Unternehmenssoftware in die Unternehmens-IT. Steinbeis-Edition (Schriftenreihe Wirtschaftsinformatik), Stuttgart (2014)

10. Schäffer, T., Beckmann, H.: Trendstudie Stammdatenqualität 2013: Erhebung der aktuellen Situation zur Stammdatenqualität in Unternehmen und daraus abgeleitete Trends. Steinbeis-Edition (Schriftenreihe Wirtschaftsinformatik), Stuttgart (2014)

11. BDI, Roland Berger: Die Digitale Transformation der Industrie Eine europäische Studie von Roland Berger Strategy Consultants im Auftrag des BDI (2015). http://www.bdi.eu/download_content/InformationUndTelekommunikation/Digitale_Transformation.pdf. Accessed 3 Nov 2015

12. Leyh, C., Bley, K., Schäffer, T.: Digitization of german enterprises in the production sector – do they know how "digitized" they are? In: Proceedings of the Americas Conferenence on Information Systems, AMCIS 2016, 11–14 August, San Diego, USA (2016)

13. Leyh, C., Schäffer, T., Bley, K.: SIMMI 4.0 – a maturity model for classifying the enterprise-wide IT and software landscape focusing on industry 4.0. In: Proceedings of the 2016 Federated Conference on Computer Science and Information Systems, FedCSIS 2016, 11–14 September, Gdansk, Poland (2016)

14. Kagermann, H., Wahlster, W., Helbig, H.: Umsetzungsempfehlungen für das Zukunftsprojekt Industrie 4.0. Abschlussbericht des Arbeitskreises Industrie 4.0. Frankfurt am Main (2013)

15. Lemke, C., Brenner, W.: Einführung in die Wirtschaftsinformatik: Band 1: Verstehen des digitalen Zeitalters. Springer, Heidelberg (2014)

16. Wendler, R.: The maturity of maturity model research: a systematic mapping study. Inf. Softw. Technol. **54**(12), 1317–1339 (2012)

17. Benguria, G., Santos, I.: SME maturity, requirement for interoperability. In: Mertins, K., Popplewell, K., Ruggaber, R., Xiaofei, X. (eds.) Enterprise Interoperability I - New Challenges and Industrial Approaches, pp. 29–40. Springer, London (2008)

18. Vom Brocke, J., Simons, A., Niehaves, B., Riemer, K., Plattfaut, R., Cleven, A., et al.: Reconstructing the giant: on the importance of rigour in documenting the literature search process. In: Proceedings of the European Conference on Information Systems, ECIS 2009, Verona, Italy (2009)

19. Kasunic, M., Anderson, W.: Measuring Systems Interoperability: Challenges and Opportunities. Software Engineering Measurement and Analysis Initiative. Carnegie Mellon University (2004)

20. Söderström, E., Meier, F.: Combined SOA maturity model (CSOAMM): towards a guide for SOA adoption. In: Enterprise Interoperability II, pp. 389–400. Springer, London (2007)

21. Guédria, W., Chen, D., Naudet, Y.: A maturity model for enterprise interoperability. In: Meersman, R., Herrero, P., Dillon, T. (eds.) OTM 2009. LNCS, vol. 5872, pp. 216–225. Springer, Heidelberg (2009). doi:10.1007/978-3-642-05290-3_32

22. Paulk, M.: Capability Maturity Model for Software. Wiley Online Library, Hoboken (1993)

23. Paulk, M.C.: How ISO 9001 compares with the CMM. IEEE Softw. **12**(1), 74 (1995)

24. CMMI Product Team: CMMI for Development, version 1.2 - Improving processes for better products. Carnegie Mellon University (2006)

25. Sonic Software: A new Service-Oriented Architecture (SOA) Maturity Model. Sonic Software Corporation, AmberPoint Inc., BearingPoint, Inc., Systinet Corporation (2005). http://www.omg.org/soa/UploadedDocs/SOA/SOA_Maturity.pdf. Accessed 10 Jan 2016

26. Becker, J., Knackstedt, R., Pöppelbuß, D.-W.I.J.: Entwicklung von Reifegradmodellen für das IT-Management. Wirtschaftsinformatik **51**(3), 249–260 (2009)

27. De Bruin, T., Freeze, R., Kaulkarni, U., Rosemann, M.: Understanding the main phases of developing a maturity assessment model. In: Proceedings of 16th Australasian Conference on Information Systems, ACIS 2005 (2005)

28. Hevner, A., March, S.T., Park, J., Ram, S.: Design science in information systems research. MIS Q. **28**(1), 75–105 (2004)

29. Boehm, M., Jasper, M., Thomas, O.: Das Further Education Maturity Model: Entwicklung und Implementierung eines Reifegradmodells zur Auswahl von Weiterbildungsveranstaltungen im Bereich IT-Management und-Consulting. In: Thomas, O. (ed.) Living Lab Business Process Management Research Report, Nr. 6. Osnabrück (2013)
30. Hecht, S.: Ein Reifegradmodell für die Bewertung und Verbesserung von Fähigkeiten im ERP-Anwendungsmanagement. Springer, Heidelberg (2014)
31. Leyh, C., Schäffer, T., Forstenhäusler, S.: SIMMI 4.0 – Vorschlag eines Reifegradmodells zur Klassifikation der unternehmensweiten Anwendungssystemlandschaft mit Fokus Industrie 4.0. In: Proceedings zur Multikonferenz Wirtschaftsinformatik (MKWI), pp. 1651–1662 (2016)
32. Industrie 4.0: Industrie 4.0 – Whitepaper FuE-Themen, Veröffentlichung der Plattform Industrie 4.0 in Zusammenarbeit mit dem Wissenschaftlichen Beirat (2015)
33. Schöning, H., Dorchhain, M.: Data mining und analyse. In: Bauernhansl, T., Ten Hompel, M., Vogel-Heuser, B. (eds.) Industrie 4.0 in Produktion, Automatisierung und Logistik: Anwendung Technologien Migrationen, pp. 543–554. Springer, Wiesbaden (2014)
34. Kappes, M.: Netzwerk-und Datensicherheit: Eine praktische Einführung. Springer, Wiesbaden (2013)
35. Krcmar, H.: Einführung in das Informationsmanagement. Springer, Heidelberg (2015)
36. Forstner, L., Dümmler, M.: Integrierte Wertschöpfungsnetzwerke-Chancen und Potenziale durch Industrie 4.0. e i. Elektrotechnik und Informationstechnik **131**(7), 199–201 (2014)
37. Wegener, D.: Industrie 4.0 – Chancen und Herausforderungen für einen Global Player. In: Bauernhansl, T., Ten Hompel, M., Vogel-Heuser, B. (eds.) Industrie 4.0 in der Produktion, Automatisierung und Logistik, pp. 343–358. Springer, Wiesbaden (2014)
38. Kaufmann, T.: Geschäftsmodelle in Industrie 4.0 und dem Internet der Dinge: der Weg vom Anspruch in die Wirklichkeit. Springer, Wiesbaden (2015)
39. BMWi: Erschliessen der Potenziale der Anwendung von "Industrie 4.0" im Mittelstand. Studie im Auftrag des Bundesministerium für Wirtschaft und Energie (BMWi). agiplan GmbH, Mülheim an der Ruhr, Germany (2015)

The Role of ICT Solutions in the Intelligent Enterprise Performance

Monika Łobaziewicz[(✉)]

Faculty of Management, Lublin University of Technology,
Nadbystrzycka 38, Lublin, Poland
ml@un.pl

Abstract. During the last years the number of innovative ICT systems, applications and tools has been growing still to support business performance. However, advanced ICT solutions are only means to the end of better process performance, not a substitute for it. Intelligent enterprises that are knowledge – driven organizations running their activity in increasingly dynamic, complex and uncertain environment. The aim of paper is the discussion about the wide spectrum of ICT solutions used by the intelligent enterprise and their meaning in the management of intelligent organization. The study results show that ICT drivers empowering the intelligent enterprise are: mobile workforce integration and management, smart virtual workplace, e- collaboration tools, business flexibility and prediction, scalability and customization, learning machines and systems, business continuity management, converting data into business intelligence. This is one of the first approach in this case that the author is going to continue in the advanced research.

Keywords: Intelligent enterprise · ICT · Enterprise management · Intelligent enterprise business model

1 Introduction

Undoubtedly, an intelligent enterprise has a high abilities to learn from experience, adapt to new situations, understand and handle abstract concepts, and use knowledge to impact on the business environment. Problem solving, comprehending complex ideas, learning quickly, and learning from experience are crucial for the intelligent enterprise. Companies today are looking to boost operational productivity and performance while addressing the full range of information requirements throughout the extended enterprise. In this case, the intelligence in the enterprise management is more than just delivering reports only from a data warehouse. It's about providing large numbers of people – executives, analysts, customers, business partners, and everyone else – secure and simple access to the right information, just in time so they can satisfy their unique reporting or analysis requirements to create a high added value.

The intelligent enterprise provides information for service-oriented purposes and for optimizing operational systems. It can be intelligent in two ways:

- it can behave intelligently or/and can "utilize" intelligence;
- it needs to maximize the extend and utility of its intellectual capital.

© Springer International Publishing AG 2017
E. Ziemba (Ed.): AITM 2016/ISM 2016, LNBIP 277, pp. 120–136, 2017.
DOI: 10.1007/978-3-319-53076-5_7

The intelligent enterprise is an organization which acts effectively in the present and is capable of dealing effectively with the challenges of the future. It meets its objectives both of the enterprise itself and those of its stakeholders and makes trade – offs between them.

Because, today it is difficult to run the business performance without the use of advanced IT systems, applications, tools – the question concerning the differences between intelligent and traditional enterprise appears.

The aim of paper is the discussion about the wide spectrum of ICT solutions used in the intelligent enterprise and their meaning in the management of intelligent organization. This is one of the first approach in this case that the author is going to continue in the advanced research.

The paper is structured as follows. Section 1 is an introduction to the subject. Section 2 explains a theoretical background of an intelligent enterprise. Section 3 presents a research review of the intelligent enterprise. Section 4 is a review of intelligent enterprise business models and presents its results as the conception of an intelligent enterprise integrated model. Section 5 presents a discussion of findings.

2   Intelligent Enterprise in the Literature Review

The concept of an intelligent enterprise has its source particularly in a few ideas: an organisation based on knowledge and information management, a self - learning organization, an organisation based on the intellectual capital.

The ideal intelligent enterprise is able to self-organizing, dynamically interacting with a distributed network of stakeholders within and external to business partners. In this organization, the intelligence is measured by the scale of innovation, knowledge creation, and the ability to generate high flexible structures, learning from the collective intelligence of the enterprise as network [1].

On the other hand, Haeckel and Nolan present the another approach defining an intelligent enterprise as an organization based on the enterprise intelligence that means "the ability to deal with complexity, that is, its ability to capture, share, and extract meaning from marketplace signals" [2]. An organization's complexity is in turn a function of how many information sources it needs, how many business elements it must coordinate, and the number and type of relationships binding these elements. According to their analysis, the organization's 'intelligence quotient' is determined by three critical attributes: the ability to access knowledge and information (connecting); the ability to integrate and share information (sharing); and the ability to extract meaning from data (structuring). Connecting means that information sources and users are linked in such a way that accurate information can be captured and made available to the right users at the right time and place. Sharing means that people in the organization can share data, interpretations of the data, as well as their understanding of the core processes of the organization. Structuring means that insight or meaning is obtained by matching and relating information from multiple sources so that some form of pattern or trend emerges. Structuring is achieved by creating information about information, for instance, how data are organized, related and used.

The results of a literature surveys conduct that from the ICT point of view, the intelligent enterprise is correlated with following terms: business intelligence, artificial intelligence, enterprise intelligence systems. The concept of the 'intelligent enterprise' was first presented by Quinn as the enterprise depending more on the development and deployment of intellectual resources than on the management of physical and fiscal assets. Its functions are disaggregated into manageable intellectual clusters that Quinn calls 'service activities'. Information technology has made it possible to delegate and outsource many of these service activities to other organizations. Instead of focusing on products, the intelligent enterprise excels in a few core knowledge-based service activities critical to its customers and surrounds these with other activities necessary to defend the core. Then it uses advanced information, management, and intelligent systems to coordinate the many other diverse and often dispersed activity centers needed to fulfill customer needs that now it has a special meaning because of the use of advanced ICT solutions [3].

Ming and Feng [4], Hopkins, Lavalle, Balboni [5], Kruschwitz and Shockley [6], Dayani [7], Quinn [8], Stubbs [9], Tan and Cao [10, 11] note that the knowledge management, wireless networking technologies, mobile devices has prompted many modern enterprises to look for management information systems to remotely monitor and control of their company operations in order to increase their flexibility and competitiveness in the market. In other words, the intelligent enterprise operates with knowledge based technologies, especially on-line systems for remote work and activities improving the effectiveness of business processes and has important role in creating competitive advantage. Szczerbicki [12] notices that a modern intelligent enterprise is able to convert intellectual resources using ICT solutions to the end product with a high level of added value.

One should be pointed that now intelligent enterprises use in their business a hybrid approach rather than using a single intelligent system or application to do activities and to make decisions. Modern IT environment includes various interfaces and components completely Web-based and uses XML extensively which can work like shared platform to be accessed by multiple users and decision makers [13]. Enterprises operate on B2B platforms with'in built' EDI technologies that integrate ERP systems and special applications of business partners, use the workflow, CRM. All of them provide a lot of data and information in the integrated way. Thus, they act like knowledge management systems [14, 15]. Nowadays the main problem for the intelligent enterprise is not be the access to information but the ability to verify it and then to transform it into a useful operational and strategic resource, necessary to create a unique added value.

Enterprise management in the uncertain 'information-rich' environment requires great understanding of the role of information and human potential. To gain this understanding, the knowledge is required [16]. In the intelligent enterprise, employees know that ICT tools enable the knowledge sharing, not only fosters collaboration but also facilitates experience and knowledge discovery. Thannhuber [17] emphasizes that IT systems supported by knowledge and intelligence paired together allow to adapt dynamically the enterprise to its environment, provide the framework for making optimal decision. Moreover, the intelligent enterprise applies automated analytics on data generated by systems and applications to better understand what resources are being used, how well they should be used to support the business processes.

The intelligent enterprises create the high ability to measure past performance for the future purposes. ICT solutions deliver knowledge to the right people when and where it is needed, and keep in mind that timeliness is an issue.

According to Dayal [18] the intelligent enterprise is characterized by being able to adapt quickly to changes in its operating environment. It monitors not only its own business processes but its interactions with customers, partners, suppliers and collaborators, as well. The intelligent enterprise understands how the exchange of information among all business participants relates to its business objectives and it acts to control and optimize its operations to meet its business objectives. In this enterprise decisions are made quickly and accurately to modify business processes on the fly, dynamically allocate resources, or change business partners (e.g., suppliers, service providers) and partnerships (e.g., establish new service level agreements).

March and Olsen [19] believes that the intelligent enterprise is built on two fundamental processes: 'rational calculation,' and 'learning from experience'. Rational calculation is the choice of alternatives based on an evaluation of their expected consequences according to preferences. It looks ahead into the future to anticipate outcomes. Learning from experience is the choice of alternatives based on rules developed from an accumulation of past experience. It looks backwards at history to find guidance for future action.

To sum up, an intelligent company integrates "what's going on out there" with "how we do things around here", "present time" with "future time" using a power of knowledge and the intellectual capital supported by integrated tools based on ICT.

3 Research Review of the Intelligent Enterprise

The study show that there is a lack of advanced surveys devoted to the intelligent enterprises. Up to date, in Poland the only research concerning intelligent enterprises was carried out by Polish Agency for Enterprise Development (PARP) in 2010 on a group of 300 small and medium-sized enterprises [23]. One of the purpose of the research was finding an answer to a question what are the characteristics of the intelligent enterprise in Poland and whether they use ICT solutions more effectively than other organisations.

In the research carried out by PARP it was assumed that an intelligent organisation has following features:

- it has a long term strategy of development to achieve goals;
- it has an advanced human resources management (HRM) policy;
- it has a company website and intra network as well as it uses specialised ICT business management tools;
- it uses the knowledge management.

Surveys have shown that 26.5% of SMEs had a long term strategy, 31.6% had the HRM policy, 47% used developed ICT tools and 38% used the knowledge management. In contrast, 63% of big companies had both the strategy and the personnel management policy well developed. Therefore, the bigger organizations meet the criteria of intelligent organization to a larger extent than SMEs.

In Poland, intelligent organizations do not have a clear innovative profile yet established. Now, when the Operational Programme Intelligent Development 2014–2020 started, it is known that a type of innovation is not a factor differentiating companies in terms of their willingness to implement solutions typical for intelligent organizations. More often are process innovations (28%), organizational innovations (24%) and product innovations (21%). The tendency to introduce the solutions adequate for intelligent organizations to the business practice increases with the size of company turnover. From the business sector point of view, intelligent organisations have the biggest share among industrial companies (14%), as well as trade and service companies.

The research indicate then a stronger focus on technological development among intelligent organizations, their better adaptation to the challenges of the knowledge based economy, the speed of access to knowledge and the possibility of its use are key competitive factors.

Intelligent organizations in Poland more often use ICT solutions to support management processes in comparison with other organizations. The most popular are e-workflow, databases and data warehouses management (83%), as well as Intranet (76%). The further are Customer Relationship Management (twice more often than organizations that do not meet criteria for intelligent organizations) and solutions supporting a team working, every fifth - HRM and every sixth - Business Intelligence (three times more often than other organizations).

The last problem concerning ICT solutions that support the management of intelligent organizations is their effectiveness assessment. The few critical comments were focused on low efficiency of databases and data warehouses. Very positively were evaluated Supply Chain Management (78%) and Customer Relationship Management (70%). As far as the effectiveness of various ICT tools by intelligent organizations is concerned, it is worth to emphasize that generally ICT tools are assessed as less effective by small businesses than by middle sized and large. This is due to the specific nature of these tools, which do not necessarily have to be effective in organizations with a low developed organizational structure and not very complicated business processes.

In 2010 MIT Sloan Management Review and the IBM Institute for Business Value conducted a research among nearly 3,000 executives, managers and analysts working across more than 30 industries and involved intelligent organizations of various sizes in more than 100 countries. There were also interviewed academic experts and subject matter experts from a number of industries and disciplines to understand the practical issues facing intelligent organizations [24]. As a result, there are following results:

- Intelligent enterprise is focused on the highest value using each business opportunity, starting with questions, not data opposite to 'traditional' organizations. It should first define the insights and questions needed to meet the big business objective and then identify data needed for targets. They can target specific subject areas, and use readily available data in the initial analytic models;
- Intelligent enterprise drives actions and delivers value. This means that new methods and tools to embed information into business processes, ICT analytics solutions, optimization, workflows and simulations are making insights more understandable and actionable;

- Intelligent enterprise develops existing capabilities adding new ones. To do this, they use sophisticated modelling and visualization tools based on ICT, but that does not mean that spreadsheets and charts should go away. On the contrary, new tools should supplement earlier ones, or continue to be used side by side, as needed;
- Intelligent enterprise uses an information agenda to do plan for the future. Big data is getting bigger. Information is coming from interconnected supply chains today;
- In the intelligent enterprise strategic information arrives through unstructured digital channels: social media, smart phone applications and an ever-increasing stream of emerging Internet-based gadgets. The information agenda identifies foundational information practices and tools while aligning IT and business goals through enterprise information plans and financially justified deployment road maps. This agenda helps establish necessary links between those who drive the priorities of the organization by line of business and set the strategy, and those who manage data and information. A comprehensive agenda also enables managers to keep pace with changing business goals. It provides a vision and high-level road map for information that aligns business needs to growth.

In 2011 MIT Sloan Management Review and the IBM Institute for Business Value conducted the next edition of the research among nearly 4,000 executives [6]. The aim of the research was the inquiry how intelligent organizations turning data and analytics into competitive advantage. As a result, there are following conclusions:

- Access to data requires improvement. Only 10% of managers have access to a good quality of data and information. The majority are not satisfied with their information access or they have limited or no access to the data they need to do good their work;
- Intelligent enterprises are looking at the analytics as a tool of strategic decision making, not as the tactical activity. Employees are starting understand the value of using analytics for strategic decision making;
- Data consistency is a key in decision making. It is more important for managers to have uniformly consistent data quality across the organization, rather than perfect data from one business unit and poor quality from another;
- Leaders behaviours should be trustworthy. They should make fact-based decisions compatible with long-term strategy, share data across 'silos';
- Enterprises are still struggling to understand how to use analytics to improve business and processes. The problem is who owns the data and who has access to it;
- There are two challenges in using analytics effectively in the enterprise: integrating data across 'silos' and their right interpretation;
- Not only the innovation is important for intelligent enterprises but the growing revenue, penetrating new markets, acquiring new customers, as well. Therefore, primary business objectives have not changed despite of macro and microeconomic changes;
- Organizational and cultural challenges are twice more difficult as technological items. In a result, leaders have their work cut out of them and underscores the need to practice what they promise before the organization is able to use analytics most effectively.

Summing up, intelligent enterprises are combining the new systems and tools based on ICT with expertise in business process management. They are still learning how to extract the precise information they need – highly relevant and contextualized – and predict the most likely outcomes of key decisions and events. They are learning to shape their own futures.

4 Business Models Conceptions of the Intelligent Enterprise

4.1 A Review of Intelligent Enterprise Business Models

An enterprise model is a high-level map of a business that guides the conception of its activities. It is clear that managers should design a business which extends beyond procedural design. It includes making strategic decisions about what market signals should be sensed, what data should be used to interpret those signals, and how an appropriate response should be executed. As Haeckel and Nolan [2] emphasize, the enterprise model should be expressed in business language, not IT terminology that can be used a support tool. Management should select and use one business design language and insist on its use throughout the organization. In order to create a unified understanding of how we do things around here, and, if it makes strategic sense, to facilitate future integration of presently autonomous organizational units, a common business language is required.

The results of literature surveys conduct that there are very little discussion about business models of the intelligent enterprise. Most of the conceptions are related to business intelligence or knowledge management models. There are a few concepts presented as white papers or presentations exposed at IT conferences.

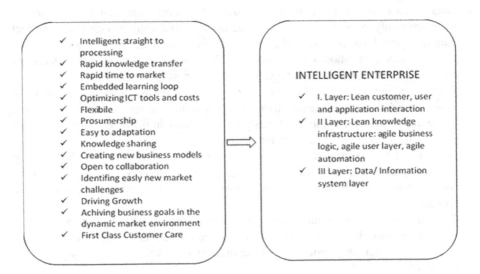

Fig. 1. Intelligent enterprise optimizing the knowledge driven organisation (Source: http:// knowledge-values.com/learning/#knowledge-academy/)

Professor Larry Lucardie [20] from Knowledge Value Institute defines the intelligent enterprise as lean, agile and learning, which a business model is based on the knowledge value (Fig. 1).

Andrew Coleman from IBM [21] notices that the business model of intelligent enterprise is based on prediction. The intelligent organisation is able to compare what is happening right now with past experience to predict the future so that it can anticipate the changes needed to proactively optimize the business. Therefore, the intelligent enterprise is a market game changer (Fig. 2).

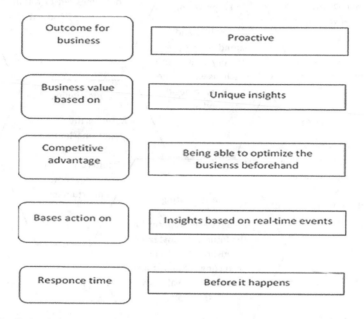

Fig. 2. Predictive intelligent enterprise model (Source: IBM Global Business Services, p. 2)

The research conducted by IBM in a group of 225 business leaders worldwide, show that enterprises are operating with bigger blind spots and that they are making important decisions without access to the right information. They recognize that new analytics, coupled with advanced business process management capabilities, signal a major opportunity to close gaps and create new business advantage. Those who have the vision to apply new approaches are building intelligent enterprises and will be ready to outperform their peers [21]. IBM have pointed the essential characteristics that describe an enterprise ready to exploit advanced analytics and optimized performance (Fig. 3).

In the digital world, success comes from speed, agility and integration. As the different sources present, the intelligent enterprise is digital- based oriented that finding entirely new ways to increase the value of every customer experience and business interaction (Fig. 4).

As Accenture Consulting research show for most companies in most industries, despite the level of their intelligence, cloud has created nearly as many complications as

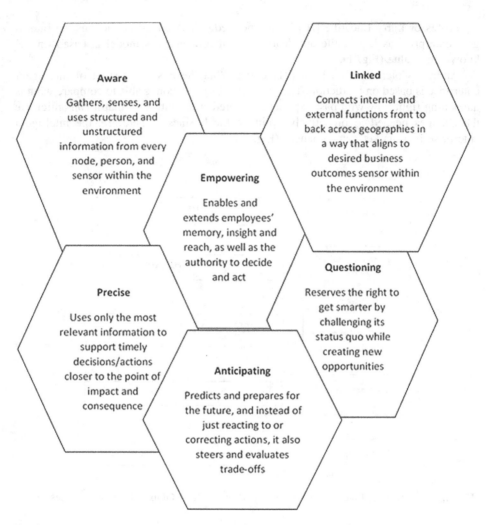

Fig. 3. Characteristics of the intelligent enterprise in IBM conception (Source: IBM Global Business Services, p. 7)

it has provided solutions. Many companies, including intelligent enterprises, are afraid of their data security. There are no automated processes to move application workloads easily among those instances of cloud. Moreover, the enterprises struggle to cope with the myriad security and privacy issues that continue to complicate cloud [22].

4.2   Conception of Integrated Intelligent Enterprise Model

As a result of the business models of intelligent enterprise analysis, one should be noticed that intelligent enterprises opposite to traditional organizations are able to

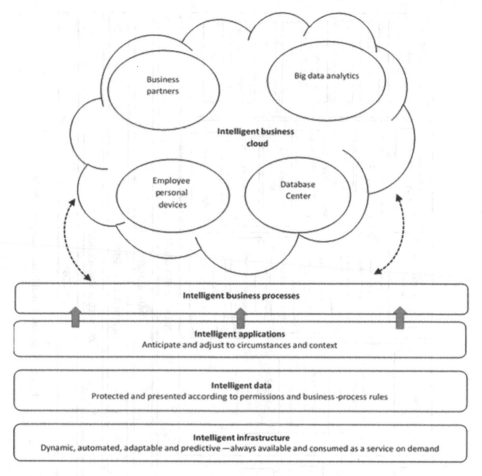

Fig. 4. Intelligent digital business (Source: Accenture Realizing the potential of the intelligent business cloud, 2015. https://www.accenture.com/us-en/insight-intelligent-business-cloud)

integrate their strategy and the knowledge management with IT systems, applications and tools (Fig. 5).

Intelligent enterprises operate in increasingly complex IT systems what is the result of business processes complexity. Autonomous subsystems are still be interrelated and embedded in larger systems.

Building the business model of the intelligent enterprise provides for a strategy and technology infrastructure that ensures that accurate and timely information is effectively incorporated into the decision making process so that the organizations can exploit this information through process, knowledge and visualization based technologies to manage their business effectively. Intelligent enterprises require an intelligent workforce and intelligent ICT tools and vice versa. The challenge is the ability to integrate them to achieve the strategic market position and to create the high added value for all groups of interests.

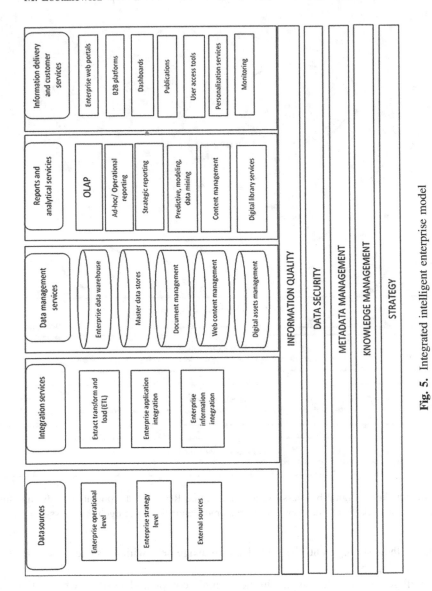

Fig. 5. Integrated intelligent enterprise model

5   ICT Drivers Empowering the Intelligent Enterprise Performance

The results of theoretical study and the research conducted by PARP, MIT Sloan Management Review, IBM Institute for Business Value and Accenture Corporate became the background to develop a scientific discussion about the intelligent enterprise and the role of ICT in this organization. Taking into account the wide spectrum of ICT solutions used in the intelligent enterprise management, there are some ICT drivers.

Mobile Workforce Integration and Management The access to professional knowledge is critical in the intelligent enterprises and mobile connections to operating systems, applications, platforms are important, especially in the fast – paced business environment. Mobile technologies drive technical innovation to improve networks, ensure employees remain fully integrated with their company and clients wherever they are. Thus, in the intelligent organization its coherency is determined by the intelligence of its network that becomes the organization with wireless tentacles spreading from it to embrace location-aware services.

The next aspect is mobile workforce management software that helps standardize tasks, it guides employees through each step in business processes, it supports a remote supervision. Decreasing the time it takes employees to become more productive. It is also an opportunity to implement new technologies that capture the best of the past while building value for the future. When different work groups have different mobile workforce management solutions, it is virtually impossible to optimize resources and processes across the enterprise.

Smart Virtual Workplace Gartner [25] notes the top 12 emerging digital workplace technologies:

- Ambient knowledge: natural language processing and machine learning will help organizations extract information from a wide array of employee sources to gather valuable knowledge;
- Read analytics: the democratization of big data analytics where dashboards and analytics functions are pushed down into the employee community to drive better, data-driven decisions;
- Production studio: organizations can seize the opportunity to create multimedia tools and production hubs for employees to bring these rich media types to their work environments;
- Immersive technology: enterprises can use technology that blurs the line between the physical world and digital world to create a sense of immersion such as video conferencing with gesture control or use of augmented reality or virtual reality technologies for simulated training situations;
- Office landscape: as more employees work remotely, enterprises can develop complex scheduling software to manage office hoteling and develop a physical environment that is optimized for employee engagement, such as advantageous collaboration spaces;
- Personal IoT: workplaces can take advantage of their employees' personal networks of beacons and sensors for scenarios such as smart badges, that show contextual digital signs; or the ability to identify people when they approach a building to schedule meeting rooms, assign desks, and order meals;
- 'Silo buster': organizations should take advantage of collaborative tools to drive ideation, crowdsourcing, etc. beyond traditional teams and organizations structures;

- Virtual personal assistants (VPA): it will perform a variety of personal tasks, eventually learning from individuals to act on their behalf;
- Personal cloud: employees in the future may bring their own personal collections of internet apps and services to use for both personal and professional purposes;
- Hackers bench: with new codeless programming tools, employees can develop and integrate their own applications. IT can lead this effort by creating a sandbox, base guidelines and communities, and provide lightweight support;
- Omni-Comms: employees will benefit from a fully mobile suite of communication and collaboration services that will be embedded in business processes;
- Organization digital university: this type of educational program will help employees acquire a wide variety of digital literacies with alternative learning methods.

As the approaches to virtualization of IT infrastructure, networks and storage devices continue to mature, infrastructures become software-driven. Smart virtual workplace provides end to end desktop virtualization allowing employees to access applications, data safely over any network from the device of any choice. New trends show that business will increasingly turn to hybrid cloud solutions to enable scalable business processes. Hybrid clouds can quickly scale to a company's needs and services can be paid for as needed. They combine the best of two worlds, offering true benefits to intelligent enterprises aiming to stay ahead in their markets.

E- Collaboration Tools E-collaboration is the standard for business communication today, nearly eliminating the need to meet face to face. While knowledge sharing increases, formal and informal groups become e- collaborative communities to reach organizational goals. Intelligent enterprises continue to integrate these into their business processes and reinvent their customer engagement models.

In the intelligent enterprise ICT tools as B2B, B2C platforms, virtual clouds allow disparate teams to work together in real-time, enabling multiple individuals to interact as efficiently and effectively with co-workers, clients, and suppliers.

Business Flexibility and Prediction The intelligent enterprise can be called as the visionary, the designer of changes where the business flexibility and prediction are crucial. They must now be highly flexible and resilient in order to seamlessly communicate and interoperate with disparate technologies and systems. ICT solutions are very helpful in this case. Now, software is becoming increasingly predictive and cognitive. It can apply learnings from data to future situations. In essence, it is capable of experience. To capture the power and potential of software intelligence, intelligent companies will find new ways to get smart software out of the lab and into as many practical scenarios as possible. Only then will their software be able to spur innovation and raise the operating-performance bar across the organization.

Scalability and Customization Intelligent enterprises align their IT infrastructure capabilities with business requirements. Modularity of systems, applications allow companies to have only what is needed at present, trimming up-front costs and leaving open the possibility of expanding or incorporating new technologies in the future. With the increase of consolidation, intensive virtualization, the traditional data center will transform to the 'hyperscale' data center. It requires a fundamentally different approach than that taken with typical enterprise IT systems. Rather than building 'monolithic' platforms, distributed architecture design is implemented around distributed processing frameworks. That requires software and ICT tools that automate node deployment, recover from failure (rerouting of workloads), and other management and monitoring tools.

Learning Machines and Systems The intelligent enterprise is making its machines smarter, embedding software intelligence into every aspect of its business to drive new levels of operational efficiency, evolution, and innovation. For the intelligent enterprise a software intelligence is not a one-off project, but as an across-the-board functionality. One that will drive new levels of evolution and discovery, propelling innovation throughout the enterprise. Apttus' Louis Columbus from Microsoft [26] notes that one of the best ways to do that is through 'app-driven' intelligence and cognitive, predictive analytics. For example, Microsoft is going to bridge these divides by blending its Cognitive Services platform with the Cortana Intelligence Suite that combines information management and scale-out storage with machine-learning analytics and dashboard visualization to turn raw data into actionable intelligence. Columbus points on applying intelligent cloud techniques to automated Quote-to-Price service to provide more proactive support to contract lifecycle management.

Business Continuity Management It is obvious that intelligent companies need to have 24 h a day access to their data. Data digitalization and rapidity of their processing require more accurate, reliable and sophisticated ICT tools converting all data into intelligence for better business outcomes. On the other hand, managers need them to be not complicated in their use. Moreover, for a high level of operational uptime, infrastructure components must be fault tolerant with the ability to recover from complex failures and data storage must be secure. To ensure the effective business continuity management ISO 22301 standard can be very useful for the intelligent enterprise because it requires to:

- Identify and manage current and future threats to business;
- Take a proactive approach to minimizing the impact of incidents;
- Keep critical functions up and running during times of crises;
- Minimize downtime during incidents and improve recovery time;
- Demonstrate resilience to customers, suppliers and for tender requests.

Converting Data into Business Intelligence Advanced ICT solutions enable extracting from huge amounts of data collected from the real cyberspace. Intelligent enterprises are able to manage Big Data to drive better business processes, product development, and customer service. The important is the fact that they enable to use effectively unstructured data captured from different systems, mobile devices, social media, log files, emails to perform real-time context analytics to understand received information, its content to make right decisions in the right time.

Business intelligence helps enterprises to answer critical questions that drive performance. In an increasingly competitive market it is vital to have intelligent information, immediately available such as financial results, market analysis, and human resource costs and to also be able to identify obstructions in productivity and to pin-point opportunities. However, as businesses grow, this information becomes increasingly difficult to extract and the processes become more complex. Enterprises generate and store more data and there is a greater need for more specialized infrastructures using a variety of technology platforms.

Therefore, intelligent enterprises are not only the users of advanced tools based on ICT technologies to optimize business practices, drive workforce engagement and create a competitive edge, but they are also able to leverage and to create value from the date and information generating by ICT solutions.

6 Conclusions

Undoubtedly, the future ready business must develop the capacity to anticipate and address emergent employee, vendor, and customer needs proactively, and eliminate problems. Thus, the discussion about intelligent enterprise is at up to date in the digital world. There are more theoretical disputes then extended and deepened surveys in this case. There are no in depth research devoted business models of these organizations or effectiveness, strategy or management in this organizations, especially with use of ICT solutions.

In the paper, there were presented a few business models and surveys that can be the good start for the future research about intelligent enterprises. Poland is at the stage of an intensive investing in the research and development, therefore Polish companies are still learning how to create the intelligence and how to be intelligent organizations. This is especially a challenge for companies from the SMEs sector. The research conducted by MIT Sloan Management Review and the IBM Institute for Business Value show that for the intelligent enterprise, the new reality is this: personal experience and insight are no longer sufficient. New analytics capabilities are needed to make better decisions. Then, Accenture Consulting research present that the intelligent enterprise is digitally–based oriented.

On the base of the literature review and surveys conducted by global IT companies there were the conception of integrated intelligent enterprise model and ICT drivers empowering the intelligent enterprise presented. These are: mobile workforce integration and management, smart virtual workplace, e- collaboration tools, business flexibility and prediction, scalability and customization, learning machines and systems, business continuity management, converting data into business intelligence.

The above premises encourage the author to continue the scientific discussion about intelligent enterprise with a special attention to ICT solutions. The advanced research will be continued that the aim will be the creation of an intelligent enterprise model operating in the intelligent development based economy.

References

1. Jones, P.H., Christakis, A.N., Flanagan, T.R.: Dialogic design for the intelligent enterprise: collaborative strategy, process, and action. In: INCOSE International Symposium, San Diego, CA 2007, vol. 17, pp. 717–732 (2007). doi:10.1002/j.2334-5837.2007.tb02906.x
2. Haeckel, S., Nolan, R.: Managing by wire. Harvard Bus. Rev. **1993**, 122–132 (1993)
3. Quinn, J.B.: The intelligent enterprise: a new paradigm. Acad. Manag. Executive **6**(4), 48–63 (1992)
4. Ming, Y.H., Feng, D.X.: Research on the intelligent enterprise based on intelligent behavior. In: Proceedings of the 7th International Conference on Innovation and Management 2010, pp. 2094–2099 (2010)
5. Hopkins, M.S., Lavalle, S., Balboni, F.: 10 insights: a first look at the new intelligent enterprise survey. MIT Sloan Manag. Rev. **52**(1), 22–31 (2010)
6. Kruschwitz, N., Shockley, R.: First look: the second annual new intelligent enterprise survey. MIT Sloan Manag. Rev. **52**(4), 87–89 (2011)
7. Dayyani, B.: The intelligent enterprise: knowledge-driven category management. In: Proceedings of the 7th International Conference on Intellectual Capital, Knowledge Management and Organisational Learning, pp. 138–145 (2010)
8. Quinn, J.B.: The intelligent enterprise a new paradigm. Acad. Manag. Executive **19**(4), 109–121 (2005)
9. Stubbs, E.: The Intelligent Enterprise, pp. 79–93. Wiley, Indianapolis (2014)
10. Tan, B., Cao, X.W.: The intelligent enterprise and the changing role of computer information systems in strategic planning. Inf. Res. Manag. J. **4**(1), 21–29 (1991)
11. Tan, B., Cao, X.W., Ahpak, D.: Achieving competitive advantage through building an intelligent organization with technological innovation: the case of a chinese enterprise. In: Proceedings of 2010 International Conference on Innovation, Management and Service, pp. 24–29 (2010)
12. Szczerbicki, E.: Intelligent enterprise management. Cybernet. Syst. **32**(7), 697–699 (2001)
13. Wang, S.G., Liu, R., Liu, X.T.: An enterprise intelligent system development and solution framework. In: Proceedings of 8th International Conference on Electronic Measurement and Instruments, Icemi 2007, vol. Iv, pp. 115–118 (2007)
14. Gupta, J.N., Sharma, S.K.: Creating knowledge based organizations, IGI Global (2004)
15. Stonehouse, G.H., Pemberton, J.D.: Learning and knowledge management in the intelligent organisation. Int. J. Participation Empowerment **7**(5), 131–144 (1999)
16. Szczerbicki, E., Gomółka, Z.: Management of information in complex systems: perspectives for new millennium. In: Intelligent Processing and Manufacturing of Materials. Proceedings of the Second International Conference IPMM 1999, vol. 2, (1999). doi:10.1109/IPMM.1999.791491
17. Thannhuber, M.J.: The Intelligent Enterprise. Springer, Heidelberg (2005)
18. Dayal, U.: Managing the intelligent enterprise, e-commerce technology. In: IEEE Proceedings International Conference CEC (2004). doi:10.1109/ICECT.2004.1319711
19. March, J.G., Olsen, J.P.: Ambiguity and Choice in Organization. Universitesforlaget, Bergen (1979)
20. Knowledge Values. http://knowledge-values.com
21. IBM Institute for Business Value: Business analytics and optimization for the intelligent enterprise. IBM Global Business Services Executive Report. USA (2009)
22. Accenture realizing the potential of the intelligent business cloud (2015). https://www.accenture.com/us-en/insight-intelligent-business-cloud

23. Kordel, P., Kornecki, J., Pylak, K., Wiktorowicz, J., Kowalczyk, A., Krawczyk, K.: Inteligentne organizacje – zarządzanie wiedzą i kompetencjami pracowników. PARP, Warszawa (2010)
24. LaValle, S., Hopkins, E., Lesser, R., Shockley, M.S., Kruschwitz, N.: Big Data, analytics and the path from insights to value. Research Feature, December 2010
25. http://www.gartner.com/smarterwithgartner/top-12-emerging-digital-workplace-technologies/
26. Cole, A.: Defining the intelligent enterprise. IT Business Edge (2016). http://www.itbusinessedge.com/blogs/infrastructure/defining-the-intelligent-enterprise.html

Evaluation of User Specific Privacy Policy Architecture for Collaborative BPaaS on the Example of Logistics

Björn Schwarzbach[1(✉)], Michael Glöckner[1], Bogdan Franczyk[1,2],
and André Ludwig[3]

[1] Leipzig University, Leipzig, Germany
{schwarzbach,gloeckner,franczyk}@wifa.uni-leipzig.de
[2] Wrocław University of Economics, Wrocław, Poland
[3] Kühne Logistics University, Hamburg, Germany
andre-ludwig@the-klu.org

Abstract. Nowadays, collaboration between multiple companies along the supply chain is one of the key factors for ensuring sustainable success. Although this fact is known by almost all companies the actual collaboration is quite low because of the fear of losing sensitive and critical data to competitors. To solve this problem an architecture for modeling and execution of privacy preserved business processes and a privacy modeling approach have been developed. This paper evaluates both artifacts. The used method is framework for evaluation in design science (FEDS).

Keywords: Privacy · BPaaS · Evaluation · Cloud computing · XACML

1 Introduction

For many years, cloud computing has been very successful since it is being applied to an increasing number of use cases [1]. The most important key factors for this success are its dynamics, its decentralized nature, and the abstraction and outsourcing of physical IT systems. These factors make cloud computing indispensable for the logistics sector with its complex supply chains and collaborative processes. In the year 2008 Thomas J. Bittman, vice president of Gartner Research, published his thoughts on the future of Cloud Computing. He stated that there are three phases of Cloud Computing. While the first phase was focused on providing mostly infrastructure services with proprietary interfaces, the second phase introduced an ecosystem of smaller cloud providers offering services for the vertical supply chain based on the dominant providers of the first phase. During the third phase, these smaller providers form horizontal federations that lead to new interoperability standards of service communication.

The next logical phase is moving the management of collaborations into the Cloud. The stakeholders of the collaboration can not only access the information needed to operate their tasks but the services provided by the stakeholders can also be easily connected and combined with each other to form complex processes. Such a process consists of several IT services of different partners which interact with each other and

© Springer International Publishing AG 2017
E. Ziemba (Ed.): AITM 2016/ISM 2016, LNBIP 277, pp. 137–154, 2017.
DOI: 10.1007/978-3-319-53076-5_8

exchange data. While the process has a global scope, the individual services are executed by the partners' local control, namely the service providers. This is called collaborative Business Process as a Service. Due to the collaborative nature with multiple involved partners, privacy, security, and confidentiality related requirements gain more and more importance [2]. Cloud service providers have to ensure that data, which is generated by a cloud service, is treated confidentially and is only stored or transmitted to other services or providers accordingly to the service providers privacy policies [3]. Therefore, a centralized trusted platform is needed that copes with these tasks. Further, it has to provide interfaces that are able to regulate and control the data flow. In addition, this platform must provide the functionality to model and execute use-case and user-specific privacy policies.

The chaining of services in a collaborative business process and the therewith resulting data exchange have to be defined in detail and have to be monitored at any time. Only that way, a high level of privacy, security, and confidentiality can be ensured [4]. Not only does confidentiality of the data have to be ensured but also the access of each process partner to the appropriate data has to comply with a specific time- and role-dependent set of policies. In [5] an architecture of a platform that enables companies to consume cloud services of providers has been introduced. The platform offers features of a business process management system in terms of orchestrating individual cloud services in business processes that have been modeled by consumers, i.e. the companies. Hence, the term for this approach and the service provided by the platform is *Business Process as a Service* (BPaaS).

Especially for companies participating in collaborative business processes, privacy is a very important topic in terms of risk and compliance [6]. In an interview, we discovered that most of the companies that do not consume cloud services are reluctant because they are afraid of losing control of their data. This is becoming even more important because of recent hack attacks on global players. Also, companies that consume at least one cloud service are concerned because of privacy issues [7].

In order to encourage companies to participate in collaborative processes, one of the main challenges is the preservation of data privacy and the compliance with privacy laws during business process execution. This is getting even more important when multiple competitors are collaborating in one business process. These competitors need to share data that is usually kept secret with each other. In [2], we have proposed an approach for secure service interaction, which has shown its feasibility in multiple tests. The architecture proposed in [5] also provides a component to annotate business processes and individual activities with privacy policies. These are evaluated and enforced by the platform during business processes execution. This paper focuses on the evaluation of these two artifacts.

The paper is structured as follows: After this introduction, the architecture of the platform for privacy preserving collaborative BPaaS and the modeling approach for privacy policies in collaborative business processes are presented. The third section outlines the applied evaluation framework, while section four discusses the artifacts' evaluation and the resulting findings. The paper closes with a conclusion featuring limitations, implications, and an outlook on future research.

2   Theoretical Background

2.1   Architecture for Privacy Preserved Business Processes

In this section we propose an architecture consisting of a central platform, third party services, and gateways to enable secure communication between these components. This architecture is depicted in Fig. 1.

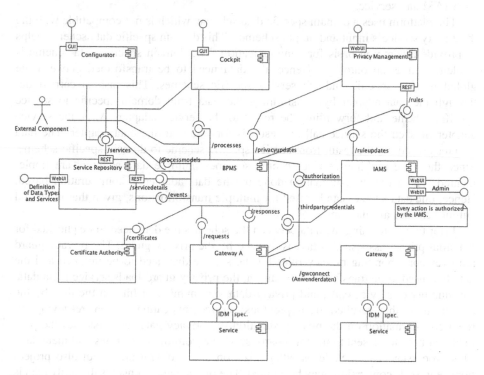

Fig. 1. Architecture of the platform and the gateways for privacy-preserving collaborative business processes

The platform comprises a user interface for the design of collaborative business processes. These collaborative business processes are composed of third party services. The third party service descriptions are stored in and managed by the service repository. The business process management system (BPMS) stores the business processes and provides features to instantiate and execute the processes. The user defines his privacy requirements in form of privacy rules with a set of privacy management tools. These privacy rules are used by the identity and access management system (IAMS) to determine whether an entity (e.g. user) is allowed to access an asset or not.

While executing a business process the BPMS has to invoke third party services. To ensure privacy during the service invocation and the whole business process we propose the use of gateways, which are similar to the proxies proposed by [8]. The core architecture of these gateways will be described in the following.

A gateway consists of four components that are organized as a stack. At the lower end of the stack the service adapter handles the current third party service consumption. To consume a third party service, the service adapter first requests authentication and authorization on behalf of the user of the platform by the service provider's identity and access management (IAM). The second step is to call the current service by using the interfaces provided by the service provider. To enable the gateway to handle multiple service providers there are multiple implementations of the service adapter, one for each IAM and service.

The platform uses a domain specific data scheme, which is not compatible with the third party service's input and output schemes. This domain specific data scheme helps to provide a common basis for communication. The domain specific data scheme is implemented as an ontology. Hence, the data need to be transformed between the global domain specific and the service specific schemes. This task is carried out through the data adapter by transforming the data from domain specific to service specific scheme and forwarding the result to the service adapter. After the service adapter finished the service call the result is forwarded to the data adapter. The data adapter transforms the result from service specific scheme to domain specific scheme. Since there are multiple service specific schemes multiple data adapters are implemented. The actual transformation done by the data adapter is configuration based. Hence, one data adapter can be used for multiple transformations, given that input and output schemes are the same.

Prior to transforming the data between the schemas the data need to be checked for potential privacy issues. This task is realized by the privacy guard. The privacy guard retrieves corresponding privacy rules for the service that need to be invoked and the data that need to be transferred. In addition, the privacy guard loads service meta data, e.g. number of service calls, and privacy data, e.g. number of hits on the data by the current user, that resulted from previous service invocations. After retrieving all required information on the privacy situation the privacy gateway processes the payload that need to be sent to the third party service according to the rules and meta data. This procession may include pseudonymization and anonymization, but also projections, e.g. scale conversion, may be applied. The privacy guard ensures that only data is transferred to the third party services that need to be transferred in order to fulfil the purpose of the current action of the business process. If the privacy guard is not able to apply all privacy rules an alert is raised in the cockpit and the business process is paused. This ensures that privacy is not violated at any time.

The communicator ensures that all payloads that need to be transferred between the actions of the business process, i.e. from one gateway to another, are encrypted with unique asymmetric keys. It also ensures that the payload of the services, both input and output data, is never loaded into the platform itself, neither encrypted nor unencrypted. The communicator's third task is to load privacy data and service meta data of the current service invocation into the platform to provide feedback for the next actions. This data is encrypted, too. To ensure that no data is kept in memory between two service invocations, gateways are for one time use only. Due to the gateway's modular structure it can be composed for different third party services and privacy rules. This ensures the maximal flexibility. Hence, the reusability, flexibility, easy adaptation and implementation are the key advantages of the gateways.

All the gateway components communicate with the neighbor units via encrypted web services. The encryption is based on a public key infrastructure (PKI) that is part of the platform. When the BPMS creates a gateway the PKI issues public and private keys to all four components. When a message reaches a component, the component checks the authenticity of the message and whether the sender is allowed to send this type of message, i.e. the sender is part of the same gateway and the component is the successor of the sender according. To enable the check of the gateway the issues keys will contain the ID of the gateway in their data. Since all components use a unique set of keys all information flows inside of the gateways are secured as long as the PKI is not compromised.

2.2   Privacy Policies for Collaborative Business Processes

This section describes in detail our approach for defining privacy policies in the context of collaborative business processes. One of our main requirements for the approach was to provide the companies with a tool that they could understand.

To define privacy policies that can be evaluated automatically and be used to decide whether a service is allowed to access some data or not we rely on use access control approaches. Basically there are four different types of access control. The mandatory access control and discretionary access control where applied in computer systems in the 70 s of the last century. While mandatory access control describes security from the system itself by policies like "access is only granted from localhost", discretionary access control assigns each identity the appropriate access rights [9]. Mandatory access control is still used nowadays, e.g. SElinux is applying this approach [10].

In the late 80 s and early 90 s more and more users where using computer systems, hence assigning each individual user, i.e. identity, the correct access rights was not feasible any more. So in the beginning of the 90 s role based access control emerged [11]. Role based access control assigns roles to identities and access rights are assigned to roles. This approach is used in Linux and Windows file systems and almost every modern software. Roles can be organized hierarchically as shown in Fig. 2 [12–14]. Because of the well established application of role based access control our first approach for defining privacy policies was to apply role based access control.

During multiple workshops with local companies we discovered that the companies do not think about privacy identically. One common thing is that all companies separated the actors who want to access data into groups. But while some companies have had a very easy and strict approach for group setup, others could not clearly tell us which companies are member of which group. Instead they used phrases like "The driver of the truck while he is in the destination city is allowed to get the recipient's phone number to call the recipient to tell him his arrival time". This simple phrase contains the following information:

- 'Driver' has to be the role of the person requesting access to the recipient's number.
- The requesting person has to be located in the area (city) of destiny.
- In addition, the driver is only permitted access to the number to announce the arrival.

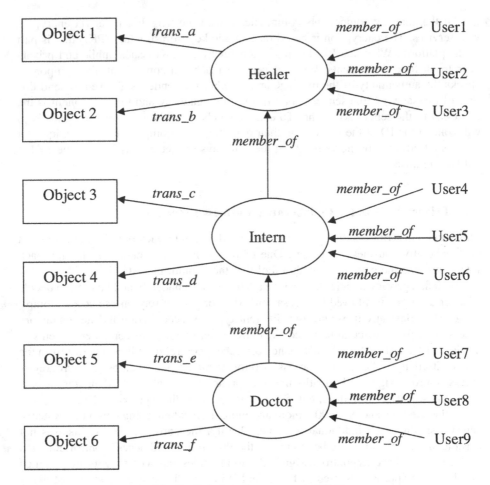

Fig. 2. Role based access control [14]

This simple policy cannot be represented easily with roles because the location of the driver is changing over time. To tackle such requirements, the research community followed two core approaches: extend role based access control with additional features, e.g. context or attributes, and creating a new access control model. [13].

Following the role based access control [15] has developed an access control model, which extends role based access control for virtual organizations. Unfortunately, this model does not cover business processes, workflows, and cloud computing. Other approaches in this direction do cover business processes but leave out the cooperation aspect. References [16–18] proposed and evaluated an extended role based access control model for team collaboration and workflows in the health sector.

All of the proposed models do not provide the flexibility in policy definition language that was needed by the participants of our workshops. To achieve a maximum flexibility, the research community developed a novel approach, the attribute based access control. In attribute access control, policies are based on attributes of subjects and objects. According to [19] attribute based access control is:

"An access control method where subject requests to perform operations on objects are granted or denied based on assigned attributes of the subject, assigned attributes of the object, environment conditions, and a set of policies that are specified in terms of those attributes and conditions." [19].

The entity requesting access is called a subject. Typical attributes of subjects are their id, e.g. username, company name, and name of the department. The data that subjects want to access is called object or resources. A policy in attribute based access control is a triple of a subject, a resource, an operation, where the operation describes what access type the subject wants to have, and a result, e.g. grant or deny access. A policy can also comprise one or more conditions. The policy "The driver of the truck while he is in the destination city is allowed to get the recipient's phone number to call the recipient to tell him his arrival time" consists of:

- *Subject:* The driver of the truck who is located in the destination city;
- *Resource:* Recipient's phone number;
- *Operation:* Read;
- *Condition:* Current workflow activity is "call recipient for dispatch notification";
- *Result:* Permit.

The remainder of this section presents our approach on applying attribute based access control for privacy preservation to collaborative business process as a service. Privacy of data is always specified to the owner of the data, i.e. the creating entity.

First of all, in our platform business processes consist of activities that call external cloud based web services. Hence, there are two very basic roles in our platform. A process designer is an entity that models the business process, that is responsible for the correctness of the process itself, and that offers the resulting business process as a service to its customers. The second role is the service provider. A service provider is an entity that provides the external services that are being orchestrated in the business process by the process designer.

Our approach enables both roles to define their privacy policies independently from each other. It also includes privacy policies defined by law. Hence, the combined privacy policy consists of three columns as shown in Fig. 3 that can be evaluated independently. The combined privacy policy results in permit if all three columns result in permit, else it results in deny.

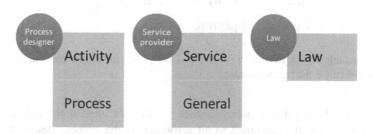

Fig. 3. Three columns of privacy policy process designer, service provider, and law

To simplify the process of policy definition and to reduce redundancy in policies we provide each role with two levels of policies. First a process designer can specify general privacy policies that are valid for the whole business process. E.g. a process designer may restrict access to all data to companies that are located in the Europe Union to ensure no data is transferred to other countries. Such privacy policies are visualized as tables where the objects are in the rows while the subjects are located in the columns. The cells contain either permit or deny depending on whether or not the subject is allowed to access the object. The subjects are defined by filters using attributes. So in this example the subject filter would be:

Companies meeting the condition: all locations have an attribute country with a value that is in a list of the countries of the European Union.

The relevant section of the table for the privacy policy "Data can only be accessed by European companies." is shown in Fig. 4. Apart from the groups created by the process designer, every table does have an additional column *Default*. The algorithm to select the correct column when the evaluation of a policy, i.e. table, takes place is select the rightmost column whose filter does accept the subject, where Default accepts every subject.

Object	Default	EU Companies
All data	deny	permit

Fig. 4. Privacy policy "Data can only be accessed by European companies" in table form

The rows of the table represent the objects, i.e. the data the policy is about. The data is organized in an object hierarchy. Objects can be expanded to define policies for child elements as shown in Fig. 5. This table also states that EU Companies have unspecified access to the object Child. The evaluation algorithm handles *t/s* as if this column does not exist. The only column that is not allowed to have *t/s* is the *Default* column since else there would be no result for the evaluation of the policy.

Object	Default	EU Companies
Parent	deny	permit
Child	permit	n/s

Fig. 5. Expandable objects in table to define a privacy policy for a child element different from the privacy policy for the parent element

The process level privacy policy applies to all data created by activities of the business process, i.e. it is assigned to all activities. If the process designer wants to define a different policy for a specific activity, he defines a privacy policy on activity level. Privacy policies on activity level are evaluated before the process level privacy policies, i.e. activity level overrides process level. On activity level even the *Default* column can be set to *n/s*. If the evaluation of activity level policy results in *n/s* the policy on process level is evaluated.

The groups of subjects of a process designer's privacy policies can use both, companies and roles of the business process, as target. In case the process designer wants to use a business process role as the subject's filter, the systems show up a list of the names of all swim lanes of the process. The process designer selects the appropriate entries and specifies the access rights as he does for company based filters.

The second role, i.e. the service providers, can define privacy roles that are applied to all data generated by their services in any business process. This is done on the level *General*. The definition of the policies follows the same concepts as for the process designer's policies. A service provider can override his general privacy policies by setting up a service specific privacy policy.

The third type of privacy policies are laws. Laws are provided by the platform provider as is and are not represented in an easy to read form as the process designer's and service provider's policy are.

3   Research Methodology

The evaluation of the presented artifacts is based on the Framework for Evaluation in Design Science Research (FEDS), developed by Venable [20]. Artifacts that have been created by a methodology based on Design Science in Information Systems Research [21] can be evaluated by this framework in order to ensure rigor. The framework offers several strategies the could be pursued depending on the characteristics of the designed artifacts. Generally, the FEDS regards evaluation as an ongoing process during design science research in order to improve the artifacts iteratively. Several characteristics influence the evaluation's purpose (why?), point of progress of the design process (when?), strategy (how?) and the artifact itself (what?). The characteristics and resulting strategies are briefly introduced. By outlining the characteristics of the current research, a strategy is chosen and the resulting methodological steps are described.

The framework distinguishes between formative and summative evaluation [22]. Formative evaluation has the main purpose to improve the results of an artifact in the ongoing research process. On the contrary, summative evaluations have the purpose to create a shared meaning of the artifact concerning distinct contexts of application. The question about the point of progress of design evaluation can be chosen ex-ante or ex-post [22] during the continuous design process. While ex-ante evaluations are more predictive in order to e.g. select a certain technology alternative, ex-post approaches are used to assess developed artifacts in terms of applicability or degree of achievements of objectives. With this, a greater likelihood of ex-post evaluation can be expected for summative evaluations but is not obligatory [20]. Goals of evaluations can be for different purpose: either achievement of environmental utility, or usefulness of solving a specific problem, or comparative advantage over existing solutions, or a complex composite of criteria (e.g. functionality, completeness, consistency), or other impacts (side effects), or reason artifact's functioning.

The framework is displayed in Fig. 6, it comprises two dimensions. On the x-axis the distinction between already described formative and summative evaluation purpose is located. The y-axis contains a distinction on how to evaluate with either artificial or naturalistic setup. While artificial setup is used to prove general functionality of a concept, naturalistic evaluations prove an artifacts functionality in real environments, i.e. real people, real systems, and real settings [23]. Different *strategies* can be pursued that are displayed in Fig. 6 as well. Depending on the needs, available resources and circumstances, a strategy is chosen for and possibly changed during evaluation. The fastest strategy with the lowest costs is found in the 'quick\&simple' approach with a very limited number of iterations bears the risk of being not reasonable. A *'Purely Technical'* approach is suitable if naturalistic data and behavior is irrelevant and human users are not focus of the artifact. The other two strategies are used for either facing *'Human Risk & Effectiveness'* or *'Technical Risk & Efficacy'*. A more detailed description of selecting a suitable strategy depending on specific circumstances can be found in Table 1.

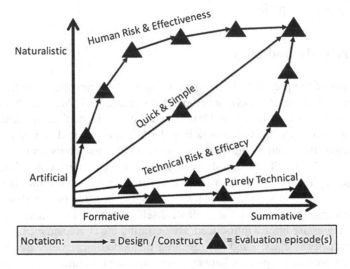

Fig. 6. Framework for Evaluation in Design Science (FEDS) with evaluation strategies [20]

The FEDS proposes 4 particular steps during the evaluation process [20]:

1. *explicate the goals:* 4 goals of the evaluation could be distinguished:
    (a) *rigor* focuses on confirming that the artifact directly produced a certain effect (more likely to be shown with artificial evaluation) or that an instantiation of the artifact works thoroughly in a real situation (more likely to be shown with naturalistic evaluation). A summative evaluation provides the greatest rigor and reliability of the produced knowledge [20].
    (b) *uncertainty and risk reduction* focuses on reducing either human and social risks or on reducing technical risks, which influences the choice of strategy (see Table 1).

Table 1. Circumstances for selecting a relevant DSR evaluation strategy [20]

DSR evaluation strategy	Circumstances selection criteria
Quick & Simple	If small and simple construction of design, with low social and technical risk and uncertainty
Human Risk & Effectiveness	If the major design risk is social or user oriented *and/or* If it is relatively cheap to evaluate with real users in their real context *and/or* If a critical goal of the evaluation is to rigorously establish that the utility/benet will continue in real situations and over the long run
Technical Risk & Efficacy	If the major design risk is technically oriented *and/or* If it is prohibitively expensive to evaluate with real users and real systems in the real setting *and/or* If a critical goal of the evaluation is to rigorously establish that the utility/benet is due to the artifact, not something else
Purely Technical Artefact	If artifact is purely technical (no social aspects) or artifact use will be well in future and not today

(c) *ethics* focuses on reduction of potential risks to animals, people, or the public society. With this especially potential stakeholders should not be put into risk.

(d) *efficiency* focuses on balancing the aforementioned goals in case of resource shortage Hence, a more formative evaluation is proposed.

2. *choose a strategy or strategies for the evaluation:* Depending on the aforementioned goals and the described circumstances of Table 1 one or more strategies have to be chosen. This can be done with a 4-step heuristic: (1) evaluate and prioritize design risks (either social/user oriented or technical or both). (2) Estimation of costs for real users, real systems and real settings. If human feedback is available for a reasonable price the *'Human Risk & Effectiveness'* strategy is suitable. If the price is to high or serious health concerns exist for users, the *'Technical Risk & Efficacy'* strategy is favorable. (3) If the artifact is purely technical and potential usage lies in remote future, the 'Purely Technical' strategy appears to be suitable or a naturalistic evaluation is just impossible. (4) If the construction that is to be evaluated is of rather small and simple extent, and none of the above mentioned risks apply, the *'Quick & Simple'* strategy is the best choice.

3. *determine the properties to evaluate:* the general set of features, goals and requirements of the artifacts that are to be evaluated are chosen. Again, a heuristic with 4 steps is proposed: (1) determine a list of potential evaluands (examples are given in [23–26]), (2) evaluands are to be aligned with the chosen goals, (3) depending on the chosen strategy of step 2, the evaluands should be of rather naturalistic or technical character and (4) determine the final list of evaluands.

4. *design the individual evaluation episode:* the 3 heuristic sub-steps comprise: (1) derived from the environmental constraints, availability of resources determines their usage. (2) Priority shall be given to essential and more important aspects and

resource are to be (re-)allocated. (3) Determination of number and structure of evaluation episodes and the according responsibility.

4 Research Findings and Discussion

This section presents the evaluation of the research artifacts. As shown in the previous section, the preparative work for the applied Framework for Evaluation in Design Science (FEDS) is structured in four steps: explicate the goals, choose a strategy or strategies for the evaluation, determine the properties to evaluate, and design the individual evaluation episodes. The evaluands are (1) the architecture and (2) the modeling approach for privacy policies. Since both artifacts can be evaluated separately the remainder of this section is split into two parts, one for each artifact.

4.1 Evaluation of the Architecture

Preparation. The first step of the evaluation is to explicate the core goals. The first goal of the architecture's evaluation is to show the architecture's *ability to model and execute* the collaborative business processes with privacy preservation. The second goal of the evaluation is *efficiency*.

The second step focuses on the selection of strategies for the architecture's evaluation. Since naturalistic evaluation involves real data from real businesses and the architectures purpose is to transfer these data between multiple partners of a business process, there is the risk of exposing data illegally. In order to avoid the exposition of real sensitive data in case of non-successful evaluation, only artificial data is used. To reduce uncertainty and risks, a formative evaluation needs to be applied first, especially to ensure that the technology is able to fulfill privacy preservation and that technical risks are reduced during design time. The architecture consists of several components which are connected with each other, as shown in Fig. 1. This leads to a high complexity. Further, the major risks are technology-driven as no manual input is necessary for the interpretation of the privacy rules. Additionally, the evaluation with real companies and real data does not provide further or deeper insight. According to Table 1, in case of absence of naturalistic evaluation, a *Purely Technical* strategy is selected to evaluate the architecture's ability to model and execute privacy preservation.

In the third step the architecture's properties that are to be evaluated, are determined. Those are partly inspired by the properties proposed by [25]. First, essential properties of the architecture are the *existence of corresponding components* that enable a user to individually model privacy rules and also components that enable the automatic execution and interpretation of privacy rules. The platform's main purpose is to ensure privacy, hence *security* and *reliability* are further crucial properties. Interoperability is crucial but also given due to the cloud computing nature of the architecture.

The last step is the design of the individual evaluation episode. The evaluation of the architecture was done after substantial changes of the components and their links. For this purpose, the architecture was discussed with teams of expert to ensure the appropriate definition, composition, and implementation of each component. The experts were selected from different research groups. Further, attendants of conferences were contributing to the architecture by discussions after the presentations of the actual status. Additionally, system tests were applied to evaluate the architecture.

Evaluation Episodes. The first part of the evaluation was done on a regular basis throughout the first iterations of the architecture's design by expert discussion with experts from the fields cloud computing, service orientation, logistics, and privacy. The discussions were initialized by brainstorming. The main ideas of the participants have been summarized and were used to improve the architecture. Examples are given in the following. In an earlier version of the architecture the same gateways were reused for the next service interactions and business data was stored in the business process management system. The experts raised some concerns that both could lead to a potential security risk in terms of data leakage or data remaining in cache. Hence, these issues were addressed in later iterations of the platform's design process. After the architecture reached a first stable state with only minor changes it was presented at two scientific conferences where additional feedback was collected during the discussion with the conferences' attendants.

After the completion of the implementation of the architecture's prototype, the technical evaluation was done mostly based on automated and semi-automated tests with artificial test cases. First, the evaluation of the components focused on the privacy related ones, which are privacy management system, identity management system, business process management system, service repository, certificate authority, and gateways. A test suite has been implemented, which executes specific test cases towards these components. The test cases comprise the execution of a task of a simulated or emulated, respectively, business process. This included the instantiation of a gateway and the third party service invocation as well as all the interpretation and testing of all related privacy policies. The tests have been executed on demand. The configurator was able to model all possible aspects according to the modeling approach for both, business processes and services. Hence, the configurator is able to model privacy policies for collaborative business processes (The evaluation of modeling approach itself by researchers and practitioners is described in the next subsection). The results confirmed the prevention of privacy violations, timing information, input messages, and output messages of the components. This way the ability of those components of the architecture to model and execute privacy rules could be positively evaluated. Further, important timing information could be collected in order to prove the efficiency of the architecture's service invocation process. Due to the certificates' characteristic of only one-time use, the time needed to create certificates is a significant portion of the tests' total time. In average the tests took 22 s each, which was evaluated as a reasonable time by the experts. Due to the use of one-time-use certificates the architecture executes the business processes slower than a normal work flow engine. The additional time needed for privacy checking is irrelevantly lower compared to the time needed for creating those certificates. On the other hand, the use of such one-time certificates results in a substantial increase of security. So efficiency of the architecture could be improved by using long-term-certificates, but this has to be paid by the price of a significantly lower level of security. The evaluation has shown that the developed architecture enables the modeling and execution of collaborative business processes with privacy preservation. It has also proven that the components of the architecture are well selected and modeled. The continually performed automated and semi-automated system tests have shown that the architecture is able to handle service calls during the business process execution with acceptable additional resource consumption under the strict condition of privacy preservation. In summary, the evaluation confirmed that the architecture fulfills the requirements and goals that were imposed. This way it was proven that the architecture possesses the ability to model and execute privacy policies of the stakeholders of the collaborative business processes (Goal 1). Further, the experts evaluated the efficiency as reasonable (Goal 2).

4.2   Evaluation of the Modeling Approach for Privacy Policies

Preparation. The overarching goal comprises the *user acceptance* as the sum of two sub goals. The first sub goal for the evaluation of the modeling approach is to prove that ability of *modeling individual privacy policies* of companies. The second sub goal is to prove that the architecture's components can understand and execute the *privacy policies as intended by the user* throughout the execution of the collaborative business processes.

The evaluation strategy implemented considers the aspect of user interaction. Again, naturalistic evaluation data appears to be not appropriate for evaluation in order not to expose sensible and confidential data. User acceptance requires to present not only incremental progress but of course the final result in order to confirm user acceptance of the final version. Hence, formative as well as subsequent summative evaluation is conducted. In order to fully analyze user acceptance, near-naturalistic data and cases are used. The modeling approach requires human interaction, hence the 'Purely Technical' strategy is not appropriate. Because of the importance of the privacy policies the 'Quick & Simple' evaluation strategy is rejected. So the 'Human Risk & Effectiveness' strategy was selected. The modification of using only a near-naturalistic setup, as real confidential data would be too sensible to be exposed in case of non-positive evaluation.

The evaluated properties comprise the privacy and not-exposition of modeled policies of companies. If the policies itself would be visible to other companies, competitors could extract confidential data. For instance, if company A would be aware of the companies that are allowed to view certain data or if the geographical zone of certain business partners would be exposed, then competitors could identify or under certain circumstances estimate a list of critical business partners of their competitors. Further, the users' satisfaction with the modeling tool is a crucial property of this evaluation. The most important properties of the modeling approach are usability, maintainability, flexibility, and comprehensibility to ensure that the modeling approach is easy to use and understandable to the companies.

The evaluation episodes again comprise tests with users after significant changes of the user interface and/or the 'look & feel' of the prototype. For this purpose, the concept was presented to and discussed with teams of experts from different fields of research and from different companies in order to ensure the appropriate usability.

Evaluation Episodes. The first iterations of the modeling approach were evaluated by researchers and practitioners in workshops. During those workshops the participants had the task to model some artificial privacy policies. After the results became satisfying and a common understanding of the principles of the modeling approach was established, the participants were asked to model some near-naturalistic cases that are close to real privacy policies from their daily business. The modeling approach was also evaluated in the course of one research project. Privacy policies were modeled according to a realistic collaborative business process. These privacy policies were interpreted successfully by the prototype of the architecture. The first workshops have shown that there is no common understanding about what exactly the concept of privacy is and although a definition was given to the participants, they had difficulties in expressing their ideas. This got even more important as the first iterations of the modeling approach offered a maximum of flexibility at the expense of big complexity. It turned out that a reduction of complexity increased the comprehensibility of the resulting modeled privacy policies but reduced the possible flexibility. As an example, the first version of the approach comprised the modeling objects of 'Subjects', 'Resources', 'Actions', 'Environment', and 'Information'. The participants could not understand these terms and their accurate meaning easily. Hence, the terms were renamed to more common ones of the logistics sector. After renaming subjects to companies or group of companies, resources to attributes (data), actions to access granted, and skipping environment and information the participants could create the privacy policies more easily. This renaming has to be applied accordingly to the specific domain where the modeling approach will be applied to.

Of course this reduction in complexity and flexibility lead to some privacy policies that could not be modeled anymore, because the environmental and object based information were not available any more. This can be addressed by adding new sub-services to the platform which contain that information so the information can be used by other tasks of the process. After this modification the participants were able to model their privacy policies easily for their business processes and their services offered to their partners with near-naturalistic data.

It turned out that the participants' privacy understanding of business processes was different to their privacy understanding of services. While the privacy policies for business process were modeled in a way that the data flow along the intended flow of goods and information was always possible, the privacy policies for services were modeled much more restrictive. This lead to tasks of business processes that could not be aligned to appropriate services. This problem was addressed by a change of the architecture. The configurator was changed to check if there is at least one possible service for every task so that the process as a whole can be executed successfully under the consideration of all privacy policies modeled. The configurator presents an alert if this condition is broken and a continuous alignment is not achievable.

Although there is a big gap between the understanding of privacy policies of researchers and practitioners, all participants were able to model their policies individually. Hence, the modeling approach is able to individually model privacy policies of different companies. Those modeled policies can be interpreted and executed by the architecture's components successfully to ensure a privacy aware collaborative business process. Users were able to conduct those steps on their own, hence, the usability was confirmed (Goal 1). General feedback of the participants was the request for a more graphical user-friendly interface.

5 Conclusion

5.1 Summary

In this paper, an architecture for modeling and execution of privacy preserving collaborative business processes and a modeling approach for privacy policies for such business processes have been introduced briefly. Both artifacts have been evaluated successfully by applying the framework for evaluation in design science (FEDS). The feasibility of the architecture has been evaluated positively by expert discussions as well as automated and semi-automated tests. Multiple workshops during the design process of the modeling approach have shown the architecture's suitability and usability.

5.2 Limitations

A high number of the practitioners that took part in the evaluation process came from the logistics sector. Also, some of the participating researchers came from the fields of cloud and logistics. Hence, the evaluation's findings are valid for logistics use cases. However, it can be assumed that the developed artifacts can be applied to other fields as well. Yet, this is still an open task for future research. During our workshops, we did not only involve experts of cloud computing and privacy but also practitioners from the logistics sector. Another limitation is the rather small number of 25 companies that participated in the interviews and the evaluation workshops. However, it is assumed that the evaluation results are valid because of their homogenous nature.

5.3 Managerial and Scientific Implications

The evaluation has proven that the modeling of privacy policies for collaborative business processes by users is reasonably practicable. Hence, there are no major obstacles for the application of the modeling approach in real use cases. Also, the architecture for modeling and execution of privacy preserved collaborative business processes was evaluated positively. Hence, the architecture is suitable for application by cloud service providers. Both artifacts are important steps towards privacy preserving collaborative business process modeling and execution in cloud environments. This will enable small companies to take part in complex supply chains.

5.4 Outlook and Further Research Steps

As the users requested in their feedback during the evaluation of the modeling approach, a graphical interface with a higher user friendliness and usability appears to be a meaningful further research step. First steps in this direction looked promising, e.g. a graphical editor for XACML was found in [27]. Additionally, further large scale experiments with real use cases and real data will be helpful to identify potential shortcomings of the artefacts' design. Finally, application to other domains than logistics is a promising aspect.

Acknowledgement. The work presented in this paper was funded by the German Federal Ministry of Education and Research under the projects PREsTiGE (BMBF 16KIS0082K) and LSEM (BMBF 03IPT504X).

References

1. Wolf, M.-B., Rahn, J., Hompel, M.T.: Cloud Computing für Logistik 2: Akzeptanz und Nutzungsbereitschaft der Logistics Mall bei Anwendern und Anbietern: [eine qualitative und quantitative empirische Analyse des Fraunhofer-Institutes für Materialfluss und Logistik IML. Fraunhofer Verlag (2013)
2. Schwarzbach, B., Pirogov, A., Schier, A., Franczyk, B.: Inter-cloud architecture for privacy-preserving collaborative BPaaS. QUIS14 (2015)
3. Takabi, H., Joshi, J.B.D., Ahn, G.-J.: Security and privacy challenges in cloud computing environments. IEEE Secur. Priv. **8**(6), 24–31 (2010)
4. Bélanger, F., Crossler, R.E.: Privacy in the digital age: a review of information privacy research in information systems. MIS Q. **35**(4), 1017–1042 (2011)
5. Schwarzbach, B., Glöckner, M., Pirogov, A., Röhling, M.M., Franczyk, B.: Secure service interaction for collaborative business processes in the inter-cloud. In: 2015 Federated Conference on Computer Science and Information Systems, pp. 1377–1386. IEEE (2015). doi:10.15439/2015F282
6. Pearson, S.: Taking account of privacy when designing cloud computing services. In: Proceedings of the 2009 ICSE Workshop on Software Engineering Challenges of Cloud Computing, pp. 44–52 (2009)
7. Bundesamt, S.: 12% der Unternehmen setzen auf Cloud Computing. https://www.destatis.de/DE/PresseService/Presse/Pressemitteilungen/2014/12/PD14\textunderscore467\textunderscore52911.html(2014)
8. Singhal, M., Chandrasekhar, S., Ge, T., Sandhu, R., Krishnan, R., Ahn, G.-J., Bertino, E.: Collaboration in multicloud computing environments: framework and security issues. Computer (2013). doi:10.1109/MC.2013.46
9. Cuppens-Boulahia, N., Cuppens, F., Garcia-Alfaro, J. (eds.): DBSec 2012. LNCS, vol. 7371. Springer, Heidelberg (2012). doi:10.1007/978-3-642-31540-4
10. Lindqvist, H.: Mandatory access control. Master's Thesis in Computing Science, Umea University, Department of Computing Science, SE-901, vol. 87 (2006)
11. Ferraiolo, D., Cugini, J., Kuhn, D.R.: Role-Based Access Control (RBAC): features and motivations. In: Proceedings of 11th Annual Computer Security Application Conference, pp. 241–248 (1995)
12. Zahid, I., Josef, N.: Towards semantic-enhanced attribute-based access control for cloud services. In: 2012 IEEE 11th International Conference on Trust, Security and Privacy in Computing and Communications, pp. 1223–1230 (2012). doi:10.1109/TrustCom.2012.280
13. Jin, X., Krishnan, R., Sandhu, R.: A unified attribute-based access control model covering DAC, MAC and RBAC. In: Cuppens-Boulahia, N., Cuppens, F., Garcia-Alfaro, J. (eds.) DBSec 2012. LNCS, vol. 7371, pp. 41–55. Springer, Heidelberg (2012). doi:10.1007/978-3-642-31540-4_4

14. Ferraiolo, D.F., Kuhn, D.R.: Role-based access controls. arXiv preprint arXiv:0903.2171 (2009)
15. Gouglidis, A., Mavridis, I.: domRBAC: an access control model for modern collaborative systems. Comput. Secur. **31**(4), 540–556 (2012)
16. Le, X.H., Wang, D.: Development of a system framework for implementation of an enhanced role-based access control model to support collaborative processes. In: Proceedings of 3rd USENIX Workshops on Health Security and Privacy (2012)
17. Le, X.H., Doll, T., Barbosu, M., Luque, A., Wang, D.: An enhancement of the role-based access control model to facilitate information access management in context of team collaboration and workflow. J. Biomed. Inform. **45**(6), 1084–1107 (2012)
18. Le, X.H., Doll, T., Barbosu, M., Luque, A., Wang, D.: Evaluation of an enhanced role-based access control model to manage information access in collaborative processes for a statewide clinical education program. J. Biomed. Inf. (2014). doi:10.1016/j.jbi.2013.11.007
19. Hu, V.C., Ferraiolo, D., Kuhn, R., Schnitzer, A., Sandlin, K., Miller, R., Scarfone, K.: Guide to Attribute Based Access Control (ABAC) definition and considerations. national institute of standards and technology (2014)
20. Venable, J., Pries-Heje, J., Baskerville, R.: FEDS: a framework for evaluation in design science research. Eur. J. Inf. Syst. (2014). doi:10.1057/ejis.2014.36
21. Hevner, A., March, S., Park, J., Ram, S.: Design science in information systems research. MIS Q. **28**(1), 75–105 (2004)
22. Wiliam, D., Black, P.: Meanings and consequences: a basis for distinguishing formative and summative functions of assessment? Brit. Educ. Res. J. **22**(5), 537–548 (1996)
23. Sun, Y., Kantor, P.B.: Cross-evaluation: a new model for information system evaluation. J. Am. Soc. Inf. Sci. Technol. (2006). doi:10.1002/asi.20324
24. Stufflebeam, D.L.: The CIPP model for evaluation. In: Kellaghan, T., Stufflebeam, D.L. (eds.) International Handbook of Educational Evaluation, vol. 9, pp. 31–62. Springer, Dordrecht (2003). Kluwer International Handbooks of Education
25. Mathiassen, L., Munk-Madsen, A., Nielsen, P.A., Stage, J., Jacksen, M.: Object-Oriented Analysis and Design. Marko, Aalborg (2000)
26. Smithson, S., Hirschheim, R.: Analysing information systems evaluation: another look at an old problem. Eur. J. Inf. Syst. (1998). doi:10.1057/palgrave.ejis.3000304
27. Nergaard, H., Ulltveit-Moe, N., Gjøsæter, T.: A scratch-based graphical policy editor for XACML. In: ICISSP 2015 Proceedings of the 1st International Conference on Information Systems Security and Privacy ESEO, Angers, Loire Valley, France, pp. 182–191 (2015)

Implementation and Evaluation of Information Systems

Examining the Antecedents and Outcomes of ERP Implementation Success: An Explanatory Study

Prodromos Chatzoglou[1,2], Dimitrios Chatzoudes[1(✉)], and Georgia Apostolopoulou[2]

[1] Democritus University of Thrace,
12 Vasilissis Sofias Street, 67100 Xanthi, Greece
pchatzog@pme.duth.gr, dchatzoudes@yahoo.gr
[2] Hellenic Open University, 18 Aristotelous Street, 26335 Patra, Greece
geapostolo84@gmail.com

Abstract. Enterprise Resource Planning (ERP) systems have transformed the way of doing business in the modern environment. More specifically, they integrate all functions of an enterprise, allowing seamless information dissemination and facilitating the decision-making process. However, the implementation of ERP systems is not always a prerequisite of operational and business success. On the contrary, companies should thoroughly investigate the critical factors that have an impact on the implementation process. Under this context, the present study aims at developing and testing a three-dimensional conceptual framework, that investigates the antecedents of "ERP implementation success", as well as the impact of the implementation itself on "organizational performance". The proposed conceptual framework was tested, using a newly-developed structured questionnaire, in a sample of 204 Greek companies that have already implemented an ERP system. Results indicate that "end-users" constitute the most significant actor for ensuring ERP implementation success. Another important empirical finding is that, among the three dimensions used to measure "ERP implementation success" (information quality, system quality, service quality), "information quality" has the strongest impact on all the dimensions of "organizational performance" (internal efficiency, competitiveness, profitability).

Keywords: Enterprise Resource Planning (ERP) · ERP implementation · Critical Success Factors (CSFs) · Structural Equation Modeling (SEM) · Greece

1 Introduction

According to Nandi and Kumar [1], during the last few decades, Enterprise Resource Planning (ERP) systems have become a global trend and organizations are investing significant resources on their implementation. ERP systems have derived from the Management Information Systems (MIS) of the 1990s, aiming to gather information from all organizational functions and assist in the decision-making process [2, 3].

© Springer International Publishing AG 2017
E. Ziemba (Ed.): AITM 2016/ISM 2016, LNBIP 277, pp. 157–178, 2017.
DOI: 10.1007/978-3-319-53076-5_9

ERP systems are, actually, customized Information Systems (IS) that integrate the business processes of a company via a common database. When using an ERP, all processes become visible and easily accessible by the management, in real-time [4, 5]. Nowadays, ERP systems are the backbone of most organizations, no matter the sector of the economy [1, 3]. According to Umble, Haft, and Umble [6], ERP systems provide an enterprise database, in which all business transactions are entered, recorded, processed, monitored and reported, in order to achieve a better cooperation and coordination among various departments.

The literature has highlighted several benefits of ERP adoption. For example, Al-Mashari, Al-Mudimigh, and Zairi [4] argued that successful ERP implementation can enhance operational efficiency and create competitive advantages. Moreover, Yang, and Su [7] found that the benefits of ERP adoption include improvements in customer service, efficient cost management and enhanced relationships between supply chain partners. Finally, Madapusi, and D'Souza [8] concluded that ERP systems have a positive influence on various measures of operational performance.

Despite the increasing popularity and the various benefits of ERP systems, the failure rates of ERP implementation are high. After all, the implementation of ERP systems requires considerable financial resources and organizational capabilities, while the whole project is considered to be complex, lengthy and challenging [4]. According to Panorama Consulting Solutions [9], 66% of the companies that have implemented an ERP system receive half the expected benefits, while the whole project tends to get out of time (in 72% of the cases) and out of budget (in 54% of the cases).

In order to facilitate the implementation of ERP projects, the empirical literature has investigated the factors increasing their success. The understanding of these factors, best known as Critical Success Factors (CSFs), can help companies sense the possible risks of ERP adoption and take the necessary actions in order to avoid them [3, 6, 10].

The present study conducted an analytical review of the ERP literature. It was concluded that the literature includes various studies investigating the factors having an impact on the effective implementation of ERP systems (CSFs or antecedents) (e.g. [3, 11, 12]). On the other hand, there are fewer studies examining the impact of ERP implementation on various measures of business success (e.g. [2, 7, 8]). Despite that, the literature review analysis failed to identify any empirical studies adopting a multidimensional approach, incorporating both antecedents and outcomes in their analysis.

The present study aspires to bridge that gap in the relevant literature, developing and testing a three-dimensional conceptual framework (research model). More specifically, the first dimension includes the antecedents of ERP successful implementation (internal environment, technology-related issues, implementation team, end-users), the second dimension the implementation itself (information quality, system quality, service quality), while the third dimension includes three measures of organizational performance (internal efficiency, competitiveness, profitability).

The examination of the proposed conceptual framework (research model) was made with the use of a newly-developed structured questionnaire that was distributed to a group of Greek companies. The Structural Equation Modelling (SEM) technique was used in order to test the research hypotheses. The present study is empirical (it is based on primary data), explanatory (examines cause-and-effect relationships), deductive (tests research hypotheses) and quantitative (analyses quantitative data collected with the use of a structured questionnaire). Its results may be useful for managers, business analysts and IT analysts in dealing with the implementation of ERP systems.

2 Literature Review

The present study conducted an analytical review of the ERP literature in an effort to better define its scope. The literature review analysis revealed that there is a lack of empirical studies investigating both the antecedents and the outcomes of ERP implementation. More specifically, a sufficient number of studies focus on the Critical Success Factors of ERP implementation (antecedents), while numerous other studies examine the impact of ERP implementation on indicators of organizational performance (outcomes). The literature review analysis will follow this dichotomous approach, examining separately the antecedents and the outcomes of ERP implementation.

2.1 Antecedents of ERP Implementation

Table 1 summarizes some of the studies that have examined the antecedents of ERP implementation. Many of these studies investigate the Critical Success Factors and the Critical Failure Factors (CFFs) of ERP implementation, and assist practitioners towards selecting the most suitable ERP software. The studies of Umble, Haft, and Umble [6], Holland and Light [13], and Al-Mashari, Al-Mudimigh, and Zairi [4] appear to be among the most cited papers in the ERP literature (734, 557, and 483 citations respectively: data acquired from the 'Scopus' database, November 2016).

In general, the relevant literature includes many studies that draw their conclusions based on a literature review analysis (e.g. [4, 6, 14, 16, 23, 25]). For example, Al-Mashari, Al-Mudimigh, and Zairi [4] developed a theoretically grounded taxonomy of ERP critical success factors, combining research studies and organizational experiences. Umble, Haft, and Umble [6], discussed their proposed CSFs in the light of a case study. These approaches, no matter how brilliant, lack coherent empirical support.

Moreover, researchers have conducted numerous case studies (e.g. [13, 17, 20]). On the other hand, empirical surveys are also frequent, but many of them follow an exploratory or qualitative approach, failing to establish cause-and-effect relationships [18, 19, 24]. Therefore, it seems that explanatory studies investigating the antecedents of ERP implementation are quite rare. The present study aspires to bridge that literature gap.

2.2 Outcomes of ERP Implementation

Table 2 provides a summary of some of the studies that have examined the outcomes of ERP implementation. In general, these studies can be grouped in two categories: (a) studies that argue that there is a direct link between ERP systems and business success, (b) studies that argue that the effect of ERP systems on business success is indirect, mediated through other factors. Moreover, the measures of business success

Table 1. Synopsis of previous studies: antecedents of ERP implementation

Study	Approach/Field	Method	Main findings
[13]: Holland and Light, 1999	Eight companies	Case study	The authors developed an CSF framework that categorized CSFs in two categories: strategic and tactical
[14]: Nah et al., 2001	Literature review analysis	Process theory approach	Eleven (11) factors were found to be critical for ERP implementation success
[15]: Hong and Kim, 2002	South Korea	Survey	ERP implementation success depends on the organizational fit of the ERP system
[4]: Al-Mashari et al., 2003	Literature review analysis	Synthesis of previous studies	The study identified twelve factors for successful ERP implementation
[6]: Umble et al., 2003	Literature review analysis	Synthesis of previous studies	The study highlighted nine factors affecting ERP implementation
[16]: Loh and Koh, 2004	Literature review analysis	Process theory approach	Three critical elements (CSFs, critical people, critical uncertainties) have an effect on successful ERP implementation
[17]: Motwani et al., 2005	Four multinational companies	Comparative case study	Change management, network relationships, and cultural readiness have a positive effect on ERP implementation success
[18]: Ehie and Madsen, 2005	Midwestern region of the USA	Survey	*CSFs*: Project management, ERP feasibility, Top management support, Business process reengineering, Consulting, Cost issues
[19]: Ifinedo and Nahar, 2006	Companies in Estonia and Finland	Survey	Informational quality is the most significant factor for ERP implementation success
[20]: Chien and Tsaur, 2007	Three Taiwanese companies	Case study	System quality, service quality and information quality are the most important factors when implementing an ERP system
[21]: Garcia-Sanchez et al., 2007	Mexican enterprises	Survey	Fourteen (14) CSFs were found to have an impact on ERP system success
[22]: Françoise et al., 2009	Panel of ERP experts	Delphi method	The study proposed a new approach for the examination of CSFs. Its results are very analytical, but quite vague

(continued)

Table 1. (*continued*)

Study	Approach/Field	Method	Main findings
[5]: Amid *et al.*, 2012	Iranian industries	Survey	Thirty five (35) CFFs are categorized into seven factors (vendor and consultant, human resources, managerial, project management, processes, organizational, technical)
[23]: Ram and Corkindale, 2014	Literature review analysis	Five-step process	The authors question the validity of many of the CSFs that have been identified in the relevant literature
[24]: Leh, 2014	German SMEs	Qualitative research	Technological factors are more important for implementation of big ERP projects
[25]: Ravasan and Mansouri, 2016	Literature review analysis	Fuzzy cognitive map	*CFFs*: Heavy customization, Poor business process reengineering, Poor consultant support, Poor top management support

used by previous studies are different in every case. More specifically, the literature investigated the impact of ERP implementation on supply chain performance [7], operational performance [8], Tobin's Q [29], organizational capabilities [2], firm performance [30], competitive advantage [33], sales performance [34], etc. The present study adopts a holistic approach, examining three of these measures, namely internal efficiency (operational performance), competitiveness and profitability.

3 Conceptual Framework

Based on the literature review analysis that was conducted prior to the development of the proposed conceptual framework, the present study classified the antecedents of ERP implementation into four distinct categories (dimensions): (1) internal environment, (2) technology-related issues, (3) implementation team, (4) end-users. Additionally, each category (dimension) was determined with the use of several factors.

The selection of all research factors was a result of a specific procedure: (1) the Scopus database was used in order to identify previous studies concerning the antecedents of ERP implementation success (65 relevant studies were identified), (2) an extensive list, including the factors used in these studies, was constructed, (c) factors were given a significance index, based on the findings of each study, (d) each factor was categorized into one of the four pre-determined categories (dimensions), (e) the factors with the highest significance index in each category were, finally, selected.

The present study adopts a unique approach on the ERP literature. Instead of, only, examining the antecedents of ERP implementation success, the outcomes of the

Table 2. Synopsis of previous studies: outcomes of ERP implementation

Study	Approach/Field	Method	Main findings
[7]: Yang and Su, 2009	Taiwanese companies	Survey	ERP benefits have a significant impact on supply chain management performance
[26]: Kale et al., 2010	130 Indian SMEs	Survey	ERP implementation has a positive effect on inventory management, customer service and communication
[27]: Nicolaou and Bajor, 2011	Financial data from 87 firms	Analysis of secondary data	Firms adopting ERP systems have higher performance during the two years following the implementation of the system
[28]: Tsai et al., 2011	110 large firms in Taiwan	Survey	The post-implementation maintenance of an ERP system has a significant influence on business performance
[8]: Madapusi and D'Souza, 2012	Indian companies	Survey	The implementation of each ERP system module has an impact on different measures of operational performance (e.g. inventory management, information quality, etc.)
[29]: Zhang et al., 2012	Financial data from 126 firms	Analysis of secondary data	Tobin's Q increases significantly in the fourth year after ERP implementation
[2]: Hassab- Elnaby et al., 2012	Financial data from 548 firms	Analysis of secondary data	ERP implementation has a positive effect on organizational capabilities, when a firm employs a prospector business strategy
[30]: Ince et al., 2013	138 Turkish companies	Survey	ERP systems have a positive impact on firm performance
[31]: Dumitru et al., 2013	One Romanian company	Longitudinal case study	The study reports a link between ERP implementation and organizational performance (the claim is insufficiently supported)
[32]: Voulgaris et al., 2014	Financial data from 88 firms	Analysis of secondary data	Firm performance of companies that have adopted ERP systems is better than the performance of companies that have not

(*continued*)

Table 2. (*continued*)

Study	Approach/Field	Method	Main findings
[33]: Ram *et al.*, 2014	Australian companies	Survey	Two CSFs (training and education and system integration) have a direct positive effect on competitive advantage
[34]: Patalas-Maliszewska and Krebs, 2014	Knowledge workers in SMEs	Survey	ERP systems enhance sales performance (ROS) (employees using ERP systems can create added value for their companies)
[35]: Roh and Hong, 2015	641 global manufacturing firms	Survey	ERP integration has a positive impact on performance improvement
[36]: Kharuddin *et al.*, 2015	Malaysian listed companies	Survey	The extensiveness of ERP adoption enhances organizational performance. System usage is a mediating factor in that relationship
[37]: Le and Han, 2016	402 Vietnamese SMEs	Survey	ERP implementation has an indirect effect (through organizational capability and competitive advantage) on firm performance
[38]: Al-Dhaafri *et al.*, 2016	Dubai Police Departments	Survey	TQM and organizational excellence mediate the relationship between ERP and organizational performance

implementation procedure were, also, taken into consideration. Thus, an original three-dimensional conceptual framework (research model) was developed (see Fig. 1).

3.1 Internal Environment

In the present study, the dimension of "internal environment" includes four factors: (a) top management support, (b) business process reengineering, (c) organizational culture, (d) change management.

(a) Top management support has been emphasized as a crucial factor in successful ERP implementation by previous studies [4, 6]. Al-Mashari, Al-Mudimigh, and Zairi [4] suggested that top management support should not only be offered during the initiation and facilitation stage, but throughout the entire ERP implementation process. Umble, Haft, and Umble [6] claimed that successful ERP implementation requires the commitment and constant participation of top management. In a

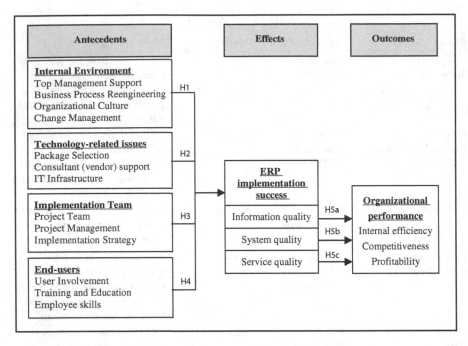

Fig. 1. The proposed conceptual framework of the study

different case, the project is most likely to fail, or fail to deliver the full range of forecasted benefits [5, 39].

(b) Business process reengineering (BPR) has been, often, proposed as a critical success factor for ERP implementation [33]. Reengineering aims at making the necessary adjustments in order to take full advantage of the new processes offered by the ERP system [40]. Therefore, organizations should be willing to adjust their processes, so as to fit with the new software and minimize the degree of customization needed [13]. After all, most experts agree that software customization results in higher implementation costs and longer implementation period [40, 41].

(c) An organizational culture of shared values and common objectives is crucial for business success [42]. Organizations should build a culture that is open to change, since openness to change plays a pivotal role in today's business environment. When organizational members have different cultures, beliefs and values, they, also, have different perceptions on various organizational changes [43]. In other words, organizational culture is a critical success factor for a project that requires significant changes.

(d) ERP projects that are supported by top management, but are not accompanied by adequate change management strategies are likely to fail [17]. An implementation process, backed with careful change management strategies and network relationships, has been found to have a positive effect on ERP implementation success

[44]. Research has shown that change management is critical to successful implementation [45].

H1:   Internal environment has a positive impact on ERP implementation success.

3.2   Technology-Related Issues

During all stages of ERP implementation, various technological-related issues need to be addressed. More specifically, (a) the appropriate ERP package should be carefully selected [45]; (b) the overall support provided by the vendor should be taken under serious consideration [3, 11]; and (c) the fit between the implemented system and the technological infrastructure of the organization should be examined [46].

(a)   The selection of an ERP system, being among the first steps of implementation, appears as a critical factor [47]. After all, the package that will be selected will determine, to a great extent, the success of the project [4, 6]. Choosing the ERP package that best suits organizational needs and processes is critical to ensure minimum modification and successful implementation [45, 47].

(b)   Organizations should, also, select the appropriate vendor that will be able to offer full support. Troubleshooting is necessary for ERP implementation, so as to prepare for unexpected circumstances or, even, crises. This is an ongoing process, since the vendor (consultant) is obligated to assist in all stages on the implementation process [4, 14]. ERP adopting companies have to work closely with ERP vendors in order to determine possible software problems. Quick response, endurance and problem solving capabilities are essential to handle any ERP implementation [14].

(c)   The appropriate IT infrastructure is necessary for the implementation of an ERP system [5, 19, 20]. Since most of ERP transactions are conducted in real-time, a reliable intranet needs to be in place [14]. A company with a satisfactory level of IT infrastructure can be expected to implement new technologies, like ERP systems, more successfully than other companies, with low degree of IT readiness [45].

H2:   Technology has a positive impact on ERP implementation success.

3.3   Implementation Team

An effective ERP implementation team is a key factor for every successful implementation project [39]. The third antecedent of ERP implementation success (implementation team) includes these three sub-factors: (a) project team, (b) project management, (c) implementation strategy.

(a)   ERP implementation projects involve all the departments of an organization [48]. According to Bhatti [49], the ERP project team includes: employees, managers, IT personnel, top management, the ERP vendor, and management consultants.

Selecting the right employees to take part in the implementation process is critical for its success. The success of ERP projects is related to the skills, knowledge, abilities and experiences of project team members [9, 11, 48].

(b) ERP implementation is a multi-level task, involving all business activities, and, often, requiring years of continuous effort [8, 27]. Therefore, an effective project management strategy should control the whole implementation process. ERP project management includes a clear definition of implementation objectives, the development of both work and resource plans, and a detailed tracking of project progress [13, 28].

(c) An ERP strategy determines how the transfer from the legacy system to the new ERP system will be organized. Adopting an efficient strategy is of vital importance, since strategy sets the whole framework of implementation [50]. According to Holland and Light [13], a clear vision is required in order to provide the project with the accurate direction and scope. Without proper strategy, implementation is likely to fail [4, 50].

H3:   Implementation team has a positive impact on ERP implementation success.

3.4   End-Users

Previous research has shown that no IT system can be successfully implemented without its users [51]. The attitude of end-users toward the ERP system has an impact on implementation success [6]. In this study, the dimension of "end-users" includes three sub-factors: (a) user involvement, (b) training and education, (c) employee skills.

(a) User involvement is one of the most cited critical success factors in ERP implementation projects [4, 52]. According to Dezdar and Ainin [39], participation in the ERP implementation process raises the understanding of the new system and helps achieving better use. Despite the level of training employees get during the implementation process, their involvement during the whole process is a very critical factor [6].

(b) ERP requires a critical mass of employee knowledge in order to solve real problems within the company [53]. Everyone who uses the ERP system should be trained and educated on how the system works and how it can be used in everyday operations [45]. Organizations should provide training opportunities, on a regular basis, in order to improve the skills and knowledge of their employees. Sufficient training and education can increase the probability of ERP implementation success [14, 41].

(c) Successful ERP implementation demands the cooperation of business experts, internal staff and external consultants, as well as the involvement of end-users [14, 49]. Employee skills are very important, since they ensure that the technical and organizational aspects of the project run efficiently [13]. Without the appropriate skills of real system users, the ERP implementation is difficult to be successful.

H4:   End-users have a positive impact on ERP implementation success.

3.5   ERP Implementation Success and Organizational Performance

Ifinedo and Nahar [19] argued that ERP implementation has a positive impact on organizational performance. Moreover, they supported that the IS success model of Delone and McLean [54] leads to improvement in organizational performance, through three key antecedents: (a) information quality, (b) system quality, and (c) service quality. The present study examined whether these three dimensions of ERP implementation have an impact on organizational performance.

(a) Information quality refers to the accuracy, timeliness, completeness and consistency of the information provided by the ERP system [20]. If the product (information provided by the ERP) is not delivered on time (timeliness) and does not conform to the needs of its customers (ERP users), then the latter will be dissatisfied and the company will lose business. On the other hand, increased information quality will have a positive organizational impact, in terms of customer satisfaction and, thus, overall organizational performance will increase.

H5a: Information quality has a positive impact on organizational performance.

(b) A well-designed ERP system is necessary for gaining organizational benefits. According to Chien and Tsaur [20], system quality is measured in terms of ease-of-use, functionality, reliability, flexibility and data quality. The expected benefits of system quality include cost reduction, enhanced performance and improved efficiency [55]. On the other hand, a system that is neither well designed nor user-friendly will, probably, create the risk of system failure [54].

H5b: System quality has a positive impact on organizational performance.

(c) Service quality is measured via the reliability, assurance and responsiveness of ERP service providers [20]. This dimension includes the overall quality of services that a particular IS provides to an organization [53, 54]. According to Roh and Hong [35], service quality is positively associated with organizational impact.

H5c: Service quality has a positive impact on organizational performance.

Figure 1 summarizes all the above hypotheses, thus, presenting the proposed conceptual framework of the present study.

4 Research Methodology

4.1 Population of the Study

The proposed conceptual framework of the present study was tested on a sample of Greek companies that have implemented an ERP system. Data concerning the target population were obtained via the web sites of various ERP system providers operating in Greece. Data concerning companies that could possibly be included in the sample were obtained via the web sites of the leading ERP system providers operating in Greece. Since no other database including companies using ERP systems exist, the use of the certain method was the only one able to provide usable information. Totally, 617 Greek companies that have implemented an ERP system were identified.

4.2 Measurement

A structured questionnaire, designed specifically for this empirical study, was used in order to collect the appropriate empirical data. All items that were used in order to measure the various research factors have been adopted exclusively by previous studies (e.g. [12, 14, 15, 17–20, 41, 45, 47, 49]). The five-point Likert scale was used for the measurement of all research factors (1 = totally disagree, 5 = totally agree). In total, ninety (90) items were used for the measurement of all research factors.

4.3 Data Collection

The questionnaire was sent to the Information Technology (IT) managers of the companies of the target population. IT managers were selected as key respondents, due to their experience and expertise. Questionnaires were sent after telephonic contact with the IT manager in each company. After making all necessary arrangements, 467 questionnaires were distributed to 467 companies that agreed to participate in the study. The research period lasted three months (October to December 2015). Initially, 213 questionnaires were returned, but after conducting all necessary controls only 204 were used for data analysis. The 204 returned questionnaires represent a very satisfactory response rate of 43.6%. This high rate is attributed to the personal contacts that were attempted.

The majority of the companies of the sample are medium-sized (51–250 employees) (42.1%), 36.5% are small (less than 50 employees), while 21.4% are large (more than 250 employees). Taking under consideration that small companies do not usually adopt ERP systems (hence, they were excluded from the sample), these results are in line with the average firm size of Greece. Moreover, most of the companies of the sample belong to three sectors: 'Food' (22.1%), 'Informatics' (19.4%), and 'Electronics' (15.4%). Finally, the majority of the companies (52.7%) have been using an ERP system for more than three years, 27.9% less than three years, and 19.4% less than one year.

4.4   Validity and Reliability

The test for the content validity of the questionnaire was conducted via a pilot study. More specifically, discussions were conducted with three practitioners and three academics, in order to test whether all questions are clear and understandable.

To test the construct validity, each research factor was evaluated: (a) for its unidimensionality and reliability, (b) for its goodness of fit to the proposed research model.

(a) The examination of the unidimensionality was conducted using Explanatory Factor Analysis (EFA), and the examination of the reliability was conducted with the use of the statistical measure 'Cronbach Alpha'. All tests concluded that the scales used, after the extraction of relatively few items, are valid and reliable (see Table 3 for the main results). More specifically, the following measures were examined [56]: (a1) Bartlett's test of Sphericity and Kaiser-Mayer-Olkin (KMO), (a2) Eigenvalue, (a3) Factor loadings, (a4) Total Variance Explained (TVE), (a5) Cronbach Alpha.

(b) The evaluation of the goodness of fit of each research factor to the proposed model was conducted using Confirmatory Factor Analysis (CFA). All tests produced satisfactory results (see Table 3 for the main results). The following measures were examined [57]: (b1) Normed X^2 (X^2/df), (b2) Construct Reliability (C.R.), (b3) Variance Extracted (V.E.), (b4) RMSEA, (b5) CFI/GFI.

5   Empirical Results

5.1   Model Valuation

The conceptual framework was tested using the "Structural Equation Modeling" (SEM) technique. The SEM approach was used because of its ability to examine a number of linear causal relationships, where one or more factors are both dependent and independent. The estimation of the structural model was conducted with the Maximum Likelihood Estimation method [57]. IBM AMOS 20.0 was used for the appropriate analysis.

After experimenting with various different models, it was decided that "ERP implementation success" and "organizational performance" will not be measured as coherent factors (structures), since the use of their various dimensions offers more in-depth information about the investigated phenomenon. More specifically, as it can be seen in Fig. 2, the model that was finally examined includes three dimensions, with a total of ten research factors.

In order to evaluate the fit of the overall model the chi-square value (X^2 = 194.61 with 73 degrees of freedom) and the p-value (p = 0.0647) were estimated. These values indicate a good fit of the data to the overall model. However, the sensitivity of the X^2 statistic to the sample size forces towards the adoption of other supplementary measures for evaluating the overall model, such as the "Normed-X^2" index (2.95), the RSMEA index (0.057) the CFI (0.973) and the GFI (0.967), that all indicate a very good fit. Moreover, for the control of the measurement model the significance of the factor loadings, the Construct Reliability (C.R.) and the Variance Extracted (V.E.) were

Table 3. Validity and reliability

Factors	KMO	TVE	Cronbach Alpha	Normed X^2	C.R.	V.E.	CFI
Top Management Support	0.834	61.77	0.88	2.24	0.69	57.7%	0.97
Business Reengineering	0.850	61.34	0.83	2.69	0.71	73.6%	0.93
Organizational Culture	0.741	56.45	0.74	3.29	0.86	78.2%	0.89
Change Management	0.818	75.91	0.89	3.45	0.87	71.6%	0.91
Internal Environment[a]	*0.692*	*55.67*	*0.73*	*2.78*	*0.76*	*58.6%*	*0.94*
Package Selection	0.658	76.24	0.69	2.11	0.77	66.8%	0.97
Consultant support	0.764	60.09	0.82	3.53	0.81	59.4%	0.95
IT Infrastructure	0.758	68.85	0.76	3.47	0.76	74.3%	0.97
Technology-related issues[a]	*0.702*	*73.11*	*0.84*	*2.26*	*0.74*	*76.8%*	*0.91*
Project Team	0.724	54.85	0.78	2.71	0.81	76.9%	0.91
Project Management	0.775	62.50	0.85	2.33	0.76	66.3%	0.97
Implementation Strategy	0.620	60.62	0.77	3.29	0.74	74.3%	0.97
Implementation Team[a]	*0.707*	*71.54*	*0.80*	*3.22*	*0.81*	*83.7%*	*0.97*
User Involvement	0.773	67.89	0.84	2.55	0.82	81.8%	0.99
Training and Education	0.705	60.65	0.78	3.55	0.84	67.3%	0.91
Employee skills	0.711	73.11	0.73	2.36	0.76	78.4%	0.95
End-users[a]	*0.637*	*60.78*	*0.69*	*3.45*	*0.71*	*69.8%*	*0.94*
Information Quality	0.762	62.18	0.80	2.14	0.83	79.3%	0.97
System Quality	0.643	67.68	0.76	2.93	0.89	78.3%	0.91
Service Quality	0.547	73.00	0.79	3.09	0.82	78.6%	0.93
Internal efficiency	0.773	79.22	0.87	2.53	0.73	79.1%	0.97
Competitiveness	0.694	59.73	0.77	2.83	0.71	66.6%	0.97
Profitability	0.732	66.16	0.74	3.66	0.84	78.3%	0.99

[a]*Second-Order EFA-CFA.*

estimated. Results indicated that all loadings are significant at the $p < 0.05$ level, while C.R. and V.E. for all factors (constructs) were satisfactory.

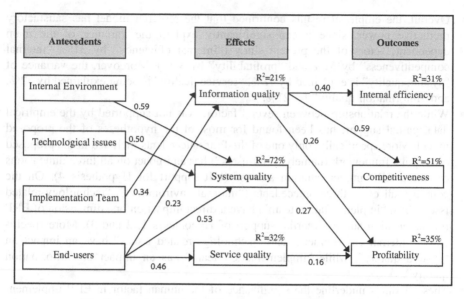

Fig. 2. Empirical results (all paths are statistically significant)

5.2 Hypothesis Testing

All research hypotheses were supported by the empirical data. As it can be seen on Table 4, two hypotheses were fully supported (H4, H5a), while all the other hypotheses were partially supported (H1, H2, H3, H5b, H5c).

Table 4. Synopsis of the empirical results

Hypotheses		Result
H1	Internal environment → ERP implementation success	Partially supported
H2	Technology-related issues → ERP implementation success	Partially supported
H3	Implementation team → ERP implementation success	Partially supported
H4	End-users → ERP implementation success	Fully supported
H5a	Information quality → Organizational performance	Fully supported
H5b	System quality → Organizational performance	Partially supported
H5c	Service quality → Organizational performance	Partially supported

Figure 2 demonstrates the overall (modified) structural model, along with the extracted path coefficients. In general, the empirical results reveal the mechanism through which the antecedents of ERP implementation are affecting the various dimensions of organizational performance. Both direct and indirect effects are being examined, thus, enhancing the understanding of the investigated phenomenon. After reviewing the empirical results (Fig. 2), various observations can be made:

- Overall, the empirical results confirmed that the research model has satisfactory predictive power, since it can significantly explain the variance of the main dependent factors of the present study ("internal efficiency" by 31%, "internal competitiveness" by 51% and "profitability" by 35%). Moreover, the variance of "system quality" is explained by 78%, "service quality" is being explained by 32%, and "information quality" by 21%.
- While the relationship between several factors was not supported by the empirical data, partial support has been found for most of the hypotheses of the proposed model. More specifically, only one of the four antecedents included in the proposed conceptual framework (namely, "end-users") has an impact on all three dimensions capturing ERP implementation success (full support for Hypothesis 4). On the contrary, all other three antecedents ("internal environment", "technology-related issues" and "implementation team") have a direct impact on one dimension of ERP implementation success (partial support of Hypotheses 1, 2 and 3). More specifically, "internal environment" and "technology-related issues" have an impact on "system quality", while "implementation team" has an impact on "information quality".
- These findings underline the significance of the human factor in ERP implementation success. It seems that the end-users of the ERP system are the cornerstones for successful implementation. Therefore, implementing organizations need to take under serious consideration the involvement of end-user in the whole implementation process, provide training and education, while focusing on increasing their overall IT skills. Bradford and Florin [41], and Dezdar and Ainin [39] found almost similar results and draw the same conclusions.
- Moreover, according to the empirical results, the antecedents of ERP implementation success should be considered as a coherent bundle of activities. Implementing companies should focus on all of these dimensions, since their simultaneous enhancement has a commutative impact on the effectiveness of the implementation process. Nevertheless, focusing on end-users should become the first priority.
- Additionally, the empirical results offer full support for hypothesis 5a, arguing that "information quality" has an impact on all dimensions measuring "organizational performance". Partial support is being offered for hypotheses 5b and 5c, since "system quality" and "service quality" have an impact on "profitability". Despite the little empirical research that has been conducted on the relationship between ERP and organizational performance, the few existing studies support these results [27, 30, 31].
- The significance of the three-dimensional approach (antecedents, effects and outcomes) introduced in the present study lies in the interrelationships between various research factors. For example, the proposed model explains 51% of the variance in "competitiveness" (outcome). As it can be seen on Fig. 2, there is only one factor having a direct positive effect on "competitiveness" ("information quality", $r = 0.19$). Despite that, two of the antecedents included in the model ("implementation team", and "end users") have an indirect effect on "competitiveness", through "information quality". Only through that mechanism, the 51% of explained variance can be justified.

- Therefore, based on the above, it can be concluded that enhanced competitiveness is a direct result of information quality, but, despite that, end-users of the ERP system and the team which is responsible for the implementation both have a significant strengthening effect on that relationship. Mapping down these complex relationships has been one of the most important contributions of the present study. Managers are urged to bear in mind the existence of these causal effects, since their main objective should be the enhancement of organizational performance.

5.3   Comparison with Previous Similar Studies

As mentioned earlier, the relevant literature has very rarely adopted a three-dimensional approach, simultaneously examining the antecedents and the outcomes of ERP implementation success. In that respect, the present study is unique.

The only close comparison can be made with the empirical study of Ram, Corkindale, and Wu [12], who conducted an explanatory research examining: (a) the impact of "project management", training and education", "business process reengineering", "system integration" on "ERP implementation" and "organizational performance", (b) the impact of "ERP implementation" on "organizational performance". They concluded that only two factors ("project management", training and education"), have an effect on "ERP implementation". Moreover, they validated the relationship between "ERP implementation" and "organizational performance". According to their findings, successful ERP implementation mediates the degree to which a critical success factor affects the performance of the organization [12]. The present study validates these results and offers the ground for future similar studies.

6   Conclusions

The present empirical study developed an original conceptual framework that has never been used in the international ERP literature. Future studies can adopt the same holistic, three-dimensional approach, further highlighting the relationship between critical factors for ERP implementation success (antecedents), ERP implementation itself (effect), and organizational performance (outcome). Its main contribution lies on its implemented methodology (synthesis of previous studies) and conceptualization (proposal of a novel, multi-dimensional research model).

The empirical results of the present study enhance the understanding of the DeLone and McLean Information System (IS) success model [54]. More specifically, a direct effect between "information quality", "system quality" and "service quality" and various measures of organization performance has been established. On the contrary, the DeLone and McLean model [54] argues that the three dimensions measuring IS quality have an indirect effect on organizational performance (through "user satisfaction" and "intention to use"). The support of a direct relationship, found in the present study, can be attributed to its conceptualization. It seems that the simultaneous examination of antecedents, effects and outcomes increases the explanatory power of the proposed model, offering a more complete picture of the ERP implementation phenomenon.

First and foremost, the empirical results highlight the significance of "end-users" in implementation effectiveness. Among all the antecedents of ERP implementation success, the dimension capturing the contribution of "end-users" on the whole process has the most significant effect. Previous studies (e.g. [58, 59]) have provided similar results, but very few have adopted such a methodological approach, using multiple factors for the measurement of each antecedent of ERP implementation success. For example, Zhang, Lee, Huang, Zhang, and Huang [59] have, also, developed an ERP implementation success framework, but their empirical analysis was qualitative (case study research).

Secondly, since all four antecedents influence, each in a different degree, the three dimensions of implementation success, it is concluded that companies should focus on their collective enhancement. After all, all of these four factors (antecedents) have an indirect effect on organizational performance. For instance, the factor measuring the characteristics of the "implementation team" has an indirect impact on "internal efficiency", "competitiveness" and "profitability", through "information quality". Such a conceptual framework, taking under consideration both direct and indirect effects between antecedents and final outcomes, has very seldom been introduced in the ERP literature.

Thirdly, "information quality" appears as the most significant aspect of the implementation process, since it has a direct effect on all measures of organizational performance. According to previous studies [4, 60, 61], enhanced information quality in the ERP implementation process leads to increased organizational performance. Information quality can help organizations choose different supply resources, hence, produce with lower costs and, therefore, develop competitive advantages, while increasing their competitiveness and internal efficiency [62, 63].

The proposed model has adequate explanatory power, since it explains a significant percentage of the variance of all three main dependent factors. More specifically, it can predict 51% of the variance in business competitiveness, underlining the effect of ERP implementation on measures that previous studies have neglected (e.g. [58, 61]). The enhanced predictive power of the model lies in its three-dimensional approach, investigating both direct and indirect effects.

6.1 Managerial Implications

On a practical level, the present study offers a comprehensive list of factors having an impact on the successful implementation of an ERP system. Managers should focus on the enhancement of the most significant of these factors, identifying specific objectives for achieving successful implementation and increased performance. Moreover, the present study underlines the mediating role of ERP implementation success in the relationship between various antecedents (critical success factors) and final outcomes (organizational performance). It seems that such an approach can better describe the hypothesized relationships, since the effects of the four antecedents need to be translated into tangible benefits (information quality, system quality, and service quality) in order to have a positive impact on organizational performance.

6.2   Limitations and Future Research

The study is somehow limited by the poor definition of its population. This limitation is inherent to all studies of the field, since a complete list of ERP implementing companies is not easy to acquire. Further research is suggested with larger samples that would, probably, offer more information and strengthen the results of the present study. Moreover, it would be interesting to examine more factors and gather primary data from all company personnel, so as to achieve a more complete view of the subject under investigation.

References

1. Nandi, M.L., Kumar, A.: Centralization and the success of ERP implementation. J. Enterp. Inf. Manag. **29**(5), 728–750 (2016). doi:10.1108/JEIM-07-2015-0058
2. HassabElnaby, H.R., Hwang, W., Vonderembse, M.A.: The impact of ERP implementation on organizational capabilities and firm performance. Bench. Inter. J. **19**(4/5), 618–633 (2012). doi:10.1108/14635771211258043
3. Garg, P., Garg, A.: Factors influencing ERP implementation in retail sector: an empirical study from India. J. Enterp. Inf. Manag. **27**(4), 424–448 (2014). doi:10.1108/JEIM-06-012-0028
4. Al-Mashari, M., Al-Mudimigh, A., Zairi, M.: Enterprise resource planning: taxonomy of critical factors. Eur. J. Op. Res. **146**(2), 352–364 (2003). doi:10.1016/S0377-2217(02),00554-4
5. Amid, A., Moalagh, M., Ravasan, A.Z.: Identification and classification of ERP critical failure factors in Iranian industries. Inf. Syst. **37**(3), 227–237 (2012). doi:10.1016/j.is.2011.10.010
6. Umble, E.J., Haft, R.R., Umble, M.M.: Enterprise resource planning: Implementation procedures and critical success factors. Eur. J. Op. Res. **146**(2), 241–257 (2003). doi:10.1016/S0377-2217(02)00547-7
7. Yang, C., Su, Y.F.: The relationship between benefits of ERP systems implementation and its impacts on firm performance of SCM. J. Enterp. Inf. Manag. **22**(6), 722–752 (2009). doi:10.1108/17410390910999602
8. Madapusi, A., D'Souza, D.: The influence of ERP system implementation on the operational performance of an organization. Intern. J. Inf. Manag. **32**(1), 24–34 (2012). doi:10.1016/j.ijinfomgt.2011.06.004
9. Panorama Consulting Solutions: ERP report (2014). http://go.panorama-consulting.com/rs/panoramaconsulting/images/2014-ERP-Report.pdf
10. Sun, H., Ni, W., Lam, R.: A step-by-step performance assessment and improvement method for ERP implementation: action case studies in Chinese companies. Comput. Ind. **68**, 40–52 (2015). doi:10.1016/j.compind.2014.12.005
11. Ahmad, M.M., Cuenca, R.P.: Critical success factors for ERP implementation in SMEs. Robot. Comput. Integr. Manuf. **29**(3), 104–111 (2013). doi:10.1016/j.rcim.2012.04.019
12. Ram, J., Corkindale, D., Wu, M.L.: Implementation critical success factors (CSFs) for ERP: do they contribute to implementation success and post-implementation performance? Inter. J. Prod. Econ. **144**(1), 157–174 (2013). doi:10.1016/j.ijpe.2013.01.032
13. Holland, C.P., Light, B.: A critical success factors model for ERP implementation. IEEE Softw. **16**(3), 30–36 (1999)

14. Nah, F.F., Lau, J.L., Kuang, J.: Critical factors for successful implementation of enterprise systems. Bus. Process Manag. J. **7**(3), 285–296 (2001). doi:10.1108/14637150110392782
15. Hong, K.K., Kim, Y.G.: The critical success factors for ERP implementation: an organizational fit perspective. Inf. Manag. **40**, 25–40 (2002). doi:10.1016/S0378-7206(01)00134-3
16. Loh, T.C., Koh, S.C.L.: Critical elements for a successful enterprise resource planning implementation in small-and medium-sized enterprises. Inter. J. Prod. Res. **42**(17), 3433–3455 (2004). doi:10.1080/00207540410001671679
17. Motwani, J., Subramanian, R., Gopalakrishna, P.: Critical factors for successful ERP implementation: exploratory findings from four case studies. Comput. Ind. **56**(6), 529–544 (2005). doi:10.1016/j.compind.2005.02.005
18. Ehie, I.C., Madsen, M.: Identifying critical issues in enterprise resource planning (ERP) implementation. Comput. Ind. **56**(6), 545–557 (2005). doi:10.1016/j.compind.2005.02.006
19. Ifinedo, P., Nahar, N.: Quality, impact and success of ERP systems: a study involving some firms in the nordic-baltic region. J. Inf. Technol. Impact. **6**(1), 19–46 (2006)
20. Chien, S.W., Tsaur, S.M.: Investigating the success of ERP systems: case studies in three Taiwanese high-tech industries. Comput. Ind. **58**(8,9), 783–793 (2007). doi:10.1016/j.compind.2007.02.001
21. Garcia-Sanchez, N., Prez-Bernal, L.E.: Determination of critical success factors in implementing an ERP system: a field study in Mexican enterprises information. Technol. Dev. **13**(3), 293–309 (2007). doi:10.1002/itdj.20075
22. Françoise, O., Bourgault, M., Pellerin, R.: ERP implementation through critical success factors' management. Bus. Process Manag. J. **15**(3), 371–394 (2009). doi:10.1108/14637150910960620
23. Ram, J., Corkindale, D.: How "critical" are the critical success factors (CSFs)? examining the role of CSFs for ERP. Bus. Process Manag. J. **20**(1), 151–174 (2014). doi:10.1108/BPMJ-11-2012-0127
24. Leyh, C.: Critical success factors for ERP projects in small and medium-sized enterprises: the perspective of selected German SMEs. In: IEEE Federated Conference on Computer Science and Information Systems, pp. 1181–1190 (2014). doi:10.15439/2014F243
25. Ravasan, A.Z., Mansouri, T.: A dynamic ERP critical failure factors modelling with FCM throughout project lifecycle phases. Prod. Plan. Control. **27**(2), 65–82 (2016). doi:10.1080/09537287.2015.1064551
26. Kale, P.T., Banwait, S.S., Laroiya, S.C.: Performance evaluation of ERP implementation in Indian SMEs. J. Manuf. Technol. Manag. **21**(6), 758–780 (2010). doi:10.1108/17410381011064030
27. Nicolaou, A.I., Bajor, L.H.: ERP systems implementation and firm performance. Rev. Bus. Inf. Syst. **8**(1), 53–60 (2011). doi:10.19030/rbis.v8i1.4504
28. Tsai, M.T., Li, E.Y., Lee, K.W., Tung, W.H.: Beyond ERP implementation: the moderating effect of knowledge management on business performance. Total Qual. Manag. **22**(2), 131–144 (2011). doi:10.1080/14783363.2010.529638
29. Zhang, L., Huang, J., Xu, X.: Impact of ERP investment on company performance: evidence from manufacturing firms in China. Tsinghua Sci. Technol. **17**(3), 232–240 (2012). doi:10.1109/TST.2012.6216752
30. Ince, H., Imamoglu, S.Z., Keskin, H., Akgun, A., Efe, M.N.: The impact of ERP systems and supply chain management practices on firm performance: case of turkish companies. Soc. Behav. Sci. **99**, 1124–1133 (2013). doi:10.1016/j.sbspro.2013.10.586
31. Dumitru, V.F., Albu, N., Albu, C.N., Dumitru, M.: ERP implementation and organizational performance: A Romanian case study of best practices. Amf. Econ. **15**(34), 518–531 (2013)

32. Voulgaris, F., Lemonakis, C., Papoutsakis, M.: The impact of ERP systems on firm performance: the case of Greek enterprises. Glob. Bus. Econ. Rev. **17**(1), 112–129 (2014). doi:10.1504/GBER.2015.066536
33. Ram, J., Wu, M.L., Tagg, R.: Competitive advantage from ERP projects: examining the role of key implementation drivers. Inter. J. Proj. Manag. **32**(4), 663–675 (2014). doi:10.1016/j.ijproman.2013.08.004
34. Patalas-Maliszewska, J., Krebs, I.: The impact of enterprises systems on sales performance: a study of ERP system implementations in Polish SMEs. Manag. Prod. Eng. Rev. **5**(2), 54–59 (2014). doi:10.2478/mper-2014-0017
35. Roh, J.J., Hong, P.: Taxonomy of ERP integrations and performance outcomes: an exploratory study of manufacturing firms. Prod. Plan. Control. **26**(8), 617–636 (2015). doi:10.1080/09537287.2014.950624
36. Kharuddin, S., Foong, S.Y., Senik, R.: Effects of decision rationality on ERP adoption extensiveness and organizational performance. J. Enterp. Inf. Manag. **28**(5), 658–679 (2015). doi:10.1108/JEIM-02-2014-0018
37. Le, M.D., Han, K.S.: Understanding the impact of ERP system implementation on firm performance-focused on Vietnamese SMEs. Inter. J. Softw. Eng. Appl. **10**(9), 87–104 (2016). doi:10.14257/ijseia.2016.10.9.09
38. Al-Dhaafri, H., Al-Dhaafri, H., Al-Swidi, A., Al-Swidi, A., Yusoff, R., Yusoff, R.: The mediating role of TQM and organizational excellence, and the moderating effect of entrepreneurial organizational culture on the relationship between ERP and organizational performance. TQM J. **28**(6), 991–1011 (2016). doi:10.1108/TQM-04-2014-0040
39. Dezdar, S., Ainin, S.: Examining ERP implementation success from a project environment perspective. Bus. Process Manag. J. **17**(6), 919–939 (2011). doi:10.1108/14637151111182693
40. Gardiner, S.C., Hanna, J.B., LaTour, M.S.: ERP and the reengineering of industrial marketing processes: a prescriptive overview for the new-age marketing manager. Ind. Mark. Manag. **31**(4), 357–365 (2002). doi:10.1016/S0019-8501(01)00167-5
41. Bradford, M., Florin, J.: Examining the role of innovation diffusion factors on the implementation success of enterprise resource planning systems. Inter. J. Account. Inf. Syst. **4**(3), 205–225 (2003). doi:10.1016/S1467-0895(03)00026-5
42. Cadden, T., Marshall, D., Cao, G.: Opposites attract: organisational culture and supply chain performance. Supply Chain Manag. Inter. J. **18**(1), 86–103 (2013). doi:10.1108/13598541311293203
43. Ke, W., Wei, K.K.: Organizational culture and leadership in ERP implementation. Decis. Support Syst. **45**(2), 208–218 (2008). doi:10.1016/j.dss.2007.02.002
44. Al-Ghamdi, A.: Change management Strategies and Processes for the successful ERP System Implementation: a Proposed Model. Inter. J. Comp. Sci. Inf. Secur. **11**(2), 36–41 (2013)
45. Somers, T.M., Nelson, K.G.: A taxonomy of players and activities across the ERP project life cycle. Inf. Manag. **41**(3), 257–278 (2004). doi:10.1016/S0378-7206(03)00023-5
46. Katerattanakul, P., Lee, J., Hong, S.: Effect of business characteristics and ERP implementation on business outcomes: an exploratory study of Korean manufacturing firms. Manag. Res. Rev. **37**(2), 186–206 (2014). doi:10.1108/MRR-10-2012-0218
47. Shehab, E.M., Sharp, M.W., Supramaniam, L., Spedding, T.A.: Enterprise Resource Planning: an integrative review. Bus. Process. Manag. J. **10**(4), 359–386 (2004). doi:10.1108/14637150410548056
48. Newell, S., Tansley, C., Huang, J.: Social capital and knowledge integration in an ERP project team: the importance of bridging and bonding. Br. J. Manag. **15**(1), 43–57 (2004). doi:10.1111/j.1467-8551.2004.00405.x

49. Bhatti, R.: Critical success factors for the implementation of Enterprise Resource Planning (ERP): empirical validation. In: The Second International Conference on Innovation in Information Technology, pp. 1–10 (2005)
50. Chien, T.K., Cheng, M.S.: The implementation strategy of key task for ERP activities. In: Proceedings of the 2014 IEEE International Conference on Industrial Engineering and Engineering Management (IEEM), Malaysia, pp. 1126–1130 (2014)
51. Chang, M., Cheung, W., Cheng, C., Yeung, J.: Understanding ERP system adoption from the user's perspective. Inter. J. Prod. Econ. 113(2), 928–942 (2008). doi:10.1016/j.ijpe.2007.08.011
52. Esteves, J., Pastor, J.A.: Organizational and technological critical success factors behavior along the ERP implementation phases. In: Seruca, I., Cordeiro, J., Hammoudi, S., Filipe J. (eds.) Enterprise Information Systems, pp. 63–71 (2006)
53. Dezdar, S.: Strategic and tactical factors for successful ERP projects: insights from an Asian country. Manag. Res. Rev. 35(11), 1070–1087 (2012). doi:10.1108/01409171211276945
54. DeLone, W.H., McLean, E.R.: Information systems success: the quest for the dependent variable. Inform. Syst. Res. 3(1), 60–95 (1992)
55. Nofal, M., Yusof, Z.: Integration of business intelligence and enterprise resource planning within organizations. Procedia Technol. 11, 658–665 (2013). doi:10.1016/j.protcy.2013.12.242
56. Hair, F., Anderson, R., Tatham, R., Black, W.: Multivariate Data Analysis with Readings. Prentice-Hall International, London (1995)
57. Schumacker, R.E., Lomax, R.G.: A beginner's guide to structural equation modeling. Routledge Academic, New York (2010)
58. Dezdar, S., Ainin, S.: The influence of organizational factors on successful ERP implementation. Manag. Decis. 49(6), 911–926 (2011). doi:10.1108/00251741111143603
59. Zhang, Z., Lee, M.K.O., Huang, P., Zhang, L., Huang, X.: A framework of ERP systems implementation success in China: an empirical study. Inter. J. Prod. Econ. 98(1), 56–80 (2005). doi:10.1016/j.ijpe.2004.09.004
60. Finney, S., Corbett, M.: ERP Implementation: a compilation and analysis of critical success factors. Bus. Process Manag. J. 13(3), 329–347 (2007). doi:10.1108/14637150710752272
61. Shang, S., Seddon, P.B.: Managing process deficiencies with enterprise systems. Bus. Process Manag. J. 13(3), 405–416 (2007). doi:10.1108/14637150710752317
62. Ziemba, E., Kolasa, I.: Risk factors relationships for information systems projects – insight from polish public organizations. In: Ziemba, E. (ed.) FedCSIS 2015. LNBIP, vol. 243, pp. 55–76. Springer, Heidelberg (2016). doi:10.1007/978-3-319-30528-8_4
63. Pawełoszek, I.: Data mining approach to assessment of the ERP system from the vendor's perspective. In: Ziemba, E. (ed.) FedCSIS 2015. LNBIP, vol. 243, pp. 125–143. Springer, Heidelberg (2016). doi:10.1007/978-3-319-30528-8_8

Examining the Critical Success Factors for ERP Implementation: An Explanatory Study Conducted in SMEs

Prodromos Chatzoglou, Dimitrios Chatzoudes[(✉)], Leonidas Fragidis, and Symeon Symeonidis

Democritus University of Thrace, Xanthi, Greece
{pchatzog, lfrangid}@pme.duth.gr,
dchatzoudes@yahoo.gr, ssymeoni@ee.duth.gr

Abstract. The contemporary business environment is characterized by intense global competition, emphasis on the use of technology and need for integrating business processes. In that context, organizations are urged to reduce their costs, increase their productivity and improve customer satisfaction. Enterprise Resource Planning (ERP) systems represent state-of-the-art information technologies that are able to integrate business processes within and beyond organizational boundaries and facilitate the flow of information across all functions. Despite that, ERP implementation projects are complicated, costly and include high failure risks. Moreover, Small and Medium Enterprises (SMEs) rarely possess the appropriate resources and expertise in order to successfully implement ERP systems. The present study aims (a) to develop and (b) empirically test a conceptual framework that investigates the factors affecting ERP system effective implementation in SMEs. The examination of the conceptual framework was made with the use of a newly-developed structured questionnaire that was distributed to a group of Greek SMEs. The reliability and the validity of the questionnaires were thoroughly examined, while research hypotheses were tested using the "Structural Equation Modeling" (SEM) technique. Results offer interesting empirical observations and managerial implications.

Keywords: Enterprise Resource Planning (ERP) · Critical Success Factors (CSFs) · SMEs · Structural Equation Modeling (SEM) · Greece

1 Introduction

Enterprise Resource Planning (ERP) systems are complex Information Systems (IS) that enable the integration of business processes and the seamless flow of information [1]. In other words, they support business operations by providing real time data [2]. An ERP system has organization-wide effects, since it integrates all necessary business functions (e.g. manufacturing, accounting, procurement, sales, human resources, etc.) into a single system with a shared database [1–3].

According to Al-Mashari, Al-Mudimigh, and Zairi [4], a successful ERP system can enhance operational efficiency and create significant competitive advantages. Tsai,

© Springer International Publishing AG 2017
E. Ziemba (Ed.): AITM 2016/ISM 2016, LNBIP 277, pp. 179–201, 2017.
DOI: 10.1007/978-3-319-53076-5_10

Li, Lee and Tung [5] argue that, since their introduction in the early 1990s, ERP systems have become the center of modern business.

The various benefits of ERP systems include: elimination of redundant information, reduction of cycle time, drastic declines in inventory, reduction of production cost, efficient management of the network of suppliers and customers, increased productivity, improved response time, enhanced relationship management (CRM) and supply chain management (SCM) [2–8]. Considering these benefits, it is not surprising that ERP systems are being treated as a major development in the world of business, and have been accepted as a standard business software over the last fifteen years [7, 9].

However, ERP implementation requires considerable financial resources, while the whole implementation project is considered complex, lengthy, and quite challenging [3, 4]. As a result, the success rate of such projects is considered to be quite disappointing [10, 11]. Moreover, Small and Medium Enterprises (SMEs) rarely have the experience and resources to effectively implement ERP systems [12]. Therefore, additional empirical studies are necessary in order to assist SMEs in increasing the success rates of ERP implementation projects.

Under that context, the aim of the present study is twofold: (a) develop an original conceptual framework (research model) examining the impact of various research factors on ERP implementation success, (b) empirically test that framework, using data from Small and Medium Enterprises (SMEs) located in Greece (empirical research).

The development of the conceptual framework was based on two methodological steps: firstly, a review of the literature identified the factors that were used by previous studies as antecedents of ERP implementation success; secondly, a panel of experts was used in order to discuss these factors and provide a list of the most significant ones. That approach was selected due to the significant number of factors that have been proposed in the relevant literature. More specifically, the members of the research team used the opinions of experienced practitioners as a criterion for selecting a specific set of factors from the extensive list that was provided from the literature review analysis. It is strongly argued that randomly selecting the research factors of the proposed conceptual framework would have resulted in the limited reliability of the present research.

The empirical examination of the conceptual framework (that was crystallized after the literature review analysis and the completion of the qualitative research) was conducted on a sample of Greek SMEs. More specifically, a newly-developed structured questionnaire was used in order to collect the appropriate primary data. The questionnaire was distributed to 421 companies, while 159 usable questionnaires were, finally, returned. Advanced statistical techniques (EFA, CFA) were used in order to enhance the validity and reliability of the results, while research hypotheses were tested using the "Structural Equation Modeling" (SEM) technique.

The present study makes an effort to point out areas that companies should emphasize in order to successfully adopt ERP systems and, therefore, harvest their potential benefits. Its contribution lies in this enhanced approach. In synopsis, the study contributes in the following areas:

- It focuses on Small and Medium enterprises (SMEs), an approach that has found limited empirical investigation in the international literature. The literature review analysis underlined that the contemporary research mostly examines the implementation of ERP systems in large organizations.
- It examines the antecedents of ERP implementation success in SMEs of a European country. The literature review analysis that was conducted failed to recognize enough similar studies.
- It uses a qualitative research in order to recognize the most important antecedents of ERP implementation success and, then, develops a conceptual framework based on these factors. According to the best of the researchers' knowledge, such an approach is unique in the relevant literature. Moreover, it is significant, since previous studies used factors that were randomly selected from the literature, without a solid empirical basis [e.g. 7, 13–15].
- It can be perceived as a reference point for future studies, since it offers a critique concerning the multitude of ERP implementation antecedents that have been examined in the international literature.
- Its results may be generalized in other developed countries with similar characteristics, and produce valuable managerial lessons for practitioners in these countries.

2 Literature Review

2.1 Critical Success Factors

Critical Success Factors (CSFs) identify key business areas that require constant management attention [16]. In plain words, CSFs assist managers to directly affect a specific outcome, by proactively taking necessary actions in certain areas [13, 16].

According to Ram, Corkindale, and Wu [13], numerous CSFs of ERP implementation have been introduced in the relevant literature. For example, Shaul and Tauber [17] conducted a literature review and identified 94 CSFs. Nevertheless, a general consensus on the CSFs of ERP implementation does not yet exist [18]. Moreover, it seems that most empirical studies focus exclusively on large organizations [18].

According to Saade and Nijher [19], despite the growth in the investigation of CSFs regarding ERP implementation, there is a long way before the empirical contribution can be considered to be substantial. Additionally, despite the wide range of CSFs proposed in the literature, many organizations continue to experience failures and difficulties in implementing ERP systems [19], thus, calling for additional research.

More significantly, according to Ram and Corkindale [16], there is a lack of an established process for the identification of CSFs. Various authors use subjective criteria in order to select the critical factors utilized in their studies, something that results in a lack of objective approaches. The present study heals that gap in the relevant literature, by developing a conceptual framework that was crystallized after a coherent two-step approach (literature review analysis and consultation with experienced practitioners/focus-group methodology).

2.2 Previous Studies

Numerous studies have investigated the critical success factors for ERP system implementation. However, most of these studies are focused on larger organizations [11, 12, 20]. ERP adoption by Small and Medium Enterprises SMEs has traditionally received less attention from the international literature. According to Poba-Nzaou, Raymond and Fabi [20], this represents an area for additional research, especially since SMEs face greater difficulties in adopting ERP systems.

The present study conducted an extensive review of the relevant literature, in an effort to grasp a spherical view of the subject and, therefore, better define its research scope. The following paragraphs present a brief analysis of a representative sample of previous empirical studies that are mostly concerned with CSFs on SMEs.

Poba-Nzaou, Raymond, and Fabi [20] adopted a single-case methodology in order to examine the factors that minimize the risk of ERP system implementation. More specifically, they tested a process model that focuses on risk minimization in all stages of ERP implementation [20]. Their approach was purely qualitative and the generalizability of their results very limited. In the same vein, Lee, Lee, and Kang [21] conducted a case study on a Korean SME. They found that ERP implementation provided numerous advantages to that specific company (e.g. reduction of material loss, improvement of corporate image, etc.) and highlighted the critical points of its implementation. Nevertheless, their study was also very hard to be generalized to other SMEs.

Sumner and Bradley [22] and Doom, Milis, Poelmans, and Bloemen [18] conducted multiple case studies in SMEs. Sumner and Bradley [22] examined eight SMEs located in the USA and concluded that most of the CSFs identified in the literature for larger organizations also apply to these companies. Doom, Milis, Poelmans, and Bloemen [18] examined four Belgian SMEs and draw the same conclusion. Nevertheless, they also identified distinct differences in the critical factors that are significant for smaller organizations [22]. Either way, both of these studies suffer from limited generalizability, according to their authors [18, 22]. The same also applies for the case studies conducted by Grandhi and Chugh [25] and Christofi, Nunes, Chao Peng, and Lin [29].

The empirical study of Shaul and Tauber [27] attempted to propose an analytical success model for ERP implementation in SMEs. More specifically, the study clustered 94 CSFs, already identified in the relevant literature, into 15 categories (factors). Moreover, the success factors were grouped across the six phases of the ERP life cycle. The results provided by Shaul and Tauber [27] were quite analytical, but relatively vague and out of focus. The same limitation applies for the findings of Ahmad and Cuenca [28], who conducted a qualitative study and identified 33 CSFs of ERP implementation.

Saini, Nigam, and Misra [11] examined the success factors for implementing ERP systems at Indian SMEs. Their argued that technological factors (e.g. IT infrastructure), people factors (e.g. cross-functional team), and organizational factors (e.g. adaptability to changes) have a direct impact on the success of ERP implementation [11]. As it can be seen on Table 1, few other empirical studies have also examined the CSFs of ERP implementation [8, 12, 24, 26, 30, 32]. For example, Awa and Ojiabo [12] utilized the

Table 1. Synopsis of previous studies concerning SMEs

Study	Field	Method	Main findings
[20]: Poba-Nzaou et al., 2008	One Canadian SME	Case study	The SME applied ten specific practices in adopting ERP
[21]: Lee et al., 2008	One Korean SME	Case study	The study provided qualitative information
[22]: Sumner and Bradley, 2009	Eight SMEs for the USA	Multiple case study	CSFs: Top management support, End-user involvement, Vanilla implementation of key business processes, Team-building
[23]: Xia et al., 2009	Chinese SMEs	Literature review analysis	CSFs: Top management support, Project team competence, Scope, Change management, Data accuracy, Education & training
[18]: Doom et al., 2010	Four Belgian SMEs	Multiple case study	Thirteen (13) CSFs were identified
[24]: Basu et al., 2012	Indian SMEs	TOPSIS method	CSFs: Top management support, Project management, Project team competence, Education and training, Change management, Package selection, Communication
[25]: Grandhi and Chugh, 2012	Two SMEs (Italy, Australia)	Case study	The study revealed three strategies that ERP vendors use in order to encourage ERP adoption from SMEs
[26]: Nikitovic and Strahonja, 2012	Croatian SMEs	Survey	The tree most significant CSFs are: Top management support, User involvement, Clear goals
[27]: Shaul and Tauber, 2012	SMEs in the Mediterranean	Survey	The study clustered 94 CSFs, already identified, into 15 categories
[28]: Ahmad and Cuenca, 2013	SMEs in North-East UK	Interviews	Thirty three (33) CSFs were identified
[11]: Saini et al., 2013	Indian SMEs	Statistical z-test	Five technological factors, four people factors and ten organizational factors have an impact on ERP implementation
[29]: Christofi et al., 2013	One Cypriot SME	Case study	ERP implementation may require changes in work practices, understanding of technology, ownership and control of business processes, organizational wide policies
[30]: Xie et al., 2014	SMEs in the UK and N. America	Simulation model	CSFs: Project management, Top management, Information technology, User and vendor support

(*continued*)

Table 1. (*continued*)

Study	Field	Method	Main findings
[8]: Chien *et al.*, 2014	Taiwanese SMEs	Explanatory approach	*CSFs*: Centripetal forces, Cohesion
[31]: Bansal and Agarwal, 2015	Indian SMEs	Regression and path analysis	The study examined the causal relationships among various CSFs
[32]: Almajali *et al.*, 2016	Jordanian SMEs	Explanatory approach	*CSFs*: Training, Supportive leadership, Ease of use, User satisfaction
[12]: Awa and Ojiabo, 2016	Nigerian SMEs	Explanatory approach	Twelve (12) CSFs were identified (six with positive and six with negative impact on ERP implementation)

TOE (Technology-Organization-Environment) framework in order to investigate how twelve factors explain the adoption of ERP systems. Empirical results provided support for most of the hypotheses of the study. The most significant conclusion of Awa and Ojiabo [12] was that ERP adoption by SMEs is more driven by technological factors, than by organizational and environmental factors.

In summary, the literature includes the following gaps: (a) There is a multitude of CSFs that have been used in order to predict ERP implementation success. Therefore, one is unable to determine which are actually the most important. The need for additional research is imperative; (b) The focus on SMEs has been limited; (c) Very few studies have utilized specific criteria for selecting certain factors, and excluding others, from their analysis. Selecting factors without justification is considered as a significant limitation; (d) Few of the published empirical studies were carried out in European countries; (e) Very few studies built on previous research. The present study was designed so as to cover these limitations (research gaps) found in the relevant literature.

3   Conceptual Framework

The literature review analysis that was conducted prior to the development of the conceptual framework of the present study revealed that numerous factors have been used in order to predict ERP implementation success. Therefore, an important challenge was to decide upon the factors that were going to be incorporated into the proposed conceptual framework. The main objective was to construct a conceptual framework that incorporates the most significant factors used in the literature. Moreover, the incorporated factors were expected to have a high degree of relevance with the overall context of the study (Greek SMEs).

In order to address that critical issue, a qualitative research was conducted prior to the quantitative research. More analytically, a 'panel of experts' was formed in order to evaluate the factors that have been used in the relevant literature and assist in selecting the most appropriate ones for the proposed conceptual framework of the present study. More specifically, the focus group methodology was used.

This approach offers certain benefits: (a) the selection of the factors that were, finally, incorporated in the proposed conceptual framework was not conducted according to the subjective judgment of the researchers, but was a result of a more coherent and objective procedure, (b) the proposed conceptual framework has a strong basis on the opinions of experienced practitioners (managers of SMEs), (c) the selection of factors with low significance was avoided. It is believed that the random selection of the research factors, without any theoretical or empirical justification, would have resulted in the limited reliability of the present study.

In order to enhance the validity of the qualitative research, two sessions held in different geographical areas were conducted. All companies were selected in random, using data from the Chamber of Commerce. Each focus group included five managers of SMEs. This approach is in line with the main principles of the focus group methodology [33], since there was an appropriate number of participants for each session, two different sessions with different participants were conducted, while the represented companies were randomly selected.

The participants of each group were given (in paper) an extensive list of factors that have been used in the literature in order to predict ERP successful implementation. Then, a detailed conversation was conducted, with two members of the research team acting as moderators [33]. Each focus group took approximately two hours. Notes were taken during each session by a second moderator, while additional notes were added after reviewing the recorded sessions. After long discussions and deliberations, each focus group unanimously chose the nine most important factors of the provided list. The two focus groups agreed, with minor exceptions, in the same factors.

The conceptual framework of the present study incorporates these nine (independent) factors, resulting from the qualitative research, and one dependent factor, namely ERP implementation success. Additionally, 'organizational impact' was added in the proposed conceptual framework, in order to investigate the effect of ERP implementation on various measures of organizational performance.

3.1 Top Management Support

Top management support could be easily defined as the involvement of business executives in the areas related with ERP implementation [34]. It has been highlighted, by several authors, as a critical factor for the successful implementation of ERP systems [10, 35 36]. Senior management has two roles during implementation: supplying funds and offering leadership [10]. Al-Mashari, Al-Mudimigh, and Zairi [4] insisted that senior management support should be offered, without disruption, during the whole implementation period. Participation, support, and senior-level sponsorship are dimensions that have been found to significantly affect ERP implementation [37].

ERP implementation does not, exclusively, evolve around software reengineering. On the contrary, it includes the extensive restructuring of business processes. Consequently, senior executives must clearly and publicly indicate their support (economic or not), in order to highlight the priority given to implementation [10, 35, 37].

H1:   Top management support has a positive effect on ERP implementation success.

3.2 Organizational Culture

Organizational culture represents the shared ideologies and convictions that have an impact on organizational attitudes and activities [38]. A common culture, shared between various organizational members, has an impact on the willingness to change, e.g. to adopt a new Information System. Research has shown that organizational culture is quite significant for the success of most organizational changes [39, 40]. Jarvenpaa and Staples [40] argue that there should be a fit between the culture of the organization and the nature of the changes that may occur from implementing an ERP system.

Additionally, according to Jones, Cline, and Ryan [39], organizational culture has an effect on employee behavior towards knowledge sharing, while knowledge sharing is crucial for the successful implementation of ERP systems. Ruppel and Harrington [41] argue that organizational culture has an effect on the implementation of intranet and other information systems used inside the organization.

H2:   Organizational culture has a positive effect on ERP implementation success.

3.3 External Pressure

Sometimes, the implementation of an ERP system does not have intrinsic motives. On the contrary, companies are being forced to implement an IS, either by their supply chain partners or by their competitors [42, 43]. In the first case, implementation becomes a prerequisite for the continuous cooperation with a partner (supplier and/or customer), while in the second case, the adoption decision is based on the need to follow the competitors, and, hence, avoid any possible downturn from not doing so [43].

In the present study, it is hypothesized that when companies find themselves under pressure from the external environment, they tend to try harder to achieve their desired goals. Therefore, the higher the external pressure, the more successful the implementation of the ERP system.

H3:   External pressure has a positive effect on ERP implementation success.

3.4 Vendor Support

Vendor support is offered from software retailers and/or consulting companies [5]. In most of the cases, the retailer is, also, the consultant during, or after, the implementation. Vendor support includes user training, extended technical assistance during and after the implementation, maintenance, updates, etc. Additionally, vendors offer analytical advice concerning the selection of the appropriate ERP software [44]. According to Wang, Lin, Jiang, and Klein [4], vendors significantly enhance the effectiveness of the implemented system, via experience sharing and knowledge transfer.

Through continuous collaboration, formal training and knowledge dissemination, consultants assist their customers in receiving the full benefits of the implemented system [45]. The trustworthiness of the vendor is extremely important in determining the success, or the failure of the whole effort [46]. Koh, Simpson, Padmore, Dimitri-adis, and Misopoulos [46] found out that the close relationship with the vendor is a critical success factor for the implementation of an ERP system.

H4:   Vendor support has a positive effect on ERP implementation success.

3.5   Project Management

The implementation of an ERP system is a risky and complex project [15]. As it is evident, such projects acquire excellent management, since numerous stakeholders (different business units, suppliers, customers, vendors/consultants) are deeply involved [14, 15]. The manager of an ERP project should bear in mind different timetables, various milestones, equipment requirements, workforce availability, and budget needs [37]. Hence, successful implementation is synonymous with the man-agement of a plethora of tasks. All these tasks should be carefully monitored and managed.

More specifically, standard meetings and reports should be provided for all project collaborators. Effective project management is very crucial, since implementation success is, usually, assessed on the basis of budget and time compliance [15]. Exec-utives expect the implementation period to be completed on time, and on budget.

H5:   Project management has a positive effect on ERP implementation success.

3.6   Training

Training is considered to be a basic parameter in every ERP implementation project [35]. Hong and Kim [47] argue that training should be provided before, during and after implementation, while both technical and procedural issues should be carefully addressed. Finally, on-the-job training appears to be the most efficient choice, between all available methods [10]. Nah, Zuckweiler, and Lau [48] found out that adequate training enhances implementation success, while lack of training undermines the whole process. Additionally, sufficient training builds a positive climate towards the imple-mented system, thus, increasing its use and overall acceptance. Moreover, training enhances the ease of use, which in turn increases the probability for system success [49].

H6:   Training has a positive effect on ERP implementation success.

3.7   User Involvement

User involvement is one of the most influential factors in ERP projects [4, 10, 47]. Numerous studies argue that users should be actively involved before and during the entire ERP implementation process [7]. This will ensure that the system has a better fit with business processes, since its development will be based on real needs [4, 7].

According to various authors [14], user involvement increases user satisfaction and user acceptance, by developing realistic expectations about the capabilities of the system. Additionally, user involvement increases the perceived level of control, through user participation in the entire project [14]. When all the above conditions are being successfully met, the implementation of the ERP system will be much more efficient.

H7:   User involvement has a positive effect on ERP implementation success.

3.8   Business Process Reengineering

Business Process Reengineering (BPR) is the radical rethinking and redesign of business processes, in order to achieve improvements in critical measures, such as cost, quality, delivery, and speed [37]. ERP implementation requires such a radical redesign of business processes, since the new ERP system is expected to drastically change several aspects of doing business [50]. Reengineering business processes in a way that makes them compatible with the implemented system appears as an important antecedent of ERP implementation success [37].

H8:   Business Process Reengineering (BPR) has a positive effect on ERP implementation success.

3.9   Implemented Modules

ERP systems may be implemented in modules. A company does not have to conduct a full scale implementation; on the contrary, certain modules could be implemented on the basis of its special needs and requirements [51]. According to Yeh, Yang, and Lin [52], it would be unwise to avoid implementing most of the available modules, since only full implementation really ensures the expected benefits. Some empirical studies have argued that there is a relationship between the number of implemented modules and the functional effectiveness of the ERP system [51]. After all, the more modules a company implements, the higher its benefits from cross-operational cooperation [52].

H9:   The number of implemented modules has a positive effect on ERP implementation success.

3.10   ERP Implementation Success and Organizational Performance

The construct of "organizational performance", as it has been captured in the present study, includes measures of multiple dimensions, such as productivity, cycle time, cost reduction, information flow, and customer satisfaction. Its main goal is to include both qualitative and quantitative measures of organizational performance. Law and Ngai [53] followed a similar approach. Many previous studies investigated the impact of

ERP implementation on firm performance [54], while its impact on organizational performance has received less empirical examination. Therefore, it is hypothesized:

H10:   ERP implementation success has a positive effect on organizational performance.

The synthesis of the hypotheses presented above formulates the proposed conceptual framework of the present study (Fig. 1). It should be underlined that, according to the best of the researcher's knowledge, such a conceptual framework (combination of factors) has never been examined before in the literature.

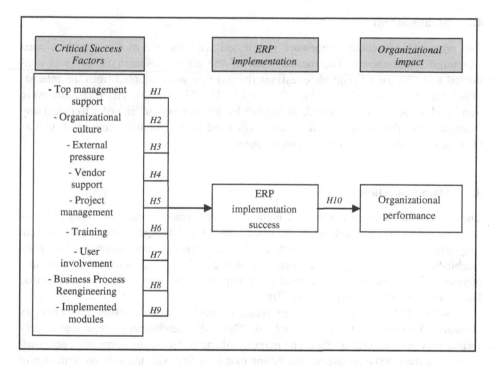

Fig. 1. The proposed conceptual framework

4 Research Methodology

4.1 Population of the Study

The population of the present study includes Greek SMEs that have implemented an ERP system. Data concerning companies that could possibly be included in the sample were obtained via the web sites of the leading ERP system providers operating in Greece. Since no other database including companies using ERP systems exist, the use of the certain method was the only one able to provide usable information. Totally, 678 Greek SMEs that have implemented an ERP system were identified.

SMEs are defined according to the number of their employees and their turnover. More specifically, "*medium-sized enterprises are those with fewer than 250 employees and a turnover of less than or equal to €50 million, or a balance sheet of less than or equal to €43 million*" [55].

SMEs are considered to be the cornerstone of the Greek economy, since they represent 99,9% of the total number of companies. In 2010, there were 742.000 SMEs, with 2.512.493 employees, which represent more than 80% of the total employment, well above the EU average. Greece has a very high share of SMEs, particularly micro enterprises, compared to the EU average [56].

4.2   Measurement

The proposed conceptual framework was tested with the use of a newly-developed structured questionnaire. The measurement of the eleven research factors was conducted with the use of multiple questions (items) that were adopted from the international literature [10, 11, 14, 39, 40, 42, 43, 45, 47, 51–53]. All questions were translated to Greek and then back to English by another person, in order to detect any discrepancies. The five-point Likert scale was used for the measurement of all factors (1 = 'strongly disagree' to 5 = 'strongly agree').

4.3   Data Collection

The questionnaire and a cover letter including clarifications, was sent to the IT managers of the companies that were identified (see Sect. 4.1). Questionnaires were sent only after a telephonic contact with the IT manager in each company has been established. After making all necessary telephone calls, 421 questionnaires were distributed to 421 companies that agreed to participate in the survey. The research period lasted three months (March to May 2015).

Totally, 165 questionnaires were returned, and after conducting all necessary controls 159 were used for data analysis. The 159 questionnaires represent a very satisfactory response rate (38%). The majority of the participating companies are small sized (less than 100 employees), something that is in line with the average firm size of the country.

The majority (21.7%) of the companies of the sample belong to the 'Informatics' industry, while 17.3% belong to the 'Food' and 14.6% to the 'Electronic' industry (sector). Moreover, the 65.4% of the companies of the sample employ 51 to 250 employees (medium-sized), 28.9% employ 11 to 50 employees (small), while only 5.7% employ less than 10 employees (micro). The majority of the companies (47.5%) have been using an ERP system for more than three years, 31.8% less than three years and 20.7% less than one year. Finally, about half of the Greek companies of the sample (51.6%) have chosen 'SAP Ltd' as their ERP system provider, 25.6% 'Oracle Ltd' and 22.8% have chosen another supplier.

4.4   Reliability and Validity

The questionnaire that was used in the present study was rigorously tested for its content and construct validity.

The test for the content validity was conducted via a pilot study. More specifically, a draft of the final questionnaire was sent to four practitioners and two academics, in order to test whether it met all theoretical and practical requirements. Specialists' comments enhanced certain aspects of the questionnaire.

To test the construct validity, each research factor was evaluated: (a) for its unidimensionality and reliability (Table 2), (b) for its goodness of fit to the proposed research model (Table 3). The examination of the unidimensionality of each research factor was conducted using Explanatory Factor Analysis (EFA). Moreover, the statistical measure 'Cronbach Alpha' was used for estimating each factor's reliability. All tests concluded that the scales used are valid and reliable (see Table 2 for the main results). More specifically, the following measures have been examined [57]:

- Appropriateness of the factor analysis: (a) 'Bartlett's test of Sphericity' (it should be statistically significant at the 0.05 level), (b) 'Kaiser-Mayer-Olkin' (KMO) (values over 0,8 are satisfactory, while values over 0.6 are acceptable).
- Number of extracted factors: 'Eigenvalue' (factors whose 'eigenvalue' is over 1 are selected).
- Item significance: Factor loadings (for a sample size of more than 150 observations, a loading over 0.45 is considered significant).

Table 2. Estimation of unidimensionality and reliability

Factors	KMO	Bartlett's test	Eigen-value	TVE	Cronbach alpha
Top management support	0.736	139.2[a]	2.546	67.3%	0.789
Organizational culture	0.894	214.9[a]	2.871	71.5%	0.823
External pressure	0.779	77.5[a]	1.371	68.4%	0.801
Vendor support	0.831	145.6[a]	2.874	81.7%	0.745
Project management	0.799	154.2[a]	1.741	84.7%	0.771
Training	0.854	95.5[a]	2.713	71.9%	0.723
User involvement	0.736	214.3[a]	2.124	76.2%	0.755
Business Process Reengineering	0.711	325.3[a]	2.587	74.1%	0.737
Implemented modules	0.857	217.6[a]	1.342	83.4%	0.741
ERP implementation success	0.839	169.7[a]	1.619	84.5%	0.901
Organizational performance	0.759	171.3[a]	2.391	88.6%	0.733

[a]$p < 0.01$

Table 3. Estimation of the goodness of fit

Factors	Normed X2	C.R.	V.E.	RMSEA	CFI/GFI
Top management support	1.57	0.78	65.6%	0.077	0.94/0.96
Organizational culture	2.67	0.74	69.4%	0.053	0.97/0.97
External pressure	3.15	0.86	0.81%	0.067	0.99/0.97
Vendor support	3.52	0.82	0.76%	0.084	0.91/0.93
Project management	2.19	0.76	0.67%	0.075	0.99/0.98
Training	1.97	0.77	0.63%	0.063	0.90/0.93
User involvement	2.37	0.69	0.57%	0.086	0.95/0.99
Business Process Reengineering	2.45	0.73	0.81%	0.059	0.90/0.90
Implemented modules	2.65	0.83	0.74%	0.061	0.91/0.96
ERP implementation success	2.77	0.77	0.64%	0.074	0.93/0.91
Organizational performance	1.61	0.74	0.61%	0.081	0.93/0.95

- Variance explained by each factor: Total Variance Explained (TVE) (it should be higher than 50%).
- Reliability: 'Cronbach Alpha' (values greater than 0.7 are considered to be valid).

The evaluation of the goodness of fit of each research factor to the proposed model was conducted using Confirmatory Factor Analysis (CFA). All tests produced satisfactory results (see Table 3 for the main results). More specifically, the following measures have been examined [58]:

- X^2: It should be statistically insignificant (p > 0.05). Since it is quite sensitive to sample size, usually the 'normed X^2' is being examined.
- Normed X^2 (X^2/df): Values between 1 and 3 are desirable, while values between 1 and 5 are acceptable.
- Construct Reliability (C.R.): It should higher than 0.7.
- Variance Extracted (V.E.): It should higher than 50%.
- RMSEA: It should be less than 0.08.
- CFI /GFI: They both should be higher than 0.9.

5 Empirical Results

5.1 Model Valuation

The examination of the proposed conceptual framework was conducted using the "Structural Equation Modeling" technique. The SEM approach was used because of its ability to examine a number of linear causal relationships, where one or more factors are both dependent and independent. The estimation of the structural model was conducted with the Maximum Likelihood Estimation method, which is the most widespread method of estimation [58]. The Covariance Matrix was used as the table of entry. The statistical package AMOS 20.0 was used for the appropriate analysis.

To evaluate the fit of the overall model the chi-square value ($X^2 = 49.7$) and the p-value ($p = 0.000$) were estimated. These values indicate a satisfactory fit of the data to the overall model. However, the sensitivity of the X^2 statistic to the sample size enforces to control other supplementary measures of evaluating the overall model, such as the "Normed-X^2" index (3.1), the RSMEA index (0.077) the CFI (0.99) and the GFI (0.97), that all indicate a very good fit. Moreover, for the control of the measurement model the significance of the factor loadings, the Construct Reliability (C.R.) and the Variance Extracted (V.E.) were estimated. Results indicated that all loadings are significant at the $p < 0.05$ level, while C.R. and V.E. for all factors (constructs) were satisfactory.

5.2   Hypothesis Testing

Seven hypotheses were found significant (H1, H2, H4, H6, H7, H8, H10), while three hypotheses were rejected by the empirical data (H3, H5, H9).

In more detail, the structural model fitted the data well, while the factors that were included can explain 72% of the variance of the dependent factor "ERP implementation success" and 26% of the dependent factor "organizational performance".

After reviewing the empirical results (and more specifically Table 4, as well as Fig. 2), the following observations can be made:

- The successful implementation of an ERP system has its roots on vendor support ($r = 0.36$), training ($r = 0.29$), and user involvement ($r = 0.26$). These three factors were found to have the strongest impact on the main dependent factor of the present study (ERP implementation success).
- No matter how important the role of vendor support, training, and user involvement, the support of top management has, also, been underlined as a significant antecedent of ERP implementation success ($r = 0.26$). Without any doubt, executives should demonstrate their belief on the implemented system, mostly by ensuring its funding and setting the example for its use.
- Moreover, the empirical data revealed that Business Process Reengineering (BPR) is a quite significant factor ($r = 0.35$). This finding adds further support to the previous observations, arguing that BPR should be a priority for vendors, employees and executives.
- Additionally, organizational culture (with emphasis on knowledge-sharing) affects implementation ($r = 0.23$). This factor cannot be easily enhanced prior or during the implementation period, since its development is, usually, a result of the unique history of the organization.
- Finally, the relationship between ERP implementation success and organizational performance has been verified by the empirical data ($r = 0.34$). Concerning the strength of that relationship ($R^2 = 26\%$, including direct and indirect effects), it should be noted that when examining complex phenomena, like organizational performance, even a relatively small predictive power seems to be satisfactory.

Table 4. Results of the structural model

Causal paths (hypotheses)		Estimate	p	Result
H1	Top management support → ERP implementation success	0.26	0.000	Accepted
H2	Organizational culture → ERP implementation success	0.23	0.000	Accepted
H3	External pressure → ERP implementation success	–	0.098	Rejected
H4	Vendor support → ERP implementation success	0.36	0.011	Accepted
H5	Project management → ERP implementation success	–	0.267	Rejected
H6	Training → ERP implementation success	0.29	0.000	Accepted
H7	User involvement → ERP implementation success	0.26	0.000	Accepted
H8	Business Process Reengineering → ERP implementation success	0.35	0.000	Accepted
H9	Implemented modules → ERP implementation success	–	0.164	Rejected
H10	ERP implementation success → Organizational performance	0.34	0.003	Accepted

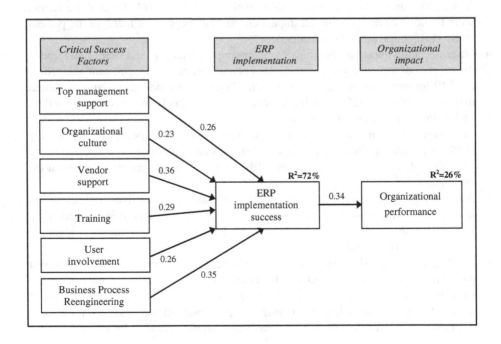

Fig. 2. Empirical results (all paths are statistically significant)

5.3   Comparison with Previous Similar Studies

As mentioned earlier, the literature of the field has failed to thoroughly examine the CSFs for ERP implementation in SMEs. Nevertheless, a comparison among the available studies should be attempted.

Saini, Nigam, and Misra [11] proposed an extensive list of factors that are categorized in three dimensions: (a) technological factors, (b) people factors and (c) organizational factors. The present study concluded that CSFs are categorized into three dimensions: (a) organizational factors (top management support, business process reengineering), (b) people factors (vendor support, training, user involvement), (c) intangible factors (organizational culture). It is argued that the technological dimension, proposed by Saini, Nigam, and Misra [11], is embedded in two of the dimensions proposed in the present study (organizational and people). For instance, vendors provide support concerning the technological issues of the implementation, while employee training is also focused on technological expertise. Moreover, organizational culture, an intangible factor (dimension), is extremely important, since it seems to enhance the other dimensions of the ERP implementation process. According to Jones, Cline, and Ryan [39], organizational culture enables the sharing of knowledge across diverse functions and perspectives during ERP implementation. Therefore, the present study argues that CSFs of ERP implementation are better categorized in the three dimensions proposed above: (a) organizational factors, (b) people factors, (c) intangible factors. Future studies are welcome to further support or criticize this approach.

In a very recent study, Nikitovic and Strahonja [26] examined the CSFs according to the phases of ERP implementation and concluded that the two most important factors are (a) top management support and (b) user involvement. Moreover, they verified the significance of most of the factors that were also highlighted in the present study. Nevertheless, the empirical study of Nikitovic and Strahonja [26] provided an extensive list of CSFs, namely thirty-two, making comparisons between studies quite impossible. Additionally, the managerial implications of such an approach are rather vague. Regretfully, the same approach has been adopted by other studies of the field. More specifically, Ahmad and Cuenca [28] identified thirty-three CSFs, Doom, Milis, Poelmans, and Bloemen [18] identified thirteen CSFs, while Shaul and Taube [17] clustered 94 CSFs, already identified in the literature, into 15 distinct categories. The present study argues that similar conclusions are of limited value for SMEs. According to their nature, SMEs lack the appropriate resources in order to take under consideration complex solutions, no matter how brilliant. Therefore, it is argued that future studies should try to limit the number of proposed CSFs. In that direction, the present study concluded that SMEs should focus on the enhancement of only six factors. The managerial implications of this approach are considered to be more useful for SMEs.

Previous studies conducted in other geographical regions of the European continent (e.g. Eastern and Central Europe) have found similar results. For example, Ziemba and Kolasa [59, 60] found that top management support, user involvement and process management have an impact on information systems projects, while Bradley [49] concluded that the determinants of ERP success are user involvement, user empowerment, system reliability and cooperation with the system supplier (vendor).

6 Conclusions

The present study was motivated by specific gaps that were recognized in the relevant literature of the specific field: (a) development of conceptual frameworks without the use of appropriate practical background, (b) lack of focus on SMEs, especially on those operating in Europe, (c) use of many different research factors predicting ERP implementation. In order to bridge these gaps, the present study used an extensive literature review and qualitative data (focus group sessions with managers of SMEs) in order to develop a conceptual framework that investigated the antecedents of ERP implementation success. Moreover, this framework was tested with the use of a newly-developed structured questionnaire (quantitative data) on a sample of Greek SMEs that have implemented and ERP system.

That specific approach offered certain advantages: focus groups offered practical knowledge concerning the factors with the most significant impact on ERP implementation, while the quantitative research revealed which of these factors are actually significant. The contribution of the study lies on this enhanced approach. More specifically, it offers the necessary ground for comparison and replication. Its conceptual framework may be replicated from future studies, while other scientists may employ its twofold approach as a basis for their future empirical investigation.

The proposed conceptual framework of the study included nine antecedents of ERP implementation success. These factors are perceived as Critical Success Factors for successful ERP implementation. Empirical data were analyzed using the "Structural Equation Modeling" technique, while the validity and the reliability of all research factors were evaluated with the use of enhanced statistical methods (EFA, CFA).

According to the results of the statistical analysis, six of the antecedents included in the research model of the present study were found to have a direct (positive) effect on successful ERP implementation. Additionally, the predictive power of the proposed model was found to be very satisfactory. More specifically, the six antecedents can explain the variance of ERP successful implementation by 72% ($R^2 = 0.72$). On the other hand, three research factors (external pressure, project management, implemented modules) were not found to have an effect on the successful implementation of an ERP system.

Therefore, it is concluded that when implementing an ERP system, organizations should focus on the following six factors: Top management support, Organizational culture, Vendor support, Training, User involvement, Business Process Reengineering. The present study argues that the enhancement of these Critical Success Factors should be conducted before, during and after ERP implementation. Partial focus will only limit their positive effect.

In general, it is concluded that ERP implementation success is a result of intangible factors (organizational culture), people-related factors (vendor support, training, user involvement), and proper leadership (organizational factors) (top management support, business process reengineering).

6.1 Managerial Implications

According to the empirical results, the present study proposes a mechanism that will drive implementation success. Various organizations may utilize this mechanism in order to experience a seamless implementation process. It includes three steps, each describing tasks that should be performed before, during and after the implementation of an ERP system.

Firstly, before the implementation, companies should spend their limited time and resources in selecting the appropriate software retailer. A good fit between the two seems to be very crucial for implementation success. Moreover, employees should be involved in the decision to adopt an ERP system. Executives should take employee attitudes and beliefs under serious consideration. In general, employees should feel like an integrated part of the whole process, while the adoption of the new system should not be understood as a decision that has been forced upon them. Only when employees feel like they have contributed to the implementation initiative, will they accept the changes that may occur. On a more practical level, the contribution of employees before the implementation is crucial for ensuring that the system will be designed in order to have a better fit with existing business practices.

Secondly, during the implementation period (that may be quite short, especially in micro-enterprises), vendors should adopt an analytical (linear) approach. Initially, the most technological-ready employees should be selected in order to test the implemented system. Then, its advantages should be underlined and communicated amongst all personnel. After that, initial training should take place. The main goal is to initiate the system after all employees have been fully involved in the whole process.

Thirdly, after the implementation period, continuous training should be offered by the vendor (or another consultant). After all, the first month following the implementation of the new ERP system is extremely crucial. Employees should feel that the new system enhances their job, while resulting in many other organizational benefits.

6.2 Limitations and Future Research

The present study is somehow limited by the poor definition of its population. This limitation is inherent to all studies of the field, since a complete list of companies that have implemented an ERP system cannot be found in most databases.

Further research is suggested with larger samples that would, probably, offer more information and strengthen the results of the present study. Moreover, it would be interesting to examine more factors and gather primary data from all company personnel, so as to achieve a more complete view of the subject under investigation.

References

1. Fadlalla, A., Amani, F.: A keyword-based organizing framework for ERP intellectual contributions. J. Enterp. Inf. Manag. **28**(5), 637–657 (2015). doi:10.1108/JEIM-09-2014-0090

2. Pawełoszek, I.: Data mining approach to assessment of the ERP system from the vendor's perspective. In: Ziemba, E. (ed.) FedCSIS 2015. LNBIP, vol. 243, pp. 125–143. Springer, Heidelberg (2016). doi:10.1007/978-3-319-30528-8_8

3. Leyh, C.: Critical success factors for ERP projects in small and medium-sized enterprises: the perspective of selected German SMEs. In: IEEE Federated Conference on Computer Science and Information Systems, pp. 1181–1190 (2014). doi:10.15439/2014F24

4. Al-Mashari, M., Al-Mudimigh, A., Zairi, M.: Enterprise resource planning: a taxonomy of critical factors. Eur. J. Oper. Res. **146**(2), 352–364 (2003). doi:10.1016/S0377-2217(02)00554-4

5. Tsai, M.T., Li, E.Y., Lee, K.W., Tung, W.H.: Beyond ERP implementation: the moderating effect of knowledge management on business performance. Total Qual. Manag. **22**(2), 131–144 (2011). doi:10.1080/14783363.2010.529638

6. Hassabelnaby, H.R., Hwang, W., Vonderembse, M.A.: The impact of ERP implementation on organizational capabilities and firm performance. Benchmarking Int. J. **19**(4/5), 618–633 (2012). doi:10.1108/14635771211258043

7. Garg, P., Garg, A.: Factors influencing ERP implementation in retail sector: an empirical study from India. J. Enterp. Inf. Manag. **27**(4), 424–448 (2014). doi:10.1108/JEIM-06-2012-0028

8. Chien, S.W., Lin, H.C., Shih, C.T.: A moderated mediation study: cohesion linking centrifugal and centripetal forces to erp implementation performance. Int. J. Prod. Econ. **158**, 1–8 (2014). doi:10.1016/j.ijpe.2014.06.001

9. Muscatello, J., Chen, I.: Enterprise resource planning (ERP) implementations: theory and practice. Int. J. Enter. Inf. Syst. **4**(1), 63–78 (2008)

10. Zhang, Z., Lee, M.K., Huang, P., Zhang, L., Huang, X.: A framework of ERP systems implementation success in China: an empirical study. Int. J. Prod. Econ. **98**(1), 56–80 (2005). doi:10.1016/j.ijpe.2004.09.004

11. Saini, S., Nigam, S., Misra, S.C.: Identifying success factors for implementation of ERP at Indian SMEs: a comparative study with Indian large organizations and the global trend. J. Mod. Manag. **8**(1), 103–122 (2013). doi:10.1108/17465661311312003

12. Awa, H.O., Ojiabo, O.U.: A model of adoption determinants of ERP within TOE framework. Inf. Technol. People **29**(4), 901–930 (2016). doi:10.1108/ITP-03-2015-0068

13. Ram, J., Corkindale, D., Wu, M.L.: Implementation critical success factors (CSFs) for ERP: do they contribute to implementation success and post-implementation performance? Int. J. Prod. Econ. **144**, 157–174 (2013). doi:10.1016/j.ijpe.2013.01.032

14. Garg, P., Chauhan, A.: Factors affecting the ERP implementation in Indian retail sector. Benchmarking Int. J. **22**(7), 1315–1340 (2015). doi:10.1108/BIJ-11-2013-0104

15. Garg, P., Agarwal, D.: Critical success factors for ERP implementation in a Fortis hospital. J. Enterp. Inf. Manag. **27**(4), 402–423 (2014). doi:10.1108/JEIM-06-2012-0027

16. Ram, J., Corkindale, D.: How "critical" are the critical success factors (CSFs)? Examining the role of CSFs for ERP. Bus. Process Manag. J. **20**(1), 151–174 (2014). doi:10.1108/BPMJ-11-2012-0127

17. Shaul, L., Tauber, D.: Critical success factors in enterprise resource planning systems: review of the last decade. ACM Comput. Surv. **45**(4), 1–39 (2013). doi:10.1145/2501654.2501669

18. Doom, C., Milis, K., Poelmans, S., Bloemen, E.: Critical success factors for ERP implementations in Belgian SMEs. J. Enterp. Inf. Manag. **23**(3), 378–406 (2010). doi:10.1108/17410391011036120

19. Saade, R., Nijher, H.: Critical success factors in enterprise resource planning implementation: a review of case studies. J. Enterp. Inf. Manag. **29**(1), 72–96 (2016). doi:10.1108/JEIM-03-2014-0028

20. Poba-Nzaou, P., Raymond, L., Fabi, B.: Adoption and risk of ERP systems in manufacturing SMEs - a positivist case study. Bus. Process Manag. J. **14**(4), 530–550 (2008). doi:10.1108/14637150810888064
21. Lee, C.K., Lee, H.H., Kang, M.: Successful implementation of ERP systems in small businesses: a case study in Korea. Serv. Bus. **2**(4), 275–286 (2008). doi:10.1007/s11628-008-0045-3
22. Sumner, M.R., Bradley, J.: CSF's for implementing ERP within SME's. In: AMCIS 2009 Proceedings, San Francisco, pp. 1–11 (2009)
23. Xia, Y., Lok, P., Yang, S.: The ERP implementation of SME in China. In: 6th International Conference on Service Systems and Service Management, pp. 135–140. IEEE Press (2009). doi:10.1109/ICSSSM.2009.5174870
24. Basu, R., Upadhyay, P., Das, M.C., Dan, P.K.: An approach to identify issues affecting ERP implementation in Indian SMEs. J. Ind. Eng. Manag. **5**(1), 133–154 (2012). doi:10.3926/jiem.416
25. Grandhi, S., Chugh, R.: Implementation strategies for ERP adoption by SMEs. In: Kim, T., Ko, D., Vasilakos, T., Stoica, A., Abawajy, J. (eds.) FGCN 2012. CCIS, vol. 350, pp. 210–216. Springer, Heidelberg (2012). doi:10.1007/978-3-642-35594-3_30
26. Nikitovic, M., Strahonja, V.: The analysis of CSFs in stages of ERP implementation? Case study in small and medium-sized (SME) companies in Croatia. In: 39th International Convention on Information and Communication Technology, Electronics and Microelectronics, pp. 1494–1499. Croatian Society MIPRO (2016). doi:10.1109/MIPRO.2016.7522375
27. Shaul, L., Tauber, D.: CSFs along ERP life-cycle in SMEs: a field study. Ind. Manag. Data Syst. **112**(3), 360–384 (2012). doi:10.1108/02635571211210031
28. Ahmad, M.M., Cuenca, R.P.: Critical success factors for ERP implementation in SMEs. Robot. Comput. Integr. Manuf. **29**(3), 104–111 (2013). doi:10.1016/j.rcim.2012.04.019
29. Christofi, M., Nunes, M., Chao Peng, G., Lin, A.: Towards ERP success in SMEs through business process review prior to implementation. J. Syst. Inf. Technol. **15**(4), 304–323 (2013). doi:10.1108/JSIT-06-2013-0021
30. Xie, Y., James Allen, C., Ali, M.: An integrated decision support system for ERP implementation in small and medium sized enterprises. J. Enterp. Inf. Manag. **27**(4), 358–384 (2014). doi:10.1108/JEIM-10-2012-0077
31. Bansal, V., Agarwal, A.: Enterprise resource planning: identifying relationships among critical success factors. Bus. Process Manag. J. **21**(6), 1337–1352 (2015). doi:10.1108/BPMJ-12-2014-0128
32. Almajali, D.A., Masa'deh, R.E., Tarhini, A.: Antecedents of ERP systems implementation success: a study on jordanian healthcare sector. J. Enterp. Inf. Manag. **29**(4), 549–565 (2016). doi:10.1108/JEIM-03-2015-0024
33. Berg, B.L., Lune, H., Lune, H.: Qualitative Research Methods for the Social Sciences. Pearson, Boston (2004)
34. Sharma, R., Yetton, P.: The contingent effects of management support and task interdependence on successful information systems implementation. MIS Q. **27**(4), 533–555 (2003)
35. Al-Mashari, M.: A process change-oriented model for ERP application. Int. J. Hum. Comput. Interact. **16**(1), 39–55 (2003). doi:10.1207/S15327590IJHC1601_4
36. Umble, J.E., Haft, R.R., Umble, M.M.: Enterprise resource planning: implementation procedures and critical success factors. Eur. J. Oper. Res. **146**(2), 241–257 (2003). doi:10.1016/S0377-2217(02)00547-7

37. Dezdar, S., Ainin, S.: Examining ERP implementation success from a project environment perspective. Bus. Process Manag. J. **17**(6), 919–939 (2011). doi:10.1108/14637151111182693

38. Cadden, T., Marshall, D., Cao, G.: Opposites attract: organisational culture and supply chain performance. Supply Chain Manag. Int. J. **18**(1), 86–103 (2013). doi:10.1108/13598541311293203

39. Jones, C.M., Cline, M., Ryan, S.: Exploring knowledge sharing in ERP implementation: an organizational culture framework. Decis. Support Syst. **41**, 411–434 (2006). doi:10.1016/j.dss.2004.06.017

40. Jarvenpaa, L.S., Staples, S.D.: Exploring perceptions of organizational ownership of information and expertise. J. Manag. Inf. Syst. **18**(1), 151–183 (2001). doi:10.1080/07421222.2001.11045673

41. Ruppel, P.C., Harrington, J.S.: Sharing knowledge through intranets: a study of organizational culture and intranet implementation. IEEE Trans. Prof. Commun. **44**(1), 37–52 (2001). doi:10.1109/47.911131

42. Liang, H., Saraf, N., Hu, Q., Xue, Y.: Assimilation of enterprise systems: the effect of institutional pressures and the mediating role of top management. MIS Q. **31**(1), 59–87 (2007)

43. Waarts, E., van Everdingen, Y.M., van Hillegersberg, J.: The dynamics of factors affecting the adoption of innovations. J. Prod. Innov. Manag. **19**(6), 412–423 (2002). doi:10.1111/1540-5885.1960412

44. Wang, G.T.E., Lin, C.L.C., Jiang, J.J., Klein, G.: Improving enterprise resource planning (ERP) fit to organizational process through knowledge transfer. Int. J. Inf. Manag. **27**(3), 200–212 (2007). doi:10.1016/j.ijinfomgt.2007.02.002

45. Wang, G.T.E., Chen, F.H.J.: Effects of internal support and consultant quality on the consulting process and ERP system quality. Decis. Support Syst. **42**(2), 1029–1041 (2006). doi:10.1016/j.dss.2005.08.005

46. Koh, S.C.L., Simpson, M., Padmore, J., Dimitriadis, N., Misopoulos, F.: An exploratory study of enterprise resource planning adoption in Greek companies. Ind. Manag. Data Syst. **10**(7), 1033–1059 (2006). doi:10.1108/02635570610688913

47. Hong, K.K., Kim, Y.G.: The critical success factors for ERP implementation: an organizational fit perspective. Inf. Manag. **40**, 25–40 (2002). doi:10.1016/S0378-7206(01)00134-3

48. Nah, F.H., Zuckweiler, K.M., Lau, L.S.: ERP Implementation: chief information officers' perceptions of CSF. Int. J. Hum. Comput. Interact. **16**(1), 5–22 (2003). doi:10.1207/S15327590IJHC1601_2

49. Bradley, J.: Management based critical success factors in the implementation of Enterprise Resource Planning systems. Int. J. Acc. Inf. Syst. **9**(3), 175–200 (2008). doi:10.1016/j.accinf.2008.04.001

50. Yusuf, Y., Gunasekaranb, A., Abthorpe, M.S.: Enterprise information systems project implementation: a case study of ERP in Rolls-Royce. Int. J. Prod. Econ. **87**, 251–266 (2004). doi:10.1016/j.ijpe.2003.10.004

51. Madapusi, A., D'Souza, D.: The influence of ERP system implementation on the operational performance of an organizational. Int. J. Inf. Manag. **32**(1), 24–34 (2012). doi:10.1016/j.ijinfomgt.2011.06.004

52. Yeh, T.M., Yang, C.C., Lin, W.T.: Service quality and ERP implementation: a conceptual and empirical study of semiconductor-related industries in Taiwan. Comput. Ind. **58**(8–9), 844–854 (2007). doi:10.1016/j.compind.2007.03.00

53. Law, H.C.C., Ngai, T.W.E.: ERP systems adoption: an exploratory study of the organizational factors and impacts of ERP success. Inf. Manag. **44**, 418–432 (2007). doi:10.1016/j.im.2007.03.004
54. Gupta, M., Kohli, A.: Enterprise resource planning systems and its implications for operations function. Technovation **26**(5–6), 687–696 (2006). doi:10.1016/j.technovation. 2004.10.005
55. EU Commission: Commission Recommendation of 6 May 2003 concerning the definition of micro, small and medium enterprises (2003). http://eur-lex.europa.eu/LexUriServ/ LexUriServ.do?uri=OJ:L:2003:124:0036:0041:en:PDF
56. European Union: Annual Report on EU SMEs 2014/2015 (2015). doi:10.2873/886211
57. Hair, F., Anderson, R., Tatham, R., Black, W.: Multivariate Data Analysis with Readings. Prentice-Hall International, London (1995)
58. Schumacker, R.E., Lomax, R.G.: A Beginner's Guide to Structural Equation Modeling. Routledge Academic, New York (2010)
59. Ziemba, E., Kolasa, I.: Risk factors framework for information systems projects in public organizations – Insight from Poland. In: Proceedings of 2015 Federated Conference on Computer Science and Information Systems, pp. 1575–1583 (2015). doi:10.15439/ 2015F110
60. Ziemba, E., Kolasa, I.: Risk factors relationships for information systems projects – Insight from Polish public organizations. In: Ziemba, E. (ed.) FedCSIS 2015. LNBIP, vol. 243, pp. 55–76. Springer, Heidelberg (2016). doi:10.1007/978-3-319-30528-8_4

Patterns of Communication Management in Project Teams

Karolina Muszyńska(⊠)

Faculty of Economics and Management, University of Szczecin,
ul. Mickiewicza 64, 71-101 Szczecin, Poland
karolina.muszynska@usz.edu.pl

Abstract. In present, dynamically developing organizations, that often realize business tasks using project-based approach, effective project management is of paramount importance. Numerous reports and scientific papers present lists of critical success factors in project management, and communication management is usually at the very top of the list. But even though the communication practices are found to be associated with most of the success dimensions, they are not given enough attention and the communication processes and practices formalized in the company's project management methodology are neither followed nor prioritized by project managers. This paper aims at supporting project managers and teams in effective managing communication and documentation processes. Its main contribution is the definition of eleven communication management patterns, which promote a context-problem-solution approach to communication management in projects, in the four complementary categories regarding project communication management practices – informational, strategical, emotional and practical, and as such can be used to deal with different types of project communication management problems.

Keywords: Project communication management · Patterns · Project success

1 Introduction

Communication influences most project activities and areas because managing any aspect of the project involves communicating within the project team or with external stakeholders. That is why communication management is considered as one of the most important knowledge areas in project management and a very complex one at the same time. It is affected by many factors, like characteristics of project stakeholders, project environment, project communication structure, communication properties, physical and psychological barriers [1]. Research has shown that there is a direct connection between communication and a project's outcome, which is determined by the design of the communication environment of the project [2]. Project communication and networking skills are considered to be the life blood of project management leadership [3] and awareness of the potential offered by efficient communication is an essential prerequisite for success in the business world [4].

Project management methodologies, frameworks and sets of principles like Project Management Body of Knowledge, Prince 2, Adaptive Project Framework, Agile

© Springer International Publishing AG 2017
E. Ziemba (Ed.): AITM 2016/ISM 2016, LNBIP 277, pp. 202–221, 2017.
DOI: 10.1007/978-3-319-53076-5_11

Software Development, Scrum, and others, include rules, hints and procedures regarding various communication management aspects, which in most cases should be sufficient to properly manage communication in a project team. The reason why this is not always the case is that, many IT companies do not actually follow any of these methodologies when realizing projects (for example, 30% of the companies surveyed in [5]) and those that do, tend to concentrate on other project management knowledge areas, which seem more important, such as scheduling, cost management, etc. There are also numerous cases of project failures [6], that could be linked to poor communication management (among others [7, 8]).

Thus it seems important to constantly promote good communication management practices and look for new ways to support project managers and team members in better realization of communication and documentation processes in their projects. That is the main goal behind the communication management patterns proposed in this paper – to give project teams an additional tool in a form of a list of patterns for controlling, managing and effective realization of communication and documentation processes. The idea behind patterns is that they provide general, reusable solutions to common problems. Communication management patterns in project teams described in this paper are based on two main sources of information - communication management best practices identified in the subject literature and results of a survey conducted among IT project managers.

The theoretical background, described in the following section of the paper, provides evidence on the significance of project communication management knowledge area based on existing literature and presents the definition of patterns and their use in other disciplines. Next, the research methodology and research findings, including eleven communication management patterns, are described. The discussion of findings highlights the most important and interesting research result, and a summary with future research directions concludes the paper.

2 Theoretical Background

2.1 The Importance of Project Communication Management

The successful implementation of a project depends on its appropriate management in a number of areas, as described in detail by e.g. Kerzner [9], Schwalbe [10], and Meredith and Mantel [11]. One of the areas of project management identified within numerous methodologies and frameworks is communication management, which is considered to be of crucial importance to the success of a project (among others [12, 13]), in particular IT projects [14] especially those carried out by dispersed teams [15–19]. It is however worth noticing that communication influences also other project management areas like managing project scope, risk, or procurement. Scope management involves one of the most difficult tasks in projects, which concerns collecting and analyzing requirements, and without effective communication proper realization of this task is impossible. Additionally, at further stages of project implementation, proper communication management is essential for managing scope changes. Managing project risk concerns identifying, analyzing, responding to and monitoring project risks. Intensive and well-planned communication is needed to timely recognize risks and respond to them appropriately. Also procurement management, involving arrangements and negotiations with external contractors, calls for applying adequate communication methods and tools.

On the one hand, importance of this knowledge area is emphasized by most stakeholders, but on the other hand, the communication processes and practices formalized in the company's project management methodology are not followed by project managers. Many project managers place communication on the bottom of their priority list [20]. For instance, recent research on utilization of project communication management methodologies in industrial enterprises in Slovak Republic revealed that 66% of the surveyed enterprises had not prepared any written document (methodology, process steps, etc.) to manage project communication [21].

Also Papke-Shields and co-authors, in their research on the use of project management practices and the link thereof to project success, discover that practices related to communication are not given enough attention, while at the same time communication practices are found to be associated with most of the success dimensions [22]. Most of the communication process in a project is usually done without proper planning, driven mostly by personalities and preferences rather than by needs, protocols and procedures [23].

Effective communication techniques and appropriate leadership styles are emphasized by Nguyen as the success factors for building and managing high performance global virtual teams [24]. Communication management is highly influenced in intercultural project teams by such factors as language, race, age, gender, religion, beliefs, habits, etc., whose analysis is essential if the project is to be accomplished with success [25].

According to PMI's Pulse research, 55% of project managers agree that effective communication with all stakeholders is the most critical success factor in project management [26]. Effective project communications ensure that the right information reaches the right person at the right time and in a cost-effective manner and it is a critical element of team effectiveness, both in traditional and virtual teams [27]. The effectiveness of project communication often determines the quality of decisions and their implementation. Without a solid communication plan, strategy and tools, it is impossible to keep everyone up-to-date and informed. More than 50% of management problems are caused by poor communication [28], which can lead to differences in expectations, people not knowing the status of the project and what is expected from them. Therefore, communication is a key element, which has to be applied effectively throughout a project's life cycle and it cannot be taken for granted, as it requires preparation and persistence.

2.2 Definition and the Use of Patterns

One of general definitions of a pattern states that it is "a regular and intelligible form or sequence discernible in the way in which something happens or is done" or "an excellent example for others to follow" [29]. Design patterns are used to represent knowledge that is based on experiences captured in several real world projects and is widely accepted. This representation is often used for describing and presenting the gained knowledge. There are similar concepts to the concept of a pattern – success factor, success models, success measures, reference architectures, best practices, worst practices, barriers, facilitators or incentives [30].

Different definitions for a pattern exist, but they all include a common ground – the patterns are general, reusable solutions to common problems and are dependent on their context [31]. They are based on the philosophy of pattern languages, first proposed by an architect Christopher Alexander, which is now widely applied in many other professional areas to encompass creative human actions ([32] and works cited therein).

Patterns have been successfully used in different disciplines, like software engineering, knowledge management, enterprise integration, enterprise architecture management, project management, etc. Below two of them are described in order to present their aim, structure and format.

Design Patterns in Software Engineering. In the software discipline a design pattern is a general reusable solution to a commonly occurring problem within a given context in software design. The pattern has four essential elements: the pattern name, the problem, which describes when to apply the pattern (it explains the actual problem and its context), the solution, which describes the elements that make up the design, their relationships, responsibilities and collaborations (this is an abstract description, a template of a solution), and the consequences – the results and trade-offs of applying the pattern.

To describe each design pattern, a consistent format has been used, including specific sections like: pattern name, intent (explains what the design pattern does, what particular issue/problem it addresses), motivation (a scenario illustrating a design problem and how the pattern solves it), applicability (situations when the design pattern can be applied, examples of poor designs where the pattern could be applied), structure (a graphical representation of classes in the pattern, accompanied with interaction diagrams), participants (classes participating in the design pattern and their responsibilities), collaborations (how the participants collaborate to carry out the responsibilities), consequences (the trade-offs and results of using the pattern), implementation (pitfalls, hints, techniques useful in pattern implementation), sample code, known uses (examples of the pattern found in real systems), related patterns (which patterns are closely related to each other). Each defined design pattern is described according to the above mentioned sections, which makes them easier to use, learn and compare [33].

Knowledge Management Patterns. Knowledge management patterns state lessons learned and best practices for the structuring of knowledge, the design of knowledge management systems, and the development of underlying ontologies. Patterns in knowledge management represent also a form of language that helps knowledge engineers to communicate about knowledge and knowledge management systems.

A knowledge pattern is defined as a general, proven, and beneficial solution to a common, reoccurring problem in knowledge design, i.e., the structuring and composition of the knowledge or the ontology defining metadata and potential relationships between knowledge components. Knowledge management patterns are described in seven groups regarding different aspects of knowledge: content, usage, ontology, presentation, transfer, knowledge management systems organization and social knowledge management. Each pattern is described according to a template including the following sections: name, issue (problem addressed by the pattern), q-effect (what knowledge quality aspects are affected by the pattern and if it is a positive, negative or neutral effect), solution (principal solutions underlining the pattern), causes (basic causes of the pattern) [30].

3   Research Methodology

The project communication management patterns described in the subsequent sections are based on two main sources of knowledge. The first source are communication management best practices described in literature [16, 34–39], and thoroughly discussed in [40], and the second source are the opinions gained from practitioners (mostly project managers of IT projects) from 10 national and international IT companies operating in Poland, chosen for the interviews because of their many-year-long diverse experience from multiple projects. A structured interview with both closed and open-ended questions was used to obtain their opinions.

The structured interviews with project managers involved presenting them the 11 project communication management patterns in their initial form, including only the first four sections (name, context, problem, solution), and asking them to answer a set of both closed- and open-ended questions concerning the respective patterns. The following four closed-ended questions were asked: "Have you experienced the presented communication management patterns?", "Has any of the presented patterns been used in your project teams?", "How would you assess the difficulty of implementation of the presented patterns?", "How would you assess the usefulness of the presented patterns?". For the last two questions an assessment scale (1–5) was used, where 1 stood for easy and very useful, while 5 – the opposite. The open-ended questions regarded the following topics: "Name possible difficulties in using the described patterns", "What facilitates the use of described patterns (tools, procedures, etc.)?", "In what contexts do you find the described patterns most adequate and why?", "In what contexts do you find the described patterns least adequate and why?". Answers provided by the respondents were used to improve and enrich the initial version of communication management patterns and the resulting enhanced patterns, arranged into categories, are presented in the research findings section.

The characteristics of patterns used in different knowledge areas, described in the theoretical background section, served as a reference for defining the structure and format of the project communication management patterns.

4   Research Findings

4.1   The Definition of a Project Communication Management Pattern

The definition of the project communication management pattern proposed in this subsection is a result of the analysis of patterns and their frameworks developed in different disciplines, and combining selected aspects of these patterns with project communication management characteristics and practices.

Project communication patterns have been grouped into four categories according to the communication management practice categories described in [37] – informational (regarding generation, collection, dissemination, storage, and disposition of project information), strategical (connected with communication planning and project environment), emotional (concerning the building of trust and relationships) and practical (connected with clear and positive communication and behavior rules). Within each category, several communication management patterns were defined. Each pattern comprises the following sections: pattern name, context, problem, solution, q-effect (what communication quality aspects are affected by the pattern and if it is a positive or a negative influence), applicability (situations, teams and projects where the communication management pattern should be applied and participants and their responsibilities), consequences (the trade-offs and results of using the pattern), implementation (pitfalls, hints, techniques useful in the pattern implementation), and related patterns.

For specifying q-effect the following communication quality aspects were considered: clearness and cohesion, adequate level of detail, timeliness, meeting needs of communicating participants, engaging the right people, guarantee of uniform understanding of the content, communication workflow supporting openness, redundancy and feedback.

Solution within a pattern describes what actions should be undertaken to realize the pattern and the communication management goal that it supports.

4.2 Communication Management Patterns in the Informational Category

Within the informational category, three communication management patterns have been specified: *Communication schedule, Project knowledge center* and *Diversity of communication means*. According to the survey carried out among practitioners, all the following patterns are recognized by almost all of them and used in their companies. In one case it was stated that the *Communication schedule* pattern is an intrinsic element of the communication plan, which is prepared at the start of the project realization.

Table 1 provides characteristics of the three project communication management patterns from the informational category, developed according to the defined template. For the sake of brevity the pattern section names were abbreviated as follows: Cx (context), Pr (problem), S (solution), Q (q-effect), A (applicability), Cq (consequences), I (implementation) and RP (related patterns).

4.3 Communication Management Patterns in the Strategical Category

Another three communication management patterns have been defined within the strategical category: *Clear rules at the start, Cultural and language competencies* and *Client's power scope*. These patterns were also acknowledged and used by most of the surveyed practitioners, although *Cultural and language competencies* pattern was not used by more than one third of them because their project teams were not culturally or

Table 1. Communication management patterns within the informational category

	Communication schedule
Cx	The project team is dispersed, some team members are in different time zones; according to the project communication plan project partners should inform each other of the project status to get feedback and encourage involvement
Pr	Communication between team members is too scarce, team members limit communication to sending reports, while direct communication takes place only in emergency situations. In consequence, issues are not resolved in due time, mutual understanding among team members is hindered due to scarce feedback, dynamics of task realization is low
S	Prepare a communication time schedule, including bilateral communication between particular team members, as well as multilateral audio/video conferences among wider forum of team members according to the anticipated communication needs; communication participants possibilities and preferences concerning communication medium and time zone shifts should be taken into account
Q	Positive on the following communication quality aspects: timeliness of information on the project tasks status; redundancy and feedback. Possibly negative on the following communication quality aspects: in case of multilateral audio/video conferences, too many participants taking part may cause the communication to be ineffective and irritating (technical problems are more likely to appear) and not engaging the right people
A	The pattern can be used for any kind of project and team, although it is especially useful for dispersed teams and bigger projects longer than three months. The pattern should regard all team members and they should be responsible for adhering to the time schedule or timely informing about any derogations
Cq	Ensures regular communication among team members, adjusted to their working day schedules and communication preferences, and keeps everybody informed about the status of project tasks and encourages instant feedback
I	Setting up a communication time schedule requires time, effort, cooperation and goodwill of team members, so that it is adhered to and beneficial; the more parties and locations the more difficult it becomes; it should be agreed upon during the project kick-off meeting, accompanied by a clear message of its goal and instructions of realization; using such tools as shared calendars and communication matrix can be useful. A very important issue in realizing this pattern is engaging only the concerned team members in multilateral conferences (thematic groups)
RP	*Clear rules at the start, Fostering direct communication, Appreciating the team*
	Project knowledge center
Cx	Communication in the project team is performed in different ways; many people use e-mail as the primary communication medium, and send various elements of the project documentation this way. Others prefer communication via Instant Messaging (IM) and attaching files to conversations. Still others would rather talk on the phone and deliver files on a pen drive
Pr	Many elements of the project documentation remain only in mailboxes, computers or pen-drives of individual team members and the project knowledge in their heads; different versions of the same documents are created and their subsequent synchronization is very cumbersome; some information is lost or finding it is time-consuming; certain project knowledge is lost when a team member leaves the team

(*continued*)

Table 1. (*continued*)

Project knowledge center	
S	Ensuring a project repository – a project knowledge center, where all project information is placed, stored and shared
Q	Positive on the following communication quality aspects: clearness and cohesion, timeliness of project documentation, adequate level of detail and communication workflow supporting openness. Possibly negative on the following communication quality aspects: in case the repository is unordered and unclear the adequate level of detail, clearness and cohesion are no longer attained
A	The pattern should be used for any kind of project and team, because even small projects and small teams produce project documentation which should be made available to the team and the cumulated knowledge may prove useful in future projects. All team members are responsible for uploading any project-related documentation in an orderly manner, established upfront or developed in the initial phase of the project realization
Cq	Ensures a common project information reference center available to all team members, taking into account given user access rights, with up-to-date project documentation and orderly history. Project documentation is not hidden in the mail boxes of individual team members and a project knowledge base is being built. Team members do not send specific information separately to all interested parties but just provide references to the appropriate place in the project repository
I	Setting up a project knowledge center requires using appropriate tools and setting certain procedures, so that the repository is easy to use and effective in storing and sharing information; it is usually a software application chosen and used by the project team for many projects, like a web portal with a wiki feature, group-work tool or project management software with the file versioning and change tracking functionalities. Problems which may arise concern effective organization of the repository and a need for training team members on how to use versioning tools. The chosen tool usually requires configuration effort and expertise and some systems are expensive. Sometimes documents sharing between the customer and the developer is not at all possible due to security issues. There may be also a problem of changing people's habits concerning sharing project documentation. To wean team members from sending project documents as attachments to e-mails, a special function could be embedded in the e-mail program, which would display a message asking the user if the attached file should not rather be placed in the repository, instead of being sent
RP	*Diversity of communication means*
Diversity of communication means	
Cx	It happens that tools used in the project team impose the way of communication among team members, limiting it mainly to written communication (mainly in order to have a permanent evidence of discussions and arrangements). Team members hardly talk to each other personally; this is particularly common in the case of international and distributed teams
Pr	Focusing mainly on one way of communication, whether oral or written, hampers the realization of the project, in the first case because of the transience of oral arrangements, in the second case, because of possible problems with understanding the intentions or the lack of instant response and feedback. In the case of written real time communication (using IM) the typing speed can be a problem, while for oral communication a poor knowledge of a foreign language can be a barrier

(*continued*)

Table 1. (*continued*)

Diversity of communication means	
S	Promoting diversity in the ways of communication, and while preserving the principles of the *Project knowledge center* pattern, emphasizing the importance of oral communication, which should support mutual understanding between team members and unite the project team
Q	Positive on the following communication quality aspects: meeting needs of communicating participants (as some team members are comfortable with written communication, while others need to communicate also orally), guarantee of uniform understanding of the content, redundancy and instant feedback (in case of oral communication). Possibly negative on the following communication quality aspects: in case of excessive diversity, project documentation consistency and cohesion is hard to maintain
A	The pattern should be used carefully, taking into account the communication culture of the project team, level of project language knowledge of team members and security issues (some communication tools may be considered as not secure). All team members should apply the pattern, and the project manager should take into account personal predispositions of each member
Cq	Diversity of communication, on the one hand enriches and facilitates communication among team members, but on the other hand, if not appropriately managed, may cause communication chaos, with some information being lost in oral conversations or time wasted during too frequent and ineffective meetings
I	The written form of communication, especially the part concerning communicating project results and producing project documentation, should be arranged at the beginning and organized into effective and easy to understand and follow procedures, which should be realized by all team members (see *Clear rules at the start* pattern). One of the most effective oral communication means are stand-up meetings, known from the agile project management approach, which are a quick and effective way to assess the status of project tasks, find out who needs help, or who is not working properly. It is also a perfect way for team members to get to know each other. It is however important that the project manager, or leader does not dominate these meetings. In case of dispersed teams video-conference stand-up meetings can be organized. In case of traditional meetings their costs (time, travel) must be taken into account and planned in advance
RP	*Clear rules at the start, Project knowledge center, Fostering direct communication*

linguistically diverse. Others argued that both *Clear rules at the start* pattern, as well as *Client's power scope* pattern, are part of the communication plan and need not to be separately described. They were however left on the list because the role of patterns is to highlight specific problematic areas to which solutions are proposed. In the case of *Clear rules at the start* pattern, preparing a high-quality communication plan is actually the suggested solution. Table 2 provides an overview of the three project communication management patterns from the strategical communication management practice category.

Table 2. Communication management patterns within the strategical category

Clear rules at the start	
Cx	It sometimes happens that while planning various aspects of the project (project tasks, responsible team members, schedule and budget), the area of communication and documentation management is neglected. There is no regular contact with the client to inform them about the progress of the project and for keeping in touch for quick reaction to possible changes and new requirements
Pr	There are no designated persons and tasks related to planning and managing communication and documentation processes. Team members feel no need to communicate the status of their tasks, nor do they feel responsible for informing the client about the status of the project
S	Development of a clear, practical and high-quality communication plan with assigned persons responsible for communication management, description of communication and documentation tasks – the ones to be carried out by specific individuals and those which are the responsibility of all members of the project team. In the case of distributed teams, it is particularly important to include the *Communication schedule* pattern. In the case of different language teams, a common project communication language should be established
Q	Positive on the following communication quality aspects: meeting needs of communicating participants. Possibly negative on the following communication quality aspects: in case of excessive formalism and bureaucracy participants may be discouraged to communicate effectively and all communication quality aspects can be threatened
A	The pattern should be used for any kind of project and team, although it is especially useful for teams with different working cultures and fixed price projects. The pattern applies to all stakeholders. All persons assigned to any communication and documentation tasks should be clearly informed of their responsibilities at the beginning of the project realization
Cq	Ensures that all team members and project stakeholders know their communication and documentation responsibilities. Client is instantly informed about the status of the project tasks. It is, however, important to let the communication plan evolve and alter throughout the project, to make it better tailored to the given project and team
I	Preparing a high-quality communication plan requires time and effort, so that it is then easy to realize and not burdensome for the project team; too much formalism may discourage the team; the communication plan should be communicated already during the project kick-off meeting, or at least during the initiation phase of the project
RP	*Communication schedule, Client's power scope, Appreciating the team, Diversity of communication means, Cultural and language competencies, Basic communication principles*
Cultural and language competencies	
Cx	Team members within one project team or members of two collaborating teams (the client's side team and the developer's side team) come from different cultural and language areas
Pr	Problem with the lack of cultural and/or language competence of team members, which hinders communication and mutual understanding, and thereby successful realization of the project

(*continued*)

Table 2. (*continued*)

	Cultural and language competencies
S	Team members should be prepared for the environment in which they are going to work and familiarized with the rules and customs prevailing in the country of other team members. Necessary language skills should also be checked to ensure comfortable communication
Q	Positive on the following communication quality aspects: clearness and cohesion, meeting needs of communicating participants, guarantee of uniform understanding of the content
A	The pattern is suitable for teams working in multicultural and international projects. It applies to all team members who are responsible for communication and documentation tasks
Cq	Culturally and linguistically competent team members facilitate communication and make the cooperation easier and more efficient
I	Having culturally and linguistically competent team members is not always possible or easy to achieve. Learning a foreign language is a long process and getting to know different cultures is difficult. If there is at least one competent person in the project team, they can train other team members. It is also a good idea to promote and use "project culture", which is above local cultures of particular team members. It should be agreed upon at the beginning of the project realization. In case of language problems in written communication, such tools as online translators or spell-checkers can be used. For oral communication a linking-person, who can freely communicate with both parties, is a solution
RP	*Clear rules at the start*
	Client's power scope
Cx	Changes to project requirements or other project related issues are communicated by different representatives of the client. After implementation of changes it turns out that the author of the communicated change was not entitled to decide about it
Pr	The project team does not know who, on the client's side, is responsible for making and communicating decisions concerning the project, as well as who to contact in problematic issues
S	Project manager must ensure that the client has appointed a person or persons who will be responsible on the client's side for making and communicating decisions throughout the project, and who should be contacted in problematic issues
Q	Positive on the following communication quality aspects: clearness and cohesion, engaging the right people, meeting needs of communicating participants, communication workflow supporting openness
A	The pattern is applicable to any team and project, because clear definition of responsibility for making decisions is always desirable
Cq	Clearly defined responsibility for certain competence areas. Clear decision-making procedure. Clearly defined deadlines for document verification and approval. Effective problem reporting

(*continued*)

Table 2. (*continued*)

Client's power scope	
I	Client's power scope should be defined at the very beginning of the project realization (communication aspects should be included in the communication plan – *Clear rules at the start* pattern). It is however important to be flexible and ready for negotiations of responsibilities and authorities. It is a good practice to assign representatives on both sides – mutual counterparts. Using the same standards for communication or process templates can also be helpful. Problems in implementing the pattern may arise in the case of dominant position of the client and reluctance to compromise, fear of making decisions, not properly chosen/prepared team on the client's side, conflicts within the client's team
RP	*Clear rules at the start, Synchronous working environments*

4.4 Communication Management Patterns in the Emotional Category

The emotional category of the communication management practices comprises another three patterns: *Fostering direct communication*, *Visits and team rotations* and *Appreciating the team*. Most of the practitioners, who were surveyed, knew all three patterns and used them in their project teams. One of them was however very sceptic towards the *Fostering direct communication* pattern, claiming that the pattern should actually be quite the contrary, because people tend to waste a lot of time on unproductive and ineffective talks and meetings. This opinion was included in the consequence section of the pattern.

The above mentioned patterns from the emotional communication management category are described in Table 3.

Table 3. Communication management patterns within the emotional category

Fostering direct communication	
Cx	Absorbed in work and rushed by deadlines, project team members often do not have time for direct talks with each other or with team members on the client's side. Additionally the management restricts such direct contacts (chats in the hallway or through IM), treating it as a waste of time and delaying tasks
Pr	Team members are alienated and feel discomfort associated with the inability to satisfy human needs, these associated with direct contact with another person. Such reduction of direct communication restrains the team from uniting, understanding each other's needs and hinders comprehension
S	Project manager should promote direct communication between team members, as well as with members of the team on the client's side
Q	Positive on the following communication quality aspects: meeting needs of communicating participants, guarantee of uniform understanding of the content, communication workflow supporting openness, redundancy and feedback
A	The pattern should be used for any kind of project and team, although in the case of distributed teams "direct" usually means audio or videoconferences, as face-to-face meetings are costly and time-consuming

(*continued*)

Table 3. (*continued*)

Fostering direct communication	
Cq	May prove very beneficial to the project and the team if properly used; both formal and informal direct communication fosters better mutual understanding, team uniting, issues resolving. It must be however properly managed and monitored to prevent team members from wasting too much time and delaying realization of tasks – this mainly concerns poorly prepared meetings
I	As far as formal communication is concerned, stand-up meetings and reviews can bring much profit, because they convey both information and emotions and let the team members get to know each other better. Informal communication can be supported by social networking tools, informal chat-rooms ("virtual water cooler") or a common meeting room (in case of local teams). The use of *Communication schedule* pattern, that takes into account the direct methods of communication, or the *Visits and team rotations* pattern also foster direct communication. Access to direct communication should be made easy by supporting a list of team members' phone numbers, instant messenger contact details, etc. Project manager should track the impact of direct communication on project performance
RP	*Communication schedule, Visits and team rotations, Diversity of communication means*

Visits and team rotations	
Cx	Project is characterized by having a distributed team and a long realization time. The direct contact of the contractor's team with the client's team is limited to the kick-off meeting and a few other project meetings
Pr	Lack of trust and willingness to communicate within the project team, because of the lack of direct contact and familiarity of team members
S	Regular visits of individual team members at the client's/contractor's site, as well as delegating team members to the client's/contractor's site for a longer period of time. In the latter solution, rotation can also be used, so that different team members can get to know each other and break the communication barrier
Q	Positive on the following communication quality aspects: meeting needs of communicating participants, communication workflow supporting openness, feedback
A	The pattern is designed for big projects with distributed teams. Only willing team members should be chosen for delegation to other locations, to avoid discontent and frustration experienced by people forced to leave their home city and family for a longer period of time. Shorter visits should be realized by all key team members
Cq	Building non-professional relations among team members fosters effective and direct communication (relation with *Fostering direct communication* pattern). Delegated team members facilitate communication between the client's team and the contractor's team
I	Realization of the pattern should be preceded by an analysis of predispositions and willingness of individual team members to delegations, so that appropriate plan of visits and team rotation can be developed and included in the budget. In reasonable circumstances bonuses or family delegations can be offered
RP	*Fostering direct communication*

Appreciating the team	
Cx	In the course of project realization team members notice errors or possibilities for solutions to various problems. However they do not have the opportunity to express their views, to give advice or share opinions, or they do not know how and where it can be done

(*continued*)

Table 3. (*continued*)

Appreciating the team	
Pr	The project management does not enable team members to share opinions, to formulate proposals or comments related to the implementation of the project. They cannot express their feelings, thoughts and remarks, and feel unappreciated and their motivation to work decreases
S	Project management should encourage team members to share their thoughts, remarks and opinions by formulating requests for support and advice, which give the team a sense of appreciation of their value and trust
Q	Positive on the following communication quality aspects: meeting needs of communicating participants, communication workflow supporting openness, feedback
A	The pattern is applicable to any team and project, because every team member should have an opportunity to share their thoughts and opinions and all team members need to feel appreciated. It is especially beneficial in long-term projects where constant improvement of work quality should take place
Cq	Appreciated project team is motivated to work towards successful realization of the project; useful remarks and suggestions are collected and may be applied to promote better project development; alarming situations are exposed and appropriate actions can be undertaken
I	The pattern may be realized in many different ways – devoting time during project meetings for team opinions, remarks, suggestions; reserving a project portal section for this purpose or a thematic mailbox; organizing surveys, retrospection sessions. Project manager should be open to remarks from the team. This pattern is connected with *Clear rules at the start*, *Communication schedule* and *Fostering direct communication* patterns, because all of them strive for letting team members communicate what they want, need or should communicate in a way which is the most suitable for them. The effort of organizing and analyzing surveys, mailboxes, retrospection sessions or portal sections should be included in the budget and schedule plan, to avoid situation that all information is collected in vain
RP	*Clear rules at the start, Communication schedule, Fostering direct communication*

4.5 Communication Management Patterns in the Practical Category

Within the last, practical category, two more communication management patterns have been identified: *Basic communication principles* and *Synchronous working environments*. Only one of the surveyed practitioners has not heard about or used the first pattern, while the second one was recognized by all, but not used by more than one third, as it was deemed suitable mainly for big projects.

In Table 4 the two remaining patterns from the practical communication management practice category have been depicted.

Table 4. Communication management patterns within the practical category

Basic communication principles	
Cx	The team consists of inexperienced members. Basic principles of communication are not respected
Pr	Misunderstandings, hostility or animosity among team members
S	Reminding team members about the basic principles of transparent, effective and positive communication, and desired behavior, that is, among others: justifying requests, asking rather than telling, keeping promises and showing up for appointments (also virtual ones), writing positive e-mails (even criticisms and dissatisfaction can be expressed in a positive way)
Q	Positive on the following communication quality aspects: clearness and cohesion, meeting needs of communicating participants
A	The pattern can be used for any kind of project and team, although it is especially useful for immature and inexperienced teams, or where there are many introverts, team members are age or culture diversified
Cq	Good atmosphere in the team, clear and positive relations among team members and their responsible behavior – all promoting successful project completion
I	Usually the basic principles of transparent, effective and positive communication is something that every person knows and feels, and it should not be required to state it explicitly, but in the cases mentioned above it may be desired to bring them to the attention of some team members. It is also a good practice to set the maximum time for response to an email, to ensure the dynamics of asynchronous communication. If possible communication rules should be agreed upon together by the whole team, preferably during the kick-off meeting
RP	*Clear rules at the start*
Synchronous working environments	
Cx	Long-term, big project, realized by two teams - the client's and the contractor's team, operating in different locations
Pr	Cooperating teams in different locations greatly differ from each other both in terms of composition and way of working, making it difficult for communication and cooperation between them
S	Providing a similar composition of the teams and work procedures in both locations in order to facilitate cooperation and communication
Q	Positive on the following communication quality aspects: engaging the right people
A	This pattern applies to big and long-term projects carried out by teams whose working environments are significantly different. To be used by team members playing similar roles in both teams
Cq	Synchronized working environments on the client's and contractor's side, with defined roles and responsibilities; easier direct communication due to existence of counterparts
I	Specifying a process with definition of roles, responsibilities, authorities and templates could be used to set up the synchronous working environments of the cooperating teams. Defining the counterparts in the cooperating teams relates this pattern with the *Client's power scope* pattern
RP	*Client's power scope*

5 Discussion of Findings

Project communication management patterns within the informational category concentrate on assuring the most effective way of communicating, storing and sharing project information. They positively influence almost all of the communication quality aspects but caution must be taken to properly implement them to avoid possible negative effects. Implementation of the patterns requires using appropriate tools as well as establishing special procedures, both of which should be agreed upon at the very beginning of the project realization. In case of tools which are new to the team members, relevant trainings should be conducted.

Communication management patterns included in the strategical category focus on the aspects of planning and establishing communication rules and providing a conducive project realization environment. Different communication quality aspects are affected by these patterns but one is common for all them: meeting needs of communicating participants. Implementation of the strategical communication management patterns involves mainly setting clear procedures and responsibilities, or as in the case of the *Cultural and language competencies* pattern, also selection of necessary communication facilitators.

Project communication management patterns grouped into the emotional category strive to meet the building of trust and relationships needs of the project teams. They also concern the appreciation and direct contacts among team members, which are very important factors in human relations. Three communication quality aspects are positively influenced by all three patterns: meeting needs of communicating participants, communication workflow supporting openness and feedback. Implementation of the emotional patterns includes utilization of certain software tools and setting appropriate procedures and planning.

The two practical project communication management patterns are aimed at supporting clear and positive communication and behavior rules and simplifying cooperation of distant teams in big projects. The first one has a positive influence on two communication quality aspects – the clearness and cohesion and meeting needs of communicating participants, while the second one favors engaging the right people. Implementation of these patterns concentrates on establishing certain rules and organizational solutions.

The interrelationship among the described communication management patterns shown on Fig. 1 reveals that one of them – *Clear rules at the start* is involved in relations with six other patterns, which indicates that solutions proposed in all these related patterns, to some extent, overlap with the solution proposed in the *Clear rules at the start* pattern. Other multi-related patterns are: *Fostering direct communication* with four related patterns and *Communication schedule*, *Diversity of communication means* and *Appreciating the team* with three related patterns.

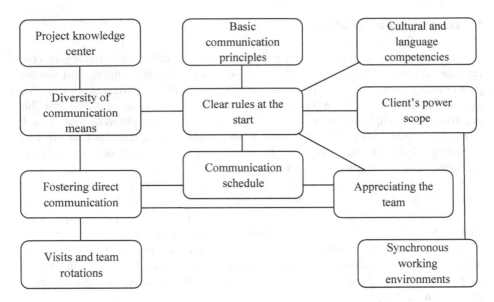

Fig. 1. Relations among project communication management patterns

6 Conclusion

The paper discussed applying the pattern-based approach to the project communication management discipline. Its main contribution is the definition of the eleven project communication management patterns (based on both prior research and opinions of practitioners in that field) that aim at supporting project managers and teams in the effective management of project communication and documentation processes. They are arranged into four groups which address various aspects of project management and types of encountered problems.

The application of the proposed patterns may bring significant advantages to the project management practice, as they can help both to solve encountered problems with communication and documentation processes as well as to avoid them.

There are at least two main future research directions that can enrich the body of knowledge on project communication patterns. The first is to assess implementation conditions, dependencies and effectiveness of the patterns specified in this paper. The second is to look for and identify additional project communication patterns. Both require conducting a more extensive survey among project-based companies and also observing implementation of respective patterns in real-life projects.

Acknowledgements. Special thanks to all the surveyed professionals from the project management field who devoted their precious time to share their experiences, knowledge and opinions on the topic of communication management patterns in project teams in their companies.

References

1. Damasiotis, V., Fitsilis, P., O'Kane, J.F.: Measuring communication complexity in projects. In: Proceedings of the Management of International Business and Economic Systems (MIBES-ESDO) 2012 International Conference, pp. 100–114. School of Management and Economics, Larissa (2012)
2. Phillips, M.M.: Reinventing Communication: How to Design, Lead and Manage High Performing Projects. Gower Publishing, Farnham (2014)
3. Burke, R., Barron, S.: Project Management Leadership: Building Creative Teams. Wiley, Chichester (2014)
4. Charles, M.: The ascent of communication: are we on board? In: Louhiala-Salminen, L., Kankaanranta, A. (eds.) The Ascent of International Business Communication, pp. 9–23. Helsinki School of Economics, Helsinki (2009)
5. Muszyńska, K.: Kształtowanie modelu komunikacji w zespole projektowym. Ph.D. dissertation. University of Szczecin (2010)
6. Al-Ahmad, W., Al-Fagih, K., Khanfar, K., Alsamara, K., Abuleil, S., Abu-Salem, H.: A taxonomy of an IT project failure: root causes. Int. Manag. Rev. 5(1), 93–104 (2009)
7. Conboy, K.: Project failure en masse: a study of loose budgetary control in ISD projects. Eur. J. Inf. Syst. 19(3), 273–287 (2010). doi:10.1057/ejis.2010.7
8. Stoica, R., Brouse, P.: IT project Failure: a proposed four-phased adaptive multi-method approach. Procedia Comput. Sci. 16, 728–736 (2013). doi:10.1016/j.procs.2013.01.076
9. Kerzner, H.R.: Project Management: A Systems Approach to Planning, Scheduling, and Controlling. Wiley, Hoboken (2013)
10. Schwalbe, K.: Information Technology Project Management. Cengage Learning Boston, Massachusetts (2013)
11. Meredith, J.R., Mantel Jr., S.J.: Project Management: A Managerial Approach. Wiley, Hoboken (2011)
12. Purna Sudhakar, G.: A model of critical success factors for software projects. J. Enterp. Inf. Manage. 25(6), 537–558 (2012). doi:10.1108/17410391211272829
13. Ofori, D.F.: Project management practices and critical success factors - a developing country perspective. Int. J. Bus. Manage. 8(21), 14–31 (2013). doi:10.5539/ijbm.v8n21p14
14. Holzmann, V., Panizel, I.: Communications management in Scrum projects. In: Proceedings of the European Conference on Information Management and Evaluation, pp. 67–74. Academic Conferences and Publishing International Limited, Reading (2013)
15. Han, J., Jung, W.: How geographic distribution affects development organizations: a survey on communication between developers. Int. J. Softw. Eng. Appl. 8(6), 241–251 (2014)
16. Niinimäki, T., Piri, A., Lassenius, C., Paasivaara, M.: Reflecting the choice and usage of communication tools in global software development projects with media synchronicity theory. J. Softw. Evol. Process 24(6), 677–692 (2012). doi:10.1002/smr.566
17. Sidawi, B.: Potential use of communications and project management systems in remote construction projects: the case of Saudi Electric Company. J. Eng. Proj. Prod. Manage. 2(1), 14–22 (2012)
18. Tone, K., Skitmore, M., Wong, J.K.W.: An investigation of the impact of cross-cultural communication on the management of construction projects in Samoa. Constr. Manage. Econ. 27(4), 343–361 (2009). doi:10.1080/01446190902748713
19. Wagstrom, P., Herbsleb, J.: Dependency forecasting in the distributed agile organization. Commun. ACM 49(10), 55–56 (2006). doi:10.1145/1164394.1164420

20. Monteiro de Carvalho, M.: An investigation of the role of communication in IT projects. Int. J. Oper. Prod. Manage. **34**(1), 36–64 (2013). doi:10.1108/IJOPM-11-2011-0439

21. Samáková, J., Sujanová, J., Koltnerová, K.: Project communication management in industrial enterprises. In: European Conference on Information Management and Evaluation, pp. 155–163. Academic Conferences International Limited, Reading (2013)

22. Papke-Shields, K.E., Beise, C., Quan, J.: Do project managers practice what they preach, and does it matter to project success? Int. J. Proj. Manage. **28**(7), 650–662 (2010). doi:10.1016/j.ijproman.2009.11.002

23. Pop, A.M., Pop, I., Dumitrascu, D.D.: An analysis model of the communication features in research project management. Rev. Economica **65**(4), 49–64 (2013)

24. Nguyen, D.S.: Success factors for building and managing high performance global virtual teams. Int. J. Sci. Basic Appl. Res. **9**(1), 72–93 (2013)

25. Isern, G.: Intercultural project management for IT: issues and challenges. J. Intercultural Manage. **7**(3), 53–67 (2015). doi:10.1515/joim-2015-0021

26. Project Management Institute: The high cost of low performance: the essential role of communications.   http://www.pmi.org/ ~ /media/PDF/Business-Solutions/The-High-Cost-Low-Performance-The-Essential-Role-of-Communications.ashx

27. Pitts, V.E., Wright, N.A., Harkabus, L.C.: Communication in virtual teams: the role of emotional intelligence. J. Organ. Psychol. **12**(3/4), 21–34 (2012)

28. Memon, S., Changfeng, W., Rasheed, S., Pathan, Z.H., Yanping, L.: Communication management of large projects in big data environment. Int. J. Hybrid Inf. Technol. **8**(11), 397–404 (2015)

29. Oxford Dictionaries: Language matters. http://www.oxforddictionaries.com/definition/english/pattern

30. Rech, J., Feldmann, R.L., Ras, E., Jedlitschka, A., Decker, B.: Knowledge patterns and knowledge refactorings for increasing the quality of knowledge. In: Jennex, M.E. (ed.) Knowledge Management, Organizational Memory and Transfer Behavior: Global Approaches and Advancements, 1st edn., pp. 281–328. IGI Global, London (2008). doi:10.4018/978-1-60566-140-7.ch017

31. Ernst, A.M.: Enterprise architecture management patterns. In: Proceedings of the 15th Conference on Pattern Languages of Programs. ACM (2008). doi:10.1145/1753196.1753205

32. Lukosch, S., Schümmer, T.: Groupware development support with technology patterns. Int. J. Hum Comput Stud. **64**(7), 599–610 (2006). doi:10.1016/j.ijhcs.2006.02.006

33. Gamma, E., Helm, R., Johnson, R., Vlissides, J.: Design Patterns: Elements of Reusable Object-Oriented Software. Pearson Education, Upper Saddle River (1994)

34. Apud, S., Apud-Martinez, T.: Effective internal communication in global organizations. http://www.iabc.com/effective-internal-communication-in-global-organizations

35. Bilczynska-Wojcik, A.: Communication management within virtual teams in global projects. Ph.D. dissertation. Dublin Business School (2014)

36. Douras, J.: Techniques to build respect and trust with a remote workforce. http://www.iabc.com/techniques-to-build-respect-and-trust-with-a-remote-workforce

37. Layman, L., Williams, L., Damian, D., Bures, H.: Essential communication practices for Extreme Programming in a global software development team. Inf. Softw. Technol. **48**(9), 781–794 (2006). doi:10.1016/j.infsof.2006.01.004

38. Ling, F.Y.Y., Low, S.P., Wang, S.Q., Egbelakin, T.K.: Foreign firms' strategic and project management practices in china. In: Proceedings of Construction Management and Economics: Past, Present and Future. University of Reading, Reading (2007)

39. Modi, S., Abbott, P., Counsell, S.: Exploring communication challenges associated with Agile practices in a globally distributed environment. http://raiseconference.org/wp-content/uploads/2012/10/ModiCounsellRAISE-paper-resubmission-final.pdf
40. Muszyńska, K.: Communication management in project teams - practices and patterns. In: Dermol, V., Trunk, A., Đaković, G., Smrkolj, M. (eds.) Proceedings of the MakeLearn and TIIM Joint International Conference on Managing Intellectual Capital and Innovation for Sustainable and Inclusive Society, pp. 1359–1366. ToKnowPress (2015)

Using PEQUAL Methodology in Auction Platforms Evaluation Process

Jarosław Wątróbski[1(✉)], Paweł Ziemba[2], Jarosław Jankowski[1],
and Waldemar Wolski[3]

[1] Faculty of Computer Science, West Pomeranian University of Technology
in Szczecin, Żołnierska 49, 71-210 Szczecin, Poland
{jwatrobski,jjankowski}@wi.zut.edu.pl
[2] The Jacob of Paradyż University of Applied Science in Gorzów Wielkopolski,
Chopina 52, 66-400 Gorzów Wielkopolski, Poland
pziemba@pwsz.pl
[3] University of Szczecin, Mickiewicza 64, 71-101 Szczecin, Poland
wwolski@wneiz.pl

Abstract. Together with the growth of e-commerce sector, companies are focusing more and more attention on website quality evaluations. Evolution along with an ever-growing set of available methods are being observed for online shopping platforms, as well as auctions, and it is creating better representations of various characteristics and parameters. The following article presents a usability study of auction websites based on the PEQUAL methodology. The used method is based on the extended version of classical EQUAL method with taken into account different aspects of preference modelling and aggregation derived from Multi-Criteria Decision Analysis (MCDA). Presented empirical verification has been conducted out for top auction websites and results show significant practical possibilities of analysis of obtained results.

Keywords: Website usability · Website evaluation · Promethee II method

1 Introduction

The growing number of online stores have brought tension among many stores on the web as competition grows. More options for the consumer means that businesses are more prone to less traffic and a lower sale rate. Apart from typical electronic shops an important area of e-commerce is the sector of online auctions with several research fields. These include the analysis of behavior of users, the optimal design, the use of data and integration auctions with business models [1]. Other research topics are related to psychological aspects such as fear and distrust [2]. Online auctions are analyzed from the perspective of learning processed and acquiring knowledge about relations between bids [3]. Quantitative methods, like structural econometric, are used for price prediction [4] and identification of determinants of prices [5]. Analysis of decisions taken by online auction users takes place [6] as well as searching for factors affecting repurchase intensions [7]. Other than process and algorithmic characteristic the usability of online auction platforms is subject to the research and results that

E. Ziemba (Ed.): AITM 2016/ISM 2016, LNBIP 277, pp. 222–241, 2017.
DOI: 10.1007/978-3-319-53076-5_12

navigation and interactions have highest importance priority [8]. Other research emphasizes the role of auction websites quality in trust and continuous usage [9]. Dedicated approaches are used for assessment of auction website quality [10] and analysis of influence of quality of auction platforms on customer loyalty [11]. To receive better results business owners use analytic software [12], web mining techniques [13] or conversion maximization systems [14]. What is even more serious is realizing what single factors are affecting the performance of online platforms and customer loyalty [15]. Some major things to establish is the building of trust [16, 17], making sure the systems are top quality [18, 19], making sure there are levels of security and privacy [20], how accessible it is [21], development or international versions [22], fixing any critical problems [23] and pushing forward new features that help consumer satisfaction and the usability of the website [24]. To help observing the website quality, different types of methods based on key factors affecting websites assessment are used [25–27]. Because the evaluation of websites is a multi-criteria issue, attempts of using Multi-Criteria Decision Analysis (MCDA) methods for evaluating the websites are observed.

Presented research is an extended version of earlier work [28]. However, the goal of this article is to make an assessment model of the most popular auction websites while implementing the PEQUAL methodology. PEQUAL methodology is based on extension of classical EQUAL method with the use MCDA methodology. It has its justification as application of the MCDA method makes it possible to carry out a broad analysis and correction of, obtained in research, website rankings, and of user's preferences. This problem has importance for various sectors and website quality evaluation methods used today will allow doing this kind of side by side analyses only to a limited extent. The article is broken down as follows: Sect. 2 includes literature review, Sect. 3 shows the methodological framework of a proposed approach, Sect. 4 presents the findings from the study with conclusions in Sect. 5.

2 Literature Review

2.1 Websites Usability and Quality

Quality and usability are concepts related to each other and they comprise a similar semantic range [29]. There are many definitions of usability. According to ISO 9241, usability "extent to which a product can be used by specified users to achieve specified goals with effectiveness, efficiency and satisfaction in a specified context of use" [30]. Next, in the norm ISO 25010:2011 concerning the software programs, usability is defined as "the ability of software to be in intelligible, easy to learn and use as well as attractive to the user in specified circumstances" [31]. According to Nielsen, on the other hand, "usability is a complex concept consisting of many factors such as: learnability, efficiency, memorability, errors and satisfaction [29]. Nielsen specifies that usability is a quality attribute describing how a user interface is easy to use [32]. One can list many papers dealing with the research into website usability. Fernandez, among other things, divides usability research methods into five groups: user testing, inspection methods, inquiry methods, analytical modelling and simulation methods

[33]. Usability testing methods can also be divided in a different way, for example, into expert methods and user inquiry methods [34].

Expert methods are obtaining research results from a group of experts or a single expert examining a website [35]. One can indicate such methods as heuristic evaluation, guideline review, Cognitive Walkthrough, Action Analysis, Analytical Modeling or Inspections [36, 37]. The methods are a collection of instructions, good practices or general rules on the basis of which experts and users evaluate a website and find out potential problems [33]. Often, the methods are based on heuristics (e.g. Nielsen's heuristics [29]). In the case of Inspections, experts carry out inspections of features and functions offered by a website as well as conformity to standards (for example reaction time) [35].

The second group dealing with user inquiry methods is characterized by the fact that research results are obtained on the basis of activity of users in a website [33]. Here, one can list the following methods: Interviews, Focus group, Surveys, Questionnaires. In the Interviews method, the expert asks the user questions concerning the website [29]. The interview may be based on questions prepared in advance. However, the expert is also able to ask additional questions. In the Focus group method, a group consisting of several people, supervised by the expert, holds a discussion [35]. The expert moderates the discussion in order to obtain essential information on the users' needs with regard to the website [36]. Thanks to Surveys one can collect users' opinions about elements of a website, acceptability of solutions adopted in the website or possible errors [34]. In a questionnaire method, users answer prepared open-ended or closed-ended questions and respondents express their opinions about the website in a verbal form or by means of a questionnaire [29].

The last group of methods is based on tests involving users. One can distinguish here methods such as Thinking Aloud, Thinking-Aloud Protocol [33], Question-Asking Protocol, Performance Measurement, Log Analysis, Web traffic analysis, [34] or Field Observation) [35]. In the Thinking Aloud method [37], by means of testing scenarios, a user shows experts his or her way of perceiving a website. It leads to the identification of key interactions and problematic elements of the website. There are different variants of this method, for example, Constructive Interaction, Codiscovery Learning, Retrospective Testing, Coaching Method, Question-Asking Protocol [33, 35]. Another method, Performance Measurement, consists in collecting numerical data while a user is using a website [35]. Next, the data is processed and performance measurements of a solution are obtained. The measurements can be, for instance, a number of tasks or time necessary for a user to do a task [33]. In the Log Analysis method, an expert or software analyses data related to a user's navigation on a website. Clicktracking or Eye Tracking can also be counted as the Log Analysis method [38, 39]. In the Field Observation method, an expert monitors a user's interaction with a website in their natural working environment [29].

2.2   Website Evaluation Methods

Website evaluation methods use different models that look at quality and because of this they are different in what they use and in their structure [40]. To obtain users thoughts on websites, most of the time the sites use surveys and then grades are put on an n-degree Likert scale [41]. In Table 1 one can see described individual quality assessment methods for websites evaluation. For techniques utilizing surveys it is expected that the quantity of clients assessing a site ought to in any event add up to 30 [37].

Table 1. Characteristics of selected methods of website quality assessment

Method	Application	No of criteria	Method determining weights of criteria	Assessment scale	Method of examining websites	No of evaluators	Theoretical basis of method	Verification of solution	Reference
eQual	e-commerce, e-government, university websites, WAP websites	22	Questionnaires	1–7	Questionnaires	min. 30	Quality Function Deployment	Consistency reliability of questionnaires (Cronbach's Alpha)	[28, 44, 45]
Ahn	e-banking, e-commerce	54	–	1–7	Questionnaires	min. 30	Technology Acceptance Model, Model of Information Systems Success	Consistency reliability of questionnaires (Cronbach's Alpha)	[28, 44]
SiteQual	e-commerce	28	–	1–9	Questionnaires	min. 30	SERVQUAL, Data Quality	Consistency reliability of questionnaires (Cronbach's Alpha)	[28, 45]
WEQ	e-government	18 + 8 (negative)	–	1–5	Questionnaires	min. 30	Website User Satisfaction	Negative criteria	[28, 46]
WPSQ	information services	19	–	1–5	Questionnaires	min. 30	Technology Acceptance Model, Model of Information Systems Success	Complex reliability tests (i.a. convergence evaluation, discriminant analysis)	[28, 47]
WQM	information services	32	Questionnaires	1–3	–	–	Kano quality model (levels of customers' expectations)	–	[28, 48]
E-S-QUAL/RecS-Qual	e-banking, e-commerce	22 + 11	–	1–5	Questionnaires	min. 30	SERVQUAL	–	[28, 49]
WAES	e-government	40	–	0–1	Expert evaluation	min. 1	–	–	[28, 50]

The EQUAL method uses Quality Function Deployment which is a method that had the job of ensuring the means of identification and providing users' thoughts on the quality of a material on different stages of it being made [42]. This method was able to look at e-commerce and government [43], websites successfully. Web Portal Site Quality appeared on the premise of a Technology Acceptance Model. The TAM is to clarify the impact of seeing, by the client, data framework qualities on his or her acknowledgment of the given framework. It depends on two quality measurements, that is, saw handiness and saw convenience [51]. The Model of Information Systems Success by DeLone and McLean incorporates data quality and framework quality [52]. The WPSQ strategy is utilized as a part of assessing entries conveying comprehensively characterized data and administrations [47].

The Ahn technique, comparatively to Web Portal Site Quality, was formulated with the utilization of Technology Acceptance Model (TAM) [53]. The primary adaptation of the Ahn method was to consider the impact of trust to bank sites on the acknowledgment by clients [54]. At the point when taking a shot at the strategy, the first TAM model was stretched out with ensuing components which were imperative from the viewpoint of the Internet: data quality, framework quality and administration quality. These components were acquired from a broadened Model of Information Systems Success of DeLone and McLean [55]. Likewise, quality attributes with respect to exchange: the nature of an item and its conveyance were included [44].

The SiteQual technique [45] appeared as a blend of the SERVQUAL and Data Quality [56] models. This model was developed on the premise of surveys concerning music online business sites [45]. While setting up the Website Evaluation Questionnaire technique, criteria utilized as a part of the Website User Satisfaction (WUS) model were utilized [57]. As in WUS, in each trademark there is one negative paradigm, which is utilized to check dependability assessment [46]. This technique appeared keeping in mind the end goal to analyse e-government sites, yet it can likewise be utilized to evaluate different sorts of websites [46]. The E-S-QUAL and E-RecS-Qual methods originate from the SERVQUAL technique utilized for contemplating and assessing administration quality [58]. They are a consequence of modifying the SERVQUAL scale to the requirements of administration quality evaluation on the Internet. Here, some assessment criteria in the SERVQUAL model were kept and new criteria basic for deciding e-benefit quality were presented. These techniques were utilized to assess quality on bank websites and also online business [49] websites. While setting up the Website Quality Model technique, Kano's quality model was utilized, in which there are characterized three levels of clients' desires with respect to the nature of an item or an administration: essential, execution, and energizing [48]. The WAES (Website Attribute Evaluation System) strategy is intended for surveying office and organization sites. It comprises of two gatherings of qualities portraying straightforwardness and intuitiveness of a site. A specialist's assessment on a parallel scale is utilized in the technique [50].

The most appropriate technique, out of every single examined one, is by all accounts eQual, which is described by the most elevated formalization level. The eQual technique uses list of criteria (Table 2) as survey inquiries. While assessing, a Likert scale, which ranges from 1 to 7, is utilized. Weights of individual criteria are resolved similarly. Aside from criterial assessment, respondents likewise give general assessment of a website. On the premise of this appraisal, the unwavering quality of incomplete conclusions of each client is checked [43]. At the point when an accumulation of poll results has been assembled, an examination of the surveys is led concerning unwavering quality and inner attachment. To decide the dependability of aftereffects of a poll in the eQual technique, Cronbach's alpha is utilized. It is accepted that the unwavering quality of results is fitting, if the estimation of coefficient alpha adds up to no less than 0.6 [43].

The issue identified with a pragmatic utilization of the strategy is to pick up weights of criteria by method for surveys, in light of the fact that unequivocal revelation of clients' inclination may produce mistakes in the exploration [59]. This is additionally affirmed by the creators' examination, in which it was shown that weights of criteria got by method for surveys prompt to inaccurate choice arrangements [60].

Table 2. Survey inquiries in eQual method

No	Main criteria	Subcriteria
1	Usability/Usability	I find the site easy to learn to operate
2		My interaction with the site is clear and understandable
3		I find the site easy to navigate
4		I find the site easy to use
5	Usability/Design	The site has an attractive appearance
6		The design is appropriate to the type of site
7		The site conveys a sense of competency
8		The site creates a positive experience for me
9	Information quality	Provides accurate information
10		Provides believable information
11		Provides timely information
12		Provides relevant information
13		Provides easy to understand information
14		Provides information at the right level of detail
15		Presents the information in an appropriate format
16	Service interaction/Trust	Has a good reputation
17		It feels safe to complete transactions
18		My personal information feels secure
19	Service interaction/Empathy	Creates a sense of personalization
20		Conveys a sense of community
21		Makes it easy to communicate with the organization

2.3   Evaluation of Websites with the Use of MCDA Methods

Aside from talked about above, in the writing there are likewise endeavours at utilizing MCDA techniques for assessment of websites. It is justified since evaluation of websites is a multi-criteria issue, in which one needs to think about many dimensions and its measurements [61]. For example, Lee and Kozar [62] utilized the AHP method to assess business and travel websites. Chmielarz broadly utilizes scoring method to asses an extensive variety of business and e-managing oriented websites [63, 64]. Sun and Lin [65] assessed online business websites with use of TOPSIS technique. Del Vasto-Terrientes et al. [66] assessed traveller websites using ELECTRE-III-H method. Besides, in progress of Lin [67] and additionally Kong and Liu [68] AHP technique was utilized. Additionally a hybrids of different MCDA techniques are additionally utilized. In the paper by Bilsel et al. [69] determining the weights of criteria was directed by AHP method, while a positioning of healing facility websites was built with the utilization of the Promethee technique. Thus, Kaya [70] utilized the AHP technique to characterize weights of criteria, and used the TOPSIS method to build an internet business websites positioning. A mix of MCDA techniques: Simple Additive Weighting, Multiplicative Exponent Weighting, TOPSIS, concordance and conflict investigation techniques was utilized by Huang et al. [71].

The examination of use of MCDA methods in website assessment demonstrates that the vast majority of them utilized surveys to gather evaluations of websites. Concerning weights of criteria, pairwise comparison and the AHP technique are frequently utilized for this reason. Most of methods use a predetermined number of criteria. Just a couple papers utilized hypothetical bases recognizing the requirement for displaying both particular quality measures and criteria [66, 70]. Additionally, just in a few papers the robustness analysis was completed [69, 71]. Even though their usage is in early stage applying MCDA methods to assess websites has a more prominent potential than simply less formalized approaches.

3   Research Methodology

3.1   PEQUAL Methodological Framework

The authors' methodology of website quality assessment named PEQUAL (Promethee – eQual) depends on the eQual method, which has its establishments in Quality Function Deployment. PEQUAL methodology is presented in details in [28]. To do observational research at initially, surveys were gathered from 32 clients. In the examination test, there were PC proficient clients who are knowledgeable about doing the shopping on the auction websites. Every one of them assessed 6 online auction websites: Allegro, Aukro, Ebay.com, Ebay.pl, Swistak and Trademe. The explanation behind selecting the above mentioned set of auction websites was the consequence of examination of legitimate rankings of top web based auction sites introduced, in addition to other things, in [72, 73]. Along these lines, 320 polls were gathered which then were checked as far as consistency unwavering quality and Cronbach's alfa was resolved. Surveys evaluation was conducted with the use of the eQual method and the results of the questionnaires were also evaluated using the Promethee II method. Using Promethee II method and GAIA plane the broad analysis of the final websites ranking was carried out. Different research scenarios were taken into consideration in the process of aggregation of partial evaluations in a final ranking. In the first scenario, using Promethee II method, the aggregation of mean criterial evaluations into a overall evaluation with the use of pseudo criteria was conducted. In the next step the analysis of the obtained ranking was carried out with the use of the GAIA method, and two dimensions of analysis were taken into account: criteria and groups of criteria. In third step, apart from GAIA analysis, a sensitivity analysis of final ranking was also conducted. In real decision situations, expert evaluations obtained in the questionnaires can be characterized by some degree of uncertainty [25]. Therefore, in fourth step new, true criteria based model was constructed. Obtained results were compared with final ranking form first scenario (Step I). In the last step, obtained rankings were compared with the group ranking. Using PROMETHEE GDSS method GAIA analysis for particular decision – makers was performed. The presented practical approach is depicted in Fig. 1.

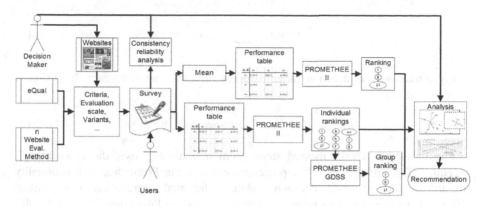

Fig. 1. Website evaluation process using PEQUAL methodology

3.2   MCDA Foundations of PEQUAL Framework

Apart from eQual technique PEQUAL framework is methodologically based on Promethee II method. The method Promethee II is very popular MCDA method and it employs pairwise comparison and a outranking relation in order to select the best decision alternative. Also, the method uses positive and negative preference flows determining to what extent a given variant outranks other ones and to what extent it is outranked by other variants [74]. In the PROMETHEE II method, the decision-maker may choose from six preference functions: a usual criterion, a quasi-criterion with an indifference threshold, a criterion with linear preference and a preference threshold, a level-criterion with indifference and preference thresholds, a criterion with linear preference and an indifference area, or, finally, a Gaussian criterion [75, 76]. Main steps of PROMETHEE II procedure are: pairwise comparison of decision alternatives with regard to criteria, applying a preference function for each criterion; determining an alternative preference index, determining positive and negative preference flows for alternatives, and determining net preference flow [77]. A preference index of alternatives calculated according formula (1):

$$\pi(a_i, b_j) = \frac{\sum_{k=1}^{n} w_k^* \varphi_k(a_i, b_j)}{\sum_{k=1}^{n} w_k} \tag{1}$$

where φ_k means a concordance factor for a pair of alternatives compared with regard to a criterion k. Positive and negative preference flows are calculated according formulas (2) and (3).

$$\phi^+(a_i) = \sum_{j=1}^{n} \pi(a_i, b_j) \tag{2}$$

$$\phi^-(a_i) = \sum_{j=1}^{n} \pi(b_j, a_i)$$ (3)

Finally, a total order of decision variants (represented by a net preference flow) should be calculated (4):

$$\phi(a_i) = \phi^+(a_i) - \phi^-(a_i)$$ (4)

The Promethee GDSS method stems from and directly uses the Promethee II procedure. The Promethee GDSS procedure extends the Promethee II functionality with the concept of group decision making. The final aggregation of individual decision-makers' evaluations takes place by means of the Promethee II method [74].

Apart from calculating a group ranking of Promethee II, in the Promethee GDSS method, the GAIA (ang. Geometrical Analysis for Interactive Assistance) analysis is also carried out. In the methodology of GAIA, information concerning a k-criterion decision problem presented in a k-dimensional space is projected on a plane, therefore, part of the information is lost. On the plane, among other things, a vector Л showing a compromise direction resulting from weights attributed to individual decision-makers (in a general case – to criteria) is presented [78]. Alternatives are represented by points and decision-makers' preferences are symbolized by vectors. If decision-makers have similar preferences, the vectors are turned in the same direction, whereas contradictory preferences result in opposite senses of the vectors. If there is no connection between experts' preferences, their vectors are turned perpendicularly to each other. The length of a vector denotes force of preferences represented by the vector. The closer the end of the vector to a given decision alternative, the more the vector supports the alternative in the ranking of results. When the analysis of GAIA points out that decision-makers' preferences are in conflict with each other, the following is recommended: a change of weights attributed to decision-makers, a change of individual evaluations, a change of criteria, a change of alternatives or adding another decision-maker [77, 78].

4   Research Findings and Discussion

4.1   EQual Based Analysis

In the first step of research, reliability analysis of obtained surveys was performed based on Cronbach's Alpha. Table 3 presents the results of these analysis. The minimum value of Cronbach's alpha, which confirms the reliability of the survey is equal to 0.6. Therefore, it can be stated that the results of the survey are reliable.

Next, a overall value of eQual Index was determined. The scores of the total value for groups of criteria are presented in Table 4.

The most preferred online auction websites, by the opinion of users, are the most popular in Poland are Allegro and Ebay.pl. This is probably since the respondents have the greatest experience in the use from these sites, and their habits related to the use of the auction platforms have their origin in these sites.

Table 3. The results of reliability analysis

Cluster of criteria	Group of criteria	Criterion	Alpha if item deleted	Alpha for group of criteria	Alpha for cluster of criteria	Global alpha
Usability	Usability	C1	0.9786	0.979	0.958	0.979
		C2	0.9787			
		C3	0.9784			
		C4	0.9784			
	Site design	C5	0.9800	0.894		
		C6	0.9791			
		C7	0.9787			
		C8	0.9786			
Information quality	Information quality	C9	0.9775	0.982	0.982	
		C10	0.9776			
		C11	0.9778			
		C12	0.9778			
		C13	0.9776			
		C14	0.9778			
		C15	0.9774			
Service interaction	Trust	C16	0.9776	0.948	0.96	
		C17	0.9778			
		C18	0.9785			
		C22	0.9786			
	Empathy	C19	0.9796	0.904		
		C20	0.9783			
		C21	0.9782			

Table 4. Assessment results (eQual index) of auction websites according to eQual method

Website	Evaluation quality index					
	Allegro	Aukro	Ebay.com	Ebay.pl	Swistak	Trademe
Usability	92.50%	59.29%	80.00%	86.79%	82.50%	78.93%
Site design	86.79%	61.43%	74.64%	79.29%	66.79%	76.07%
Information quality	84.69%	57.14%	74.08%	80.41%	51.84%	76.73%
Trust	85.36%	61.79%	73.57%	79.64%	48.93%	73.93%
Empathy	73.81%	54.76%	72.38%	71.90%	40.00%	66.19%
Global	85.13%	58.83%	74.94%	80.06%	57.99%	75.06%
Rank	1	5	4	2	6	3

4.2 Promethee II Based Analysis of Solution

In the next step, Promethee II method was applied. The averaged data from survey results are the source for calculations of Promethee II. Table 5 presents performance table of considered alternatives.

Table 5. Performance table for Promethee II

Group of criteria	Criterion	Website					
		Allegro	Aukro	Ebay.com	Ebay.pl	Swistak	Trademe
Usability	C1	6.5	4.4	5.7	6.1	5.8	5.7
	C2	6.5	3.7	5.5	6.1	5.8	5.5
	C3	6.4	4.1	5.5	6.1	5.8	5.4
	C4	6.5	4.4	5.7	6.0	5.7	5.5
Site design	C5	5.9	4.4	5.4	5.5	5.2	5.1
	C6	6.4	4.6	5.4	5.7	4.7	5.6
	C7	6.2	4.2	5.2	5.8	5.2	5.2
	C8	5.8	4.0	4.9	5.2	3.6	5.4
Information quality	C9	6.0	4.0	4.9	5.8	3.6	5.2
	C10	6.0	4.0	5.4	5.5	3.6	5.4
	C11	5.9	4.2	5.2	5.7	3.7	5.4
	C12	5.9	4.2	5.2	5.7	3.7	5.6
	C13	6.1	3.7	5.2	5.8	3.7	5.3
	C14	5.9	3.8	5.0	5.4	3.7	5.3
	C15	5.7	4.1	5.4	5.5	3.4	5.4
Trust	C16	6.1	4.1	5.2	5.8	3.5	5.1
	C17	6.1	4.2	5.2	5.7	3.2	5.1
	C18	6.2	4.7	5.4	5.4	3.6	5.5
	C22	5.5	4.3	4.8	5.4	3.4	5.0
Empathy	C19	5.4	3.8	4.9	4.8	2.5	4.4
	C20	4.8	3.4	4.7	4.6	2.5	4.2
	C21	5.3	4.3	5.6	5.7	3.4	5.3

In the Promethee II method for each criterion a preference model with a linear preference function, with an indifference threshold $q = 1$ and a preference threshold $p = 5$ was used. A preference direction was maximized. The selected preference model was assumed in order to reflect, as accurately as possible, the model used in the eQual method. The final ranking of the decision varies, the preference values of input and output and net flows are presented in Table 6.

Table 6. The final ranking and performance of decision variants (linear preference function with thresholds)

Website	Allegro	Aukro	Ebay.com	Ebay.pl	Swistak	Trademe
ϕ^+	0.0907	0.0009	0.0339	0.0611	0.0057	0.0364
ϕ^-	0.0000	0.0920	0.0002	0.0000	0.1364	0.0000
ϕ_{net}	0.0907	−0.0911	0.0336	0.0611	−0.1307	0.0364
Rank	1	5	4	2	6	3

On the basis of comparison, Tables 4 and 6, we can note that the ranking of variants obtained using the Promethee II is identical with the ranking eQual. This indicates the correctness of the usage MCDA method in the website evaluation field. This also confirms correctness of usage with the Promethee II method as the alternative to eQual.

4.3 Graphical Analysis of Promethee II Solution

Additionally, the results obtained by the Promethee II were analysed using the GAIA methodology. Figure 2 shows the results of the individual criteria analysis carried out by GAIA plane.

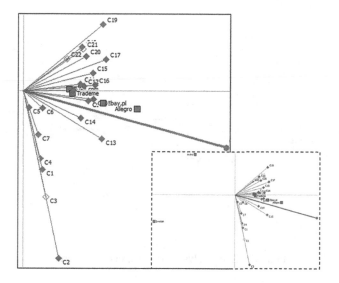

Fig. 2. GAIA analysis for criteria

The analysis of Fig. 2 demonstrates that all criteria support the four leading variants in varying degrees. The nearest alternatives to compromise the solution are Allegro, Ebay.pl, Trademe and Ebay.com. This sequence is in accordance with the ranking obtained using EQUAL method. The biggest impact on the final ranking have the criteria, where vectors in the plane GAIA are the longest, i.e., C2, C3, C19, C1, C13 and C17. In addition, a small conflict is observed between two sets of criteria, the first set is in the beginning of the first and the second in the second quarters of the system of coordinates. The first group include the criteria belonging to the group Empathy (C19–C21) and partially group Trust (C18, C22). The second set of criteria are assigned to the group Usability (C1–C4) and partly to the criteria Site Design (C5, C7). This observation was confirmed by the GAIA analysis carried out for groups of criteria, shown in Fig. 3, which is represented by a conflict between groups Usability and Empathy. This means that high ratings of an auction platform in terms of the criteria belonging to the group Usability are associated with low assessment of the same platform in terms of criteria from Empathy group. Since the criteria of the groups Usability and Site design conflict with the criteria of belonging to groups Empathy and Trust, a compromise is supported by the criteria belonging to the group Information quality. In addition, Fig. 3 expresses the similarity of evaluations about the Trust and Empathy criteria groups, because their vectors are located quite close to each other. In other words, if the auction website receives high ratings in terms of the criteria of Empathy group, it is usually also highly rated in terms of the criteria of a group Trust.

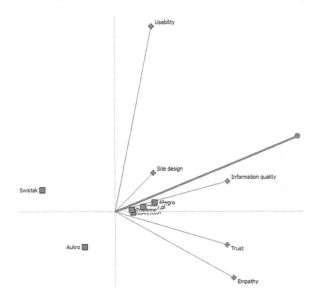

Fig. 3. GAIA analysis for the group of criteria

4.4 Sensitivity Analysis of Solution

Apart from GAIA analysis, a sensitivity analysis was also conducted. The analysis results indicate that the obtained rankings are very stable, because only changes for weights criterion C21 can cause shift in the first position in the ranking. However, the change to the second position can occur only in the case of changing the weights of criteria: C8, C18–C20. The ranges of stability for the weights of individual criteria are included in Table 7.

4.5 Reliability Analysis of Solution

To verify the assurance of the resulting solution, the new ranking was determined, New model was based on true criterion preference model (without thresholds). As a result, it was observed that even a small advantage of one variant over another in terms of a specific criterion C1–C22 causes that variant is considered as globally preferred. The

Table 7. Sensitivity analysis - the ranges of stability for the weights of criteria

Group of criteria	Criterion	Weight [%]	Min weight [%]	Max weight [%]
Usability	C1	4.55	0	23.46
	C2	4.55	0	14.24
	C3	4.55	0	19.09
	C4	4.55	0	25.00
Site design	C5	4.55	0	58.82
	C6	4.55	0	80.73
	C7	4.55	0	36.12
	C8	4.55	0	57.36
Information quality	C9	4.55	0	100
	C10	4.55	0	100
	C11	4.55	0	100
	C12	4.55	0	100
	C13	4.55	0	100
	C14	4.55	0	100
	C15	4.55	0	100
Trust	C16	4.55	0	25.00
	C17	4.55	0	38.24
	C18	4.55	0	83.97
	C22	4.55	0	100
Empathy	C19	4.55	0	12.50
	C20	4.55	0	10.64
	C21	4.55	0	12.50

obtained ranking using the true criterion is presented in Table 8. This ranking coincide with rankings presented in Tables 4 and 6 for the first two positions. There was a shift of variants in positions 3–4 and 5–6. The result from Table 8 is not also the same as ranking obtained by eQual method. It should be assumed that the application of the true criterion causes that the resulting ranking, GAIA analysis and sensitivity analysis for such rankings do not reflect exactly the preferences of the users. This is important, because many MCDA methods use only true criterion function, e.g., Melchior, Regime, Qualiflex Electre I, Electre II. It's worth to notice that the application of these methods should be done very carefully with focus on proper preference modelling and avoiding its oversimplifying.

4.6 Comparison of Averaged Rankings with Group Ranking

In the last step of research the group ranking using PROMETHEE GDSS method was determined. Based on individual rankings for each user and with the use linear preference function and thresholds $q = 1$ and $p = 5$, the individual rankings were aggregated in the group ranking. The result of using the PROMETHEE GDSS method is shown in Table 9.

Table 8. The final ranking and performance of decision variants (true criterion function)

Website	Allegro	Aukro	Ebay.com	Ebay.pl	Swistak	Trademe
ϕ^+	0.9727	0.1273	0.4545	0.7636	0.1364	0.4455
ϕ^-	0.0182	0.8636	0.4727	0.2273	0.8273	0.4909
ϕ_{net}	0.9545	−0.7364	−0.0182	0.5364	−0.6909	−0.0455
Rank	1	6	3	2	5	4

Table 9. PROMETHEE GDSS based ranking

Website	Allegro	Aukro	Ebay.com	Ebay.pl	Swistak	Trademe
ϕ^+	0.1253	0.0462	0.0733	0.1055	0.0397	0.0554
ϕ^-	0.0086	0.1473	0.0455	0.0230	0.1477	0.0733
ϕ_{net}	0.1167	−0.1012	0.0278	0.0825	−0.1080	−0.0179
Rank	1	5	3	2	6	4

Analysis of the final ranking from PROMETHEE GDSS indicates that results are similar to the rankings contained in Table 6 and ranking of eQual method (Table 4). Positions of Ebay.com and Trademe are reversed, and it is associated with a change in the value ϕ_{net} Trademe site. Values of ϕ_{net} other sites are close to the values shown in Table 6. However, the difference in the rankings indicates that the ranking GDSS does not reflect the exact preferences of users. Therefore, on the basis of analysis may lead to erroneous conclusions regarding the ranking embodiment, however, the results PROMETHEE GDSS are sufficient for the analysis of conflict between users in carrying out embodiments using Gaia plane. This plane is shown in Fig. 4. It indicates the existence of small conflicts of opinion, i.e., decision makers DM1, DM3, DM5, DM7,

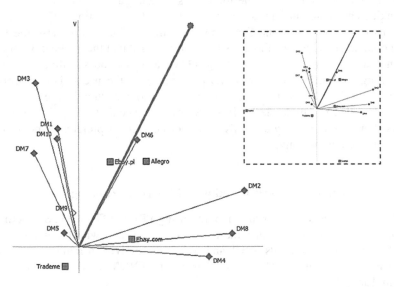

Fig. 4. GAIA analysis for the group ranking

DM9, and DM10, whose vectors have been placed in the fourth quarter of the system of coordinates, with the opinion of DM4, whose vector is located in quarter II. In addition, it must be noted that the most consistent with the final ranking of GDSS is assessment of user DM6.

5 Conclusions

Online auctions are one of the most explored e-commerce sector. Growing competition requires improvements in terms of pricing models, purchasing processes and overall website quality and usability. Dedicated methods are required to include various preferences and often conflicting interests. While several methods were used earlier they lack of multi-criteria approach and preferences aggregation.

In the proposed approach the multi-stage development of the model was acknowledged as to the criteria taken from the eQual technique with the utilization of the Promethee method (PEQUAL). It broadens prior methodologies by presenting MCDA based multi organize assessment and investigations. In the article, 6 well known auction sites were assessed. On the basis of the presented research, one can state that e-commerce websites most highly valued by users are: Allegro, Ebay and Trademe The conclusions were affirmed by stability study of obtained ranking, especially in the terms of its sensitivity and robustness analysis.

Besides, the utilization of the Promethee GDSS technique and the GAIA investigation, which is an essential part of the Promethee strategy, made it conceivable to show clients' individual inclinations. Likewise, the GAIA examination permitted inspecting shared conditions between individual gatherings and bunches of criteria on the premise of realistic information. The understanding of the GAIA plane is less tedious and simpler than the investigation of number estimations of assessments, and the conclusions drawn on its premise are similarly basic.

The examination structure of websites exhibited in the article can be the reason for their assessment alongside the rightness check of acquired assessments and inclinations of the respondents. As it has been exhibited in the introduced inquire about, this arrangement is practically wealthier than established MCDA-based techniques for site assessment strategies which have been utilized as a part of the writing to date.

References

1. Pinker, E.J., Seidmann, A., Vakrat, Y.: Managing online auctions: current business and research issues. Manage. Sci. **49**(11), 1457–1484 (2003). doi:10.1287/mnsc.49.11.1457. 20584
2. Bewsell, G.R.: Distrust, fear and emotional learning: an online auction perspective. J. Theor. Appl. Electron. Comer. Res. **7**(2), 1–12 (2012). doi:10.4067/S0718-18762012000200002
3. Blum, A., Kumar, V., Rudra, A., Wu, F.: Online learning in online auctions. Theor. Comput. Sc. **324**(2), 137–146 (2004). doi:10.1016/j.tcs.2004.05.012
4. Paarsch, H.J., Hong, H.: An Introduction to the Structural Econometrics of Auction Data. MIT Press Books (2006)

5. Lucking-Reiley, D., Bryan, D., Prasad, N., Reeves, D.: Pennies from eBay: the determinants of price in online auctions. J. Ind. Econ. **55**(2), 223–233 (2007). doi:10.1111/j.1467-6451. 2007.00309.x

6. Ariely, D., Simonson, I.: Buying, bidding, playing, or competing? value assessment and decision dynamics in online auctions. J. Consum. Psychol. **13**(1), 113–123 (2003). doi:10. 1207/S15327663JCP13-1&2_10

7. Yen, C.H., Lu, H.P.: Factors influencing online auction repurchase intention. Internet Res. **18**(1), 7–25 (2008). doi:10.1108/10662240810849568

8. Calisir, F., Elvan Bayraktaroglu, A., Altin Gumussoy, C., Ilker Topcu, Y., Mutlu, T.: The relative importance of usability and functionality factors for online auction and shopping web sites. Online Inform. Rev. **34**(3), 420–439 (2010). doi:10.1108/14684521011037025

9. Gregg, D.G., Walczak, S.: The relationship between website quality, trust and price premiums at online auctions. Electron. Commer. R. **10**(1), 1–25 (2010). doi:10.1007/ s10660-010-9044-2

10. Barnes, S.J., Vidgen, R.T.: Assessing the quality of auction web sites. In: Proceedings of the 34th Annual Hawaii International Conference on System Sciences, pp. 10. IEEE (2001). doi:10.1109/HICSS.2001.927087

11. Yen, C.H., Lu, H.P.: Effects of e-service quality on loyalty intention: an empirical study in online auction. Manag. Serv. Qual. Int. J. **18**(2), 127–146 (2008). doi:10.1108/09604520810 859193

12. Hasan, L., Morris, A., Probets, S.: Using google analytics to evaluate the usability of e-commerce sites. In: Kurosu, M. (ed.) HCD 2009. LNCS, vol. 5619, pp. 697–706. Springer, Heidelberg (2009). doi:10.1007/978-3-642-02806-9_81

13. Yadav, J., Mallick, B.: Web Mining: Characteristics and application in ecommerce. Int. J. IJECSE. **1**(4), 2020–2025 (2012)

14. Wu, X., Bolivar, A.: Predicting the conversion probability for items on C2C ecommerce sites. In: Cheung, D., Song, I.-Y. (eds.) Proceedings of the 18th ACM Conference on Information and Knowledge Management, pp. 1377–1386. ACM, New York (2009). doi:10. 1145/1645953.16461274567

15. Srinivasan, S.S., Anderson, R., Ponnavolu, K.: Customer loyalty in e-commerce: an exploration of its antecedents and consequences. J. Retailing. **78**(1), 41–50 (2002). doi:10. 1016/S0022-4359(01)00065-3

16. Manchala, D.W.: E-commerce trust metrics and models. IEEE Internet Comput. **4**(2), 36–44 (2000). doi:10.1109/4236.832944

17. Koohang, A., Paliszkiewicz, J.: E-Learning courseware usability: building a theoretical model. J. Comput. Inform. Syst. **56**(1), 55–61 (2016). doi:10.1080/08874417.2015. 11645801

18. Ziemba, E., Papaj, T., Żelazny, R.: A model of success factors for e-government adoption– the case of Poland. Issues Inf. Syst. **14**(2), 87–100 (2013)

19. Cao, M., Zhang, Q., Seydel, J.: B2C e-commerce web site quality: an empirical examination. Ind. Manage. Data Syst. **105**(5), 645–661 (2005). doi:10.1108/02635570510600000

20. Ghosh, A.K.: E-commerce Security and Privacy. Springer, New York (2012)

21. Sohaib, O., Kang, K.: The importance of web accessibility in Business to-Consumer (B2C) websites. In: 22nd Australasian Software Engineering Conference (ASWEC 2013) (2013)

22. Lituchy, T.R., Barra, R.A.: International issues of the design and usage of websites for e-commerce: Hotel and airline examples. J. Eng. Technol. Manage. **25**(1), 93–111 (2008). doi:10.1016/j.jengtecman.2008.01.004

23. Sohaib, O.: Usability and cultural issues in global e-commerce. J. Eng. Technol. Manage. **25** (1), 156–166 (2012)

24. Belanche, D., Casaló, L.V., Guinalíu, M.: Website usability, consumer satisfaction and the intention to use a website: the moderating effect of perceived risk. J. Retail. Consum. Serv. **19**(1), 124–132 (2012). doi:10.1016/j.jretconser.2011.11.001

25. Jankowski, J., Kolomvatsos, K., Kazienko, P., Wątróbski, J.: Fuzzy modeling of user behaviors and virtual goods purchases in social networking platforms. J. Univers. Comput. Sci. **22**(3), 416–437 (2016)

26. Koohang, A., Paliszkiewicz, J.: Empirical validation of an learning courseware usability model. Issues Inf. Syst. **15**(2), 270–275 (2014)

27. Ziemba, P., Jankowski, J., Wątróbski, J., Wolski, W., Becker, J.: Integration of domain ontologies in the repository of website evaluation methods. In: Ganzha, M., Maciaszek, L., Paprzycki, M. (eds.) Proceedings of the Federated Conference on Computer Science and Information Systems. ACSIS, vol. 5, pp. 1585–1595. (2015). doi:10.15439/2015F297

28. Wątróbski, J., Ziemba, P., Jankowski, J., Wolski, W.: PEQUAL-E-commerce websites quality evaluation methodology. In: Ganzha, M., Maciaszek, L., Paprzycki M. (eds.) Proceedings of the Federated Conference on Computer Science and Information Systems. ACSIS, vol. 8, pp. 1317–1327 (2016). doi:10.15439/2016F46

29. Nielsen, J.: Usability Engineering. Morgan Kaufmann, San Francisco (1993)

30. ISO 9241-11:1998(E). http://www.iso.org/iso/catalogue_detail.htm?csnumber=16883

31. ISO/IEC 25010:2011. http://www.iso.org/iso/home/store/catalogue_ics/catalogue_detail_ics.htm?csnumber=35733

32. Usability 101: Introduction to Usability. http://www.nngroup.com/articles/usability-101-introduction-to-usability/

33. Fernandez, A., Insfran, E., Abrahão, S.: Usability evaluation methods for the web: a systematic mapping study. Inform. Softw. Tech. **53**(8), 789–817 (2011). doi:10.1016/j.infsof.2011.02.007

34. Albert, B., Tullis, T., Tedesco, D.: Beyond The Usability Lab: Conducting Large-scale Online User Experience Studies. Morgan Kaufmann, Elsevier, Amsterdam (2010)

35. The Usability Methods Toolbox Handbook. http://www.idemployee.id.tue.nl/g.w.m.rauterberg/lecturenotes/UsabilityMethodsToolboxHandbook.pdf

36. Rubin, J., Chisnell, D.: Handbook of Usability Testing, How to Plan, Design, and Conduct Effective Tests. Wiley, Hoboken (2008)

37. Holzinger, A.: Usability engineering methods for software developers. Commun. ACM **48** (1), 71–74 (2005). doi:10.1145/1039539.1039541

38. Jankowski, J., Kazienko, P., Wątróbski, J., Lewandowska, A., Ziemba, P., Zioło, M.: Fuzzy multi-objective modeling of effectiveness and user experience in online advertising. Expert Syst. Appl. **65**, 315–331 (2016). doi:10.1016/j.eswa.2016.08.049

39. Jankowski, J., Ziemba, P., Wątróbski, J., Kazienko, P.: Towards the tradeoff between online marketing resources exploitation and the user experience with the use of eye tracking. In: Nguyen, N.T., Trawiński, B., Fujita, H., Hong, T.-P. (eds.) ACIIDS 2016. LNCS (LNAI), vol. 9621, pp. 330–343. Springer, Heidelberg (2016). doi:10.1007/978-3-662-49381-6_32

40. Ziemba, P., Piwowarski, M., Jankowski, J., Wątróbski, J.: Method of criteria selection and weights calculation in the process of web projects evaluation. In: Hwang, D., Jung, J.J., Nguyen, N.-T. (eds.) ICCCI 2014. LNCS (LNAI), vol. 8733, pp. 684–693. Springer, Heidelberg (2014). doi:10.1007/978-3-319-11289-3_69

41. Ziemba, P., Wątróbski, J., Jankowski, J., Wolski, W.: Construction and restructuring of the knowledge repository of website evaluation methods. In: Ziemba, E. (ed.). LNBIP, vol. 243, pp. 29–52 Springer, Heidelberg (2016). doi:10.1007/978-3-319-30528-8_3

42. Barnes, S.J., Vidgen, R.: Measuring web site quality improvements: a case study of the forum on strategic management knowledge exchange. Ind. Manage. Data Syst. **103**(5), 297–309 (2003). doi:10.1108/02635570310477352

43. Barnes, S.J., Vidgen, R.T.: Data triangulation and web quality metrics: a case study in e-government. Inform. Manage. **43**(6), 767–777 (2006). doi:10.1016/j.im.2006.06.001

44. Ahn, T., Ryu, S., Han, I.: The impact of the online and offline features on the user acceptance of Internet shopping malls. Electron. Commer. R. A. **3**(4), 405–420 (2005). doi:10.1016/j.elerap.2004.05.001

45. Webb, H.W., Webb, L.A.: Business to consumer electronic commerce website quality: integrating information and service dimensions. In: Association for Information Systems AIS Electronic Library. AMCIS 2001 Proceedings, vol. 111, pp. 559–562 (2001)

46. Elling, S., Lentz, L., Jong, M.: Website evaluation questionnaire: development of a research-based tool for evaluating informational websites. In: Wimmer, M.A., Scholl, J., Grönlund, Å. (eds.) EGOV 2007. LNCS, vol. 4656, pp. 293–304. Springer, Heidelberg (2007). doi:10.1007/978-3-540-74444-3_25

47. Yang, Z., Cai, S., Zhou, Z., Zhou, N.: Development and validation of an instrument to measure user perceived service quality of information presenting web portals. Inform. Manage. **42**(4), 575–589 (2005). doi:10.1016/j.im.2004.03.001

48. Ping Zhang, G.M.: User expectations and rankings of quality factors in different web site domains. Int. J. Electron. Comm. **6**(2), 9–33 (2001)

49. Parasuraman, A., Zeithaml, V.A., Malhotra, A.: ES-QUAL a multiple-item scale for assessing electronic service quality. J. Serv. Res-US. **7**(3), 213–233 (2005). doi:10.1177/1094670504271156

50. Demchak, C.C., Friis, C., La Porte, T.M.: Webbing governance: national differences in constructing the face of public organizations. In: Garson, G.D. (ed.) Handbook of Public Information Systems, pp. 179–196. Marcel Dekker, New York (2000)

51. Shih, H.P.: Extended technology acceptance model of Internet utilization behaviour. Inform. Manage. **41**(6), 719–729 (2004). doi:10.1016/j.im.2003.08.009

52. Seddon, P.B.: A respecification and extension of the DeLone and McLean model of IS success. Inform. Syst. Res. **8**(3), 240–253 (1997). doi:10.1287/isre.8.3.240

53. Ahn, T., Ryu, S., Han, I.: The impact of Web quality and playfulness on user acceptance of online retailing. Inform. Manage. **44**(3), 263–275 (2007). doi:10.1016/j.im.2006.12.008

54. Suh, B., Han, I.: Effect of trust on customer acceptance of Internet banking. Electron. Commer. R. A. **1**(3), 247–263 (2003). doi:10.1016/S1567-4223(02)00017-0

55. Jafari, S.M., Ali, N.A., Sambasivan, M., Said, M.F.: A respecification and extension of DeLone and McLean model of IS success in the citizen-centric e-governance. In: 2011 IEEE International Conference on Information Reuse and Integration, pp. 342–346. IEEE (2011)

56. Wang, R.Y., Strong, D.M.: Beyond accuracy: What data quality means to data consumers. J. Manage. Inform. Syst. **12**(4), 5–33 (1996). doi:10.1080/07421222.1996.11518099

57. Muylle, S., Moenaert, R., Despontin, M.: The conceptualization and empirical validation of web site user satisfaction. Inform. Manage. **41**(5), 543–560 (2004). doi:10.1016/S0378-7206(03)00089-2

58. Parasuraman, A., Zeithaml, V.A., Berry, L.L.: SERVQUAL: a multiple-item scale for measuring consumer perceptions of service quality. J. Retailing. **64**, 12–40 (1988)

59. Zenebe, A., Zhou, L., Norcio, A.F.: User preferences discovery using fuzzy models. Fuzzy Set. Syst. **161**(23), 3044–3063 (2010). doi:10.1016/j.fss.2010.06.006

60. Ziemba, P., Jankowski, J., Wątróbski, J., Piwowarski, M.: Web projects evaluation using the method of significant website assessment criteria detection. In: Nguyen, N.T., Kowalczyk, R. (eds.). LNCS, vol. 9655, pp. 167–188 Springer, Heidelberg (2016). doi:10.1007/978-3-662-49619-0_9

61. Kim, S., Stoel, L.: Dimensional hierarchy of retail website quality. Inform. Manage. **41**(5), 619–633 (2004). doi:10.1016/j.im.2003.07.002

62. Lee, Y., Kozar, K.A.: Investigating the effect of website quality on e-business success: an analytic hierarchy process (AHP) approach. Decis. Support Syst. **42**(3), 1383–1401 (2006). doi:10.1016/j.dss.2005.11.005
63. Chmielarz, W., Zborowski, M.: Comparative analysis of electronic banking Websites in selected banks in Poland in 2014. Ann. Comput. Sci. Inf. Syst. **5**, 1499–11504 (2015). doi:10.15439/2015F43
64. Chmielarz, W.: Evaluation of selected mobile applications stores from the user's perspective. Online J. Appl. Knowl. Manag. **3**, 21–36 (2015)
65. Sun, C.C., Lin, G.T.: Using fuzzy TOPSIS method for evaluating the competitive advantages of shopping websites. Expert Syst. Appl. **36**(9), 11764–11771 (2009). doi:10.1016/j.eswa.2009.04.017
66. Del Vasto-Terrientes, L., Valls, A., Slowinski, R., Zielniewicz, P.: ELECTRE-III-H: an outranking-based decision aiding method for hierarchically structured criteria. Expert Syst. Appl. **42**(11), 4910–4926 (2015). doi:10.1016/j.eswa.2015.02.016
67. Lin, H.F.: An application of fuzzy AHP for evaluating course website quality. Comput. Educ. **54**(4), 877–888 (2010). doi:10.1016/j.compedu.2009.09.017
68. Kong, F., Liu, H.: Applying fuzzy analytic hierarchy process to evaluate success factors of e-commerce. Int. J. Inf. Syst. Sci. **1**(3–4), 406–412 (2005)
69. Bilsel, R.U., Büyüközkan, G., Ruan, D.: A fuzzy preference-ranking model for a quality evaluation of hospital web sites. Int. J. Intell. Syst. **21**(11), 1181–1197 (2006). doi:10.1002/int.20177
70. Kaya, T.: Multi-attribute evaluation of website quality in E-business using an integrated fuzzy AHPTOPSIS methodology. Int. J. Comput. Intell. Syst. **3**(3), 301–314 (2010). doi:10.1080/18756891.2010.9727701
71. Huang, J., Jiang, X., Tang, Q.: An e-commerce performance assessment model: Its development and an initial test on e-commerce applications in the retail sector of China. Inform. Manage. **46**(2), 100–108 (2009). doi:10.1016/j.im.2008.12.003
72. The top 500 sites on the web. http://www.alexa.com/topsites/category;3/Business/Shopping
73. Mobile and Tablet e-Commerce: Is Anyone Really Ready? https://www.mitx.org/files/zmags-top100-web.pdf
74. Wątróbski, J., Ziemba, P., Jankowski, J., Zioło, M.: Green energy for a green city—A multi-perspective model approach. Sustain. **8**(8), 702 (2016). doi:10.3390/su8080702
75. Brans, J.P., Vincke, P., Mareschal, B.: How to select and how to rank projects: The PROMETHEE method. Eur. J. Oper. Res. **24**(2), 228–238 (1986). doi:10.1016/0377-2217(86)90044-5
76. Wątróbski, J., Jankowski, J.: An Ontology-Based Knowledge Representation of MCDA Methods. In: Nguyen, N.T., Trawiński, B., Fujita, H., Hong, T.-P. (eds.) ACIIDS 2016. LNCS (LNAI), vol. 9621, pp. 54–64. Springer, Heidelberg (2016). doi:10.1007/978-3-662-49381-6_6
77. Brans, J.P., Mareschal, B.: PROMETHEE methods. In: Multiple Criteria Decision Analysis: State of the Art Surveys. International Series in Operations Research & Management Science, vol. 78, pp. 163–186. Springer, New York (2005). doi:10.1007/0-387-23081-5_5
78. Brans, J.P., Mareschal, B.: The PROMETHEE methods for MCDM; the PROMCALC, GAIA and BANKADVISER software. In: Bana e Costa, C.A. (ed.) Readings in Multiple Criteria Decision Aid, pp. 216–252. Springer, Heidelberg (1990). doi:10.1007/978-3-642-75935-2_10

Author Index

Apostolopoulou, Georgia   157

Bley, Katja   103

Chatzoglou, Prodromos   157, 179
Chatzoudes, Dimitrios   157, 179
Chmielarz, Witold   77

Dudycz, Helena   35

Eisenbardt, Monika   49

Feng, Fan   3
Forstenhäusler, Sven   103
Fragidis, Leonidas   179
Franczyk, Bogdan   137

Glöckner, Michael   137

Hunka, Frantisek   20

Jankowski, Jarosław   222

Kaźmierczak, Adrian   35
Korczak, Jerzy   35

Leyh, Christian   103
Łobaziewicz, Monika   120
Lodewijks, Gabriel   3
Ludwig, André   137

Matula, Jiri   20
Mullins, Roisin   49
Muszyńska, Karolina   202

Nita, Bartłomiej   35

Oleksyk, Piotr   35

Pang, Yusong   3

Schäffer, Thomas   103
Schwarzbach, Björn   137
Symeonidis, Symeon   179
Szumski, Oskar   77

Wątróbski, Jarosław   222
Wolski, Waldemar   222

Ziemba, Ewa   49
Ziemba, Paweł   222

Printed in the United States
By Bookmasters